ISSUE 02
Contents

LEE BRACKSTONE AND RICHARD KING
Editorial

Much, too much, far far too much, has been written about the premature passing of Michael Jackson. King of Pop or King of Plop, *après* Michael *le deluge*, but it seemed obvious to us that Morley would cut through the hagiographical crap and yet still see the chronic pity of the man at the heart of the myth. We encouraged him to write fearlessly and at length. The essay featured here in issue two of *Loops* clocks in at 36,000 words and offers perhaps the first sober perspective on those sixty-nine days between Jackson's death and burial.

Jackson dominates our cover but another diminutive figure is unmistakable. Prince, as Jackson's immediate peer, rival, sometime nemesis, has unsurprisingly offered no comment on Jackson's death, his legacy and his posthumous deification. But in his own sweet way Prince has been paying tribute: listening to a bootleg of a recent Paris show some four tracks in we were surprised to hear a loose and happy jam through 'I Want You Back' led by Prince on rhythm guitar. A tribute of sorts. But then again, it's intriguing and amusing to notice Prince doesn't sing a note of the song himself . . .

Matt Thorne is engaged in an epic survey of Prince's thirty-year output (the first of its kind) and the essay featured here examines, uncovers and celebrates a half-decade of lunatic levels of song-writing, producing and performing. In 1983 Jackson shared a stage with Prince for the only time at a James Brown gig at the Apollo (watch it on YouTube). Jackson's performance is slick and sublime. Prince responds with sick squeals and a guitar solo so awful it has prompted debate about his psychotropic intake at the time.

Perhaps the crowning irony of these parallel, yin-yang careers is that Jackson crumbled and finally expired in preparation for an improbable fifty-night residency at O2. Prince's legendary twenty-one nights and aftershows in 2007 live on in bootleg form; those looking forward to Jackson's response must make do with an unspoiled, redeemable-on-eBay-only ticket stub for a show bathetically titled, This Is It.

OWEN HATHERLEY
So Much to Answer For
Post Punk Urbanism in Manchester

The Los Angeles-based property developer John Lydon recently opined that he'd seen what a failure socialism was because he'd lived in a council flat. This squares with the idea that punk was a sort of counter-cultural equivalent to Thatcherism – a movement for individualism, cruelty and discipline, against the woolly solidarity and collectivism of the post-war consensus. Council flats were always one of the emblems of punk, at least in its more socialist–realist variants. There was a sort of delayed cultural reaction to the cities of tower blocks and motorways built in the '60s, to the point where their effect only really registered around ten years later, when a cultural movement defined itself as having come from those towers and walkways. It wasn't always actually true, of course, but when it was – Mick Jones's mum's flat looking over the Westway, for instance – it led to a curious kind of bad faith, where, on the one hand, the dehumanising effect of these places was lamented, but, on the other, the vertiginous new landscape was fetishised and aestheticised.

Although post punk was always a great deal more aesthetically sophisticated, not bound by nostalgia for the old streets, this bad faith features here, too. Post-punk is usually represented in terms of concrete and piss, grim towers and blasted wastelands. This is best exemplified in the poster to Anton Corbijn's woeful Ian Curtis hagiography *Control*, where Sam Riley, fag dangling from mouth, looks wan and haunted below gigantic prefabricated tower blocks (which were shot in Nottingham, not the gentrified-out-of-recognition Manchester). Decades ago, when asked by Jon Savage why Joy Division's sound had such a sense of loss and gloom, Bernard Sumner reminisced about his Salford childhood, where 'there was a huge sense of community where we lived . . . I guess what happened in the '60s was that someone at the Council decided that it wasn't very healthy, and something had to go, and unfortunately it was my neighbourhood that went. We were moved over the river into a tower block. At the time I thought it was fantastic – now, of course, I realise it was a total disaster.' This is often quoted as if it's obvious. Well, of course it was a disaster. This is the narrative about modernist architecture that exists in numerous reminiscences and histories – we loved it at first, in the '60s, then we realised how appalling it was, so we knocked them down and rebuilt simulations of the old streets instead.

Decades on from the victories of punk and Thatcherism, after thirty years where the dominant form of mass housing has been the achingly traditionalist Barratt Home or perhaps an inner-urban 'loft' rather than a concrete maisonette, this yearning for old certainties, cobbles and the aesthetics of Coronation Street

Kevin Cummins

has a rather different sound. The places punk and Thatcherism wanted to destroy were, in so many cases, swept away, particularly over the last fifteen years, in favour of 'urban regeneration'. Yet the effect on the regenerated cities has been, in musical terms, unimpressive to say the least. In the 'oos, the very few areas to have retained a distinctive musical presence – forgotten estates in east and south-east London, depressed Yorkshire cities like Bradford or Sheffield – are those which have largely escaped regeneration. Meanwhile, Manchester – capital of regeneration, the UK's would-be Barcelona, with its loft apartments, its towering yuppie-dromes, its designated cultural quarters – has produced virtually no innovative music since A Guy Called Gerald's *Black Secret Technology* in 1995. Jungle, garage, grime – all largely bypassed Manchester, while 'alternative' music degen-

erated into the homilies of Badly Drawn Boy into innumerable 'landfill indie' acts, with or without attendant macho Manc swagger. You could blame this on the Stone Roses, or on Oasis – or it could be blamed on the new city created by an enormous and now pricked property bubble.

New Emerging Manchester

The late Tony Wilson was a fierce propagandist for what the property billboards on Great Ancoats Road call 'New Emerging Manchester', and was evidently pleased that Richard Florida had designated the Manchester of young media professionals and loft conversions as a centre of 'the creative class', a 'cultural capital', irrespective of the conspicuous lack of worthwhile film, art, architecture or pop music created in the regenerated city – save for the self-hagiographies

Owen Hatherley

like *Control* or *24-Hour Party People*. At the end of the most recent of these, Grant Gee's Joy Division documentary, Wilson reflected on how Manchester had gone from being the first industrial city in the early nineteenth century to, today, Britain's first successful post-industrial city – after the blight of the '70s it is now a modern metropolis once again, this time based on media and property rather than something so unseemly as industrial production. The old entrepreneurs built the mills where workers toiled at twelve-hour shifts and died before they were forty; the new entrepreneurs sold the same mills to young urban professionals as industrial–aesthetic luxury housing.

Wilson squarely credited Joy Division and Factory Records with a leading role in this transformation. He is by no means alone in this – Nick Johnson, one of the directors of the Manc property developer Urban Splash, has given presentations where he dates the beginnings of his company to the Sex Pistols gig at the Free Trade Hall. The company's boss and one of Britain's richest men, Tom Bloxham MBE, is an ex-bootleg poster salesman based in the former 'alternative' enclave of Affleck's Palace. This is a narrative which has no room for the post-war years, decades of decline which just happened to coincide with the most fertile and exciting popular culture ever produced in the city. When Manchester is profiled or reminisced over, it most often – and unsurprisingly – through a narrative which leaps from the Victorian city of 'Manchester liberalism' – a laissez-faire doctrine with distinct similarities to Thatcherism – to the city recreated and regenerated after the IRA bomb in 1996. The horrendous poverty of nineteenth-century Manchester and the gaping inequalities of today are entirely effaced. In between is a no-man's-land.

New Babylon

Both approaches have an essentially nineteenth-century idea of the city, as a place that should be unplanned and rise out of the activities of entrepreneurs and businessmen. The unplanned cities of that era have long been a touchstone of a certain school of psychogeography – a term originally derived from the Situationist International, which has, under the influence of English writers Iain Sinclair and Peter Ackroyd, come to refer to an archaeological, vaguely occult, approach to the city, where that which already exists is walked through at random, with the rich historical connections leading to recondite, occasionally critical, chains of association and reflections on the nebulous spirit of certain areas. Although this school of psychogeography is fiercely hostile to the glassy, security-obsessed cities created by regeneration, they share a hostility to planning and to the planned cities of social democracy. Both, though they come from political antipodes, can agree with each other about the ghastliness of council estates and the deficient aesthetics of '60s tower blocks. If a certain strain in punk continues in much psychogeographical writing, it is the element that laments the destruction of Victoriana, the punk and psychogeographical preservation societies.

Psychogeography, as originally defined by the Situationist International, meant something rather different. While it certainly had an interest in those areas untouched by renewal, regeneration or prettification, the SI in the '50s dared to imagine a new urbanism, an entirely new approach to the city which wasn't based on two-up/two-downs or on spaced-out, rationalist tower blocks. To have an idea of what the Situationist City would have been like, you could read Ivan Chtcheglov's 'Formulary for a New Urbanism', an elliptical prose-poem imagining a self-creating world of grottoes and Gothic spaces, which inadvertently found its way into the annals of Manchester history through the declaration, 'You'll never see the Hacienda. It doesn't exist. The Hacienda must be built.'

Or you could find it in New Babylon, a proposal for a genuinely new city, designed by the Dutch architect, painter and early Situationist Constant Nieuwenhuis as a proposal for the towns that could exist when automation has eliminated the problem of work – a ludic city, dedicated to play, where 'creativity' becomes its own reward rather a means for the accumulation of capital. There are no Le Corbusier tower blocks here, which Constant called 'cemeteries of reinforced concrete, in which great masses of the population are condemned to die of boredom'. But then you won't find here any homilies on behalf of back-to-backs, redbrick mills or outside privies, nor on the glories of the entrepreneurial city either. If punk was obsessed with the 'realness' of the streets, New Babylon doesn't even have streets, in the old sense – it is a construction based entirely on multiple levels: walkways, skyways. It was a city in motion for a population in motion, 'a nomadic town' that functioned as a 'dynamic labyrinth' entirely through means of modern technology and construction. Models of New Babylon show tentacles of elevated bridges above the existing city linking together megastructures sometimes the size of a whole town in 'a continuous spatial construction, disengaged from the ground'. The most important part of it seemed to be this element of circulation, the walkways and bridges themselves, designed to create accidents and chance encounters. Fairly obviously, for all the Situationist pretensions of Manchester's regenerators, neither the Hacienda nor New Babylon have been built there.

New Brutalism

Except, in a particularly accidental and ad hoc manner, Manchester may have had a fragment of New Babylon within it without noticing, in the form of its only example of the architecture known as the New Brutalism. The idea of the multi-level city that Constant and the Situationists were arguing had the potential to create a new city based on chance and on play was very much in the air in the '50s, particularly through the international architectural group Team 10. Though, as practising architects, none of Team 10 was ever likely to be accepted by the Situationists, there is evidence that they had some contacts with Dutch members of the group such as Constant. Team 10 was an oppositional grouping which set itself up against the mainstream of modernist architecture and planning, and the structure that they set up as their emblem of what they wanted, as opposed to the serried ranks of tower blocks that mainstream modernism was erecting en masse, was a scheme based on walkways and the elevation of the street above the ground – the Golden Lane project of the English New Brutalist architects Alison and Peter Smithson, designed in 1956, two years before New Babylon. A project for a London bombsite, this was turned from picturesque rubble into an exercise in hypermodern pop montage. To illustrate their idea, they produced a photomontage of their prospective building with its internal streets and angular, austere forms, and imposed on them discrete cut-out figures. Some seem to be having gun-fights, others are running, all seem possessed by a distinct energy, far from the calm contemplation of high modernism. Among the montaged figures are those of mid-twentieth century hyper-celebrity. In the foreground Marilyn Monroe and Joe DiMaggio are ducking, huddled as if running from paparazzi; in front of another, more domestic figure, a man is playing with a small child. Running through the whole project was a series of elevated walkways, a system of pedestrian circulation linking blocks seemingly placed at random. This street-deck, as it was called, would in principle become a new kind of community, not replicating the old but recapitulating it at a higher level – the Smithsons wrote that the 'decks would be places, not corridors or balconies; thoroughfares where there are shops, postboxes, telephone kiosks . . . the refuse chute takes the place of the village pump.' The streets in the sky would be dense, they would be urban, and while they would unashamedly house the working class as part of a Welfare State, they would also be glamorous. In short, this would be Pop.

Golden Lane would not be built, but the nearest thing to it to be erected is Park Hill, in Sheffield. This scheme cleared a notoriously violent slum by Sheffield's Midland Station nicknamed 'little Chicago', but rather than re-housing the residents in isolated towers as was then the norm, the architects – Jack Lynn and Ivor Smith, under the supervision of the city architect, Lewis Womersley – attempted to replicate in the air the tightly packed street life of the area. As associates of the Smithsons, Lynn and Smith were enthusiasts for the close-knit working-class life supposedly being broken up by the new estates and new towns. As in their Golden Lane, claustrophobic walk-ups or corridors were rejected in favour of 12-foot wide 'streets in the sky'. These 'streets' were almost all connected with the ground, on steeply sloping land. Street corners were included where the winding building twisted around, with the spaces around the blocks filled with shops, schools and playgrounds. This was a step back from Golden Lane, and from New Babylon – the walkways were for circulation only, while both the Smithsons and Constant dreamed of

entire cities threading themselves along the walkways – but it stands as the nearest thing to it ever constructed, a social democratic approximation of this ludic utopia that, while it would not have impressed any Situationist, was far, far closer to their ideas than anything produced in the post punk city. Accordingly, it, and its two successors – Kelvin and Hyde Park, both demolished in the '90s – had a major presence in the music that emerged from Sheffield's post punk scene, being referenced by the early Human League – their shimmering, proto-techno instrumental 'Dancevision' features as its sleevenote a pointed 'recorded opposite Kelvin Flats, Sheffield'.

After leaving Sheffield, Lewis Womersley set up a private practice with another architect, Hugh Wilson, and together Wilson and Womersley designed two enormous structures in Manchester at the turn of the '70s. One of them, the Arndale Centre, swallowing up a huge swathe of the inner city and sucking it into a private shopping centre under one roof, is the antithesis both of New Babylon – dedicated as it is to work and consumption – and of his work at Park Hill, with montage and walkways replaced by a lumpen, grounded space, topped by a lone office block, and the only use of multiple levels being for the benefit of the car rather than the pedestrian. The other structure designed by Wilson and Womersley was the Hulme redevelopment, particularly the Hulme Crescents. These were a shadow, a memory of Park Hill, a series of labyrinthine blocks accessed by street decks. The relative conservatism of the Crescents can be ascertained from their names – John Nash, Charles Barry, etc., all taken from architects of the Regency period, to whose work in Bath and London this was intended to be the modern equivalent – and their prefabricated concrete construction was markedly less solidly built than Park Hill.

Nonetheless, in the context of Greater Manchester, where seemingly hundreds of blocks from Pendleton to Collyhurst rose up from the Victorian slums, gigantic spaced-out tombstones that amply made Constant's point about the boredom of post-war redevelopment, the Crescents provided a modernist labyrinth, with its street decks winding round and interconnecting four vast, semicircular blocks enclosing a seeming no-man's-land of indeterminate pedestrian space. Within a couple of years of its 1971 completion, it was vermin-ridden and leaky, as a result of costs cut during the construction.

'Up the 10th floor, down the backstairs, into no-man's land'

Hulme Crescents and its surrounding area were demolished in the early '90s, seemingly yet another example of the failures of British Modernism, and its demolition is seen as being nearly as pivotal as the Commonwealth Games and the IRA bomb for Manchester's regeneration. 'Now, of course, I realise it was a total disaster.' There's another story about what went on within the street decks, which suggests that post punk was not as conservative in its urbanism as we might think. Nonetheless, the early incarnations of Brutalist Hulme fully support the 'concrete & piss' version of punk history. A 1978 *World in Action* documentary set out its stall early on by describing the deck-access, streets-in-the-sky system of the estate, then proclaiming, 'It doesn't work'. The documentary depicts the new Hulme as a rabbit warren, Constant's labyrinth turned into a hotbed for crime, fear and paranoia, a place whose tortuous planning makes the seemingly simple experience of getting a pram into your flat an ordeal, a place where rates of crime and suicide are off the national scale. Yet at the exact point that this documentary was being shot,

Hulme was becoming something else entirely. Manchester City Council, which had at that point a surplus of council housing, was implementing a policy of re-housing the families that found Hulme so unnerving on estates of houses with gardens in Burnage or Wythenshawe, leaving many empty flats. The Russell Club, which was home to the Factory nightclub, opened in 1978 by the embryonic record label, was surrounded by the estate's concrete walkways – and the club's clientèle would follow suit.

Liz Naylor, fanzine editor and scriptwriter of the Joy Division-soundtracked *No City Fun*, and whose *Various Times*, a far-from-boosterist history of the area to be published next year, remembers how, after running away from home at 16 in 1978, she asked the council for a flat. First of all, she was housed in Collyhurst, then an area with a heavy National Front presence. She asked for a flat in Hulme instead, because it had already acquired 'a population of alternatives', but 'by then the *Manchester Evening News* had been running stories for years about how awful it was'. Not only was the Factory based there, but so were many of the bands, along with fanzines like *City Fun* and recording studios. One of the most famous images of Joy Division was taken from one of the bridges over the motorway that bisected the new Hulme. Photographer Kevin Cummins later recalled how 'the heavy bombing, along with an ill-conceived '60s regeneration programme, conspired to make Manchester redolent of an eastern European city. Revisiting my photographs, I see the bleakness of a city slowly dying. A single image taken from a bridge in Hulme of Princess Parkway, the major road into Manchester, features no cars.' Yet this image of a depopulated, Brutalist Manchester as a sort of English Eastern Europe resonated in a less clichéd manner with those who chose to live in Hulme – it was welcomed. Naylor remembers

Owen Hatherley

Kevin Cummins

that the entire scene was obsessed with Berlin – 'we weren't sure whether east or west Berlin' - something that also dictated what they listened to: 'Iggy Pop's *The Idiot* and Bowie's *Heroes*, was the music.' This then extended to the films they saw at the Aaben, the estate's arthouse cinema, where Fassbinder or *Nosferatu* would be eagerly consumed by the area's overcoated youth.

There was an attendant style to go with the Germanophilia. In *Various Times* Naylor writes that 'during the early 1980s there was a "Hulme look" when the whole male population of Hulme seemed to be wearing the clothes of dead men and everyone looked as if they had stepped out of the 1930s with baggy suits and tie-less shirts.' The early '80s scene in Hulme, where Factory bands like A Certain Ratio or 'SWP types' like Big Flame and Tools You Can Trust

were based in the area, was perhaps a romanticisation of these surroundings, of the stark, 'eastern European' aesthetic, the sense of a Modernist utopia decaying, gone crumbled and decadent. Naylor remembers it being very comfortable in this period, 'not scary', an arty scene rather than the macho Mancunia that has dominated since the late '80s. Although post-punk Hulme could be seen as a sort of slumming, with the families long since de-camping to more hospitable areas, Naylor argues that rather than being just a form of urban tourism, this Hulme 'became almost an independent city, another town within a town with a shifting stream of young, single people with their own dress codes'. What is especially intriguing, however, is that this scene constituted itself here, in this bastardised approximation of

New Babylon, this space of walkways, streets in the sky and vertiginous pedestrian bridges, rather than amid old terraces or in between serried tower blocks. Partly this is happenstance, due to the fact that the City Council were essentially giving away the empty flats left by the families who escaped – but also surely to do with the possibilities of the structure itself. All the things bemoaned in the *World in Action* documentary as deleterious to family life – the labyrinthine complexity of the blocks, the noise and sense of height and dynamism, the lack of a feeling of 'ownership' in the communal areas – were perfect for the purposes of a self-creating urbanism. Naylor warns me that this might be coloured by nostalgia, but says that Hulme 'became functional for people in a way that hadn't been anticipated by the planners'. Or rather, in a way that was anticipated by the people the planners had drawn their ideas from, like Constant or the Smithsons, but which they had long since forgotten.

Gentrifying the Streets in the Sky
Naylor remembers the overriding feeling of Hulme being a sense of itself as an enclave, embattled but cohesive: 'There's no future, but if we stay here we'll be all right.' Nonetheless, from the mid-'80s, the drugs had shifted from speed to heroin, muggings had become more common, Tory election landslides led to despair and many of those associated with the post-punk scene moved on. Yet the New Brutalist Hulme went on to become a (fairly crusty, by many accounts) centre for the rave scene in Manchester, with the Kitchen, a club made by knocking through three council flats, being the Hacienda's hidden reverse. When in the mid-1990s the Crescents were demolished as a ritual sacrifice to New Emerging Manchester, there was another television documentary made about the place, this time for *The Late Show*. Only just over a decade later, and we're miles from the hand-wringing of the *World in Action* documentary, with no condemnations of the idiocies of planners from the inhabitants, but instead a fierce defence from them of the possibilities of the streets in the sky, of the light, air and openness of the Crescents, and of the richly creative community that had established itself there, even in a context where crime and deprivation was still rife. One comments that a friend's daughter 'only found out she lived in a slum when she heard it on the news'. Meanwhile, if the streets in the sky had come full circle, back to New Babylon, then this is entirely supported by the documentary, which features images of travellers' caravans in the open space between the blocks, reminding that the hypermodernist Situationist urbanism of New Babylon was originally inspired by gypsy camps.

When brutalist Hulme was demolished, what was built in its stead was a mix of social and private housing, with styles ranging from Barratt Home hutches to small but undeniably deck-access blocks – to the planners' surprise, when former Crescents residents were consulted they insisted on this much-derided feature. It's another (perhaps slightly less gentrified than most) enclave of a city which has dedicated itself to the service industry and the property market, bolstered by the propagation of an ideology of culture and creativity, where it matters little what actual cultural products are produced, as the glories of the past can be lived off seemingly indefinitely. The Beetham Tower, the skyscraping and now hard-to-let emblem of Manchester's regeneration, features in its twentieth storey 'skybar' a selection of drinks named after famous Manc bands and songs – fancy a 'Hand in Glove'? – while the city's self-presentation as a centre for pop music can be found in every tourist brochure, even if there's a sense of bathos when the current equivalents to Joy Division or The Fall are proclaimed to be the Ting Tings and Jim Noir.

Owen Hatherley

What, though, if instead of calling in the bulldozers, Manchester City Council had tried to regenerate the Crescents too? An indication of what might have been can be found in the form of Mancunia's favourite property developer Urban Splash's scheme for the redevelopment of Park Hill, Womersley's far superior first attempt at streets in the sky. This provides a warped mirror image of the re-letting of Hulme Crescents to penniless 'bohemians' at the end of the '70s. In both cases, the streets in the sky are declared to be unsuitable for the families for whom they were originally intended, and aimed instead at those with the time and inclination to explore a labyrinth of reinforced concrete. This time though it isn't skint musicians that are the 'creatives' in question, but young media workers who can afford to buy loft apartments off-plan, and instead of being rehoused in homes with gardens, its tenants are being dumped on a heaving council waiting list. Urban Splash's brochure for their redevelopment of these council homes into yuppie lofts transfers their apparently successful use of Manchester's pop cultural history to Sheffield's context. Opening with the question, 'Don't you want me baby?', as it goes on it cites ABC, the Human League and Pulp, in an infantile music-press-cum-Innocent Smoothie idiom – a reminder, once again, of just how important 'the creative industries' are to Blairism and its pet schemes – the redevelopment was recently bailed out by millions of pounds in public money. Yet in making these links between architecture and pop, they inadvertently make the point that the music of the late '70s and the buildings of the '60s are symbiotically linked – and that as much as they could produce wastelands, modernist architects could produce environments which were a spur to actual creativity, spaces of vertiginous possibilities for new ways of living, proposing a *homo ludens* no longer reliant on capital and graft. Instead, today these places are redeveloped into alibis for gentrification.

MIRIAM LINNA
Cramps Confidential 1976
Girl Drummer Bares Some but Not All

Erick Purkhiser, better known as Cramps leader Lux Interior, died on 4 February 2009. Long ago, and for one year, he was my friend. I was the drummer in the first Cramps line-up which played forty-odd dates over an eight-month period from the first show on All Saints Night 1976 until 13 July 1977, the date of the NYC blackout. With his passing came a mess of calls asking about the early days. After years of avoiding a backward glance, I was suddenly dropped headlong into the well. A mouldering box of old stuff materialised from deep in the closet, and old friends began sending in decades-old snapshots, clippings, bits of correspondence. That first year in New York was my coming of age, at least in calendar years. It was also my first year behind the traps, on the flipside of fandom. It provided a hazing that alternately galvanised and confused my head. I hope this helps clear the cobwebs for those who care. Walking through my dreams, like the Pretty Things would say. RIP, Lux.

Stuff started seeping out of the woodwork before the paint was dry. Phone calls, remember-whens, faded pictures, a couple of grainy super-8s, old letters, a stop-by. 'Lux is dead,' they'd say. 'He's gone.' So I get a call from my first big-town room-mate, Pam, sister of the great and also late Bryan Gregory, and we ruminate, a shot of white light into one hell of a mouldy basement, and it's with that conversation that I begin this slow descent into a year that time forgot. Round one is shot out of the cannon, a random blast. It was a lifetime ago – everything's changed, and nothing's changed. Like when you spin around real fast and stop, and you're digging your heels in, and everything around you is a whirling blur.

I suppose it started a year earlier, while going to school in Kent, a small college town in north-east Ohio, some thirty-five miles south of Cleveland and twelve miles east of Akron. In August 1975, I wrote a teenage letter to my Detroit pen pal Nikki Lorenz (future popster Nikki Corvette) telling her I'd made some kooky new pals on an NYC road trip with my sister Helen. 'Got asked to be a drummer in an avant-gard [*sic*] band, they want someone who's never touched a drum kit. These people say they're better than anyone, truly bizarre. Tux [*sic*] is twenty-nine, Ivy like twenty-six, both beautiful young college graduate Californians (!) who finally want to get a band together in the Big Apple.'

That first run-in was at a small Sixth Avenue eatery called Chicken & Burger World, located right by Bigelow's Pharmacy and a stone's throw from Village Oldies and Discophile, where Helen and I had been trawling for records. A familiar-looking tall guy with long hair and a velvet jacket had sidled over to our table to say that he'd seen us at a show at the

Piccadilly Inn in Cleveland a few weeks earlier, and then he told us that he and his girlfriend Ivy (who waved from their table and then came over to say hi, a tiny lady with billowing sandy curls) were in the middle of moving to New York to form a band, and that I should play drums with them. I was shocked. I told him I'd never played at all and that seemed to be a selling point. I'm guessing they had come from California to Ohio not long before that to see Lux's family – he was originally from Stow, five miles from Kent, and I understood his family was in Akron. As he was talking, I realised that I had seen him at a Kinks show – the Schoolboys tour – I remembered he had been wearing turquoise shoes. Subtle. We exchanged addresses and soon after I got back home to Ohio there was a letter from Lux saying that they'd be stopping by when they came back to move their stuff to NYC. At the time, I was going to Kent State, living on Main Street in the Town House, a rather dilapidated old hotel that housed a hippy-dippy health food store on the ground floor. My second-floor window looked directly across to a used record shop. Conveniently, I could look directly into the store and knew all its comings and goings. The downtown area was somewhat off campus and comfortably run down. There was a greasy diner a couple of blocks away, and one street over there was a folkie dive called the Blind Owl where Brewer had supposedly met Shipley. Yes, Kent was a garden spot. Four dead students had put it on the map in 1970 and legend had it that KSU had made the Top Party School list in *Playboy* at some point, but you could have fooled me. One day not long after the NYC trip, Lux and Ivy did come by ye olde Town House. We started going through stacks of mags and records and talked about music and about the band they wanted to start. In retrospect, I don't think they had a name yet, nor was Bryan Gregory even in the picture at

that time. I know they met him working in an uptown NYC record store soon after they relocated. At the time I had no intention of moving to New York – I was nineteen and in my senior year with vague plans to move in with my sister in Cleveland. I had become friends with a couple of musicians there, Peter Laughner and Crocus Behemoth, who had a fantastic band called Rocket from the Tombs, which would soon evolve into Pere Ubu. Another fab local band was the Electric Eels – I was good pals with their lawnmower-playing leader Davie. Our small bunch of rock'n'roll fans in Kent were all old record nuts, all our spare time was spent reading magazines and fanzines, writing letters, listening to the radio, and playing records (and Seeds 8-tracks). I loved going to school, crazy as that sounds, and worked full time on campus, at the library and at the admissions office. I was a mad corres-pondent, scribbling (and typing on the rusty Royal manual) reams of excitable fluff to pen pals wherever they would erupt. I was a card-carrying member of the Iggy Fan Club and wrote regularly to Creem, Back Door Man, Who Put The Bomp, Rock Scene and the Purple Warp and sent fan letters to anybody whom I felt deserved comment from the peanut gallery. These were the horse-and-buggy days when you got out a pen and scribbled your thoughts out on paper because you couldn't afford long-distance phone calls and the only option was sending a telegram! Much as I hate nostalgia, those stone-age days were pretty idyllic. Those teenage Midwest pals were all perfect rock'n'roll characters, great full-time fans and noise-makers. Remember these were still the days of extreme jocks on one side and goofy hippies on the other. Digging the Stooges was not a popular idea.

Subsequent pen-pal letters to Nikki throughout 1975 have me stating that I could never in a million years live in New York, that I

Miriam Linna

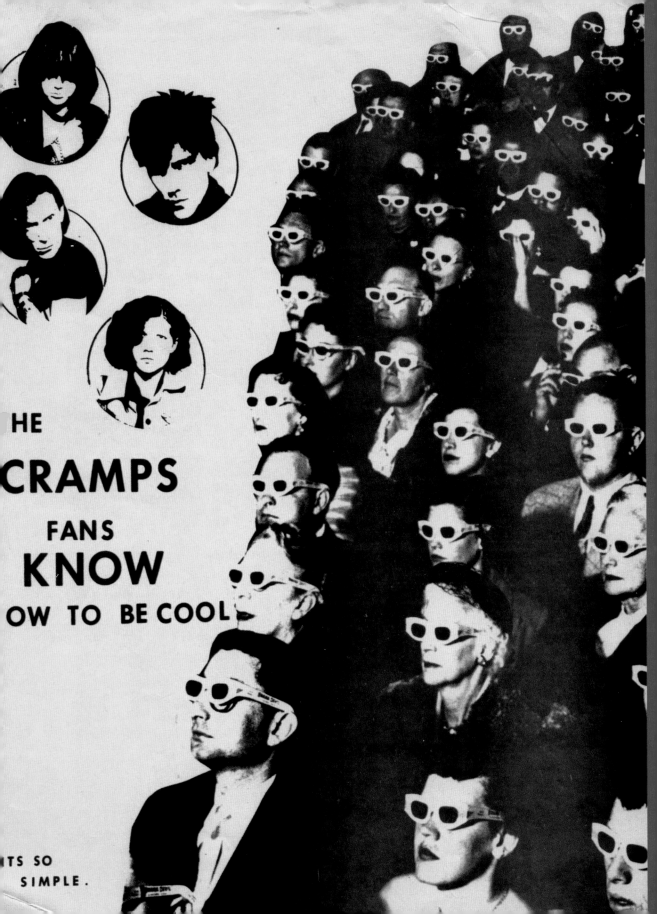

HE

CRAMPS

FANS

KNOW

OW TO BE COOL

TS SO

SIMPLE.

needed a truly shlubby city like Cleveland or Detroit. I describe seeing a dog running on a Cleveland street with a frozen rat in his mouth, with other dogs chasing him. 'Only in Cleveland,' I add, with a degree of solemnity. The next New York trip, oddly enough, was with a pack of people including the future Nick Knox, to whom I would later forfeit my throne – drum throne, that is. I describe Nick to Nikki as 'Nick, who looks like a Kink'. Strange, small world. I haven't seen Nick since 1976. He was the coolest guy back then, a talented drummer who surely had to be severely dumbed-down to bash moronically – like some people we know.

So then, in a nutshell and on a whim, again neglecting parts of the story to keep it snappy, there was another road trip to NYC with Cleveland pals which also included James Sliman (future Run DMC/Dodi Fayed press cat), delightfully zany Babs Fraley and Wildman Stiv Bator of Frankenstein fame. We all ganged up and went to see the New York Dolls, I swear, in a shopping centre on Long Island, or New Jersey, whatever – a total teenage weekend bash, Cleveland/Detroit versus the world. I'd met up with Lux and Ivy and had stayed over at their place, a small, low ceiling walk-up [apartment without a lift] on East 73rd Street. A cool old jukebox took up a good chunk of the living room – Lux said he paid a guy five bucks to carry it up the stairs, strapped to his back! There was only one window in the apartment, facing into a back alley. There was a mess of records on shelves facing the jukebox, a walk-through bedroom with a massive old bed that took up the entire room, a tiny bathroom with a sink and shower, and a miniscule kitchenette, but it was homey, and bits of velvety Victorian style bric-a-brac decorated what was in essence, Cramps HQ. The first night, I met their soft-spoken new guitar player, Bryan Gregory. The threesome had put it into first use in April, with a cool handbill (indicating a fan club – now that's confidence for a band that existed in name only!) – it would still be six months before the band would play live. The night of the fourth, we went to see the fireworks downtown, the four of us. The streets were packed with surging crowds, the noise level was insane, the big ships were in. It was simply as exciting as life could get for a kid from the boonies. I was in a band and I had yet to find a pair of drumsticks, let alone a job and a place to live.

Fortunately, my pal James wanted to move to New York right away, too. We found a two-bedroom (plus living room) walk-up in an old tenement on East Ninth Street and plonked down a deposit. I think we got one month free with a sob story about having to go back to Ohio to wrap up loose ends. At any rate, the rent worked out to forty bucks each if we got a third room-mate. Back in Cleveland, local maniac Bradley Field immediately volunteered to fill the void. Then, we got news that the Ramones and Groovies were going to be playing in Los Angeles. This was the ultimate double bill, and we decided to head to our new home in New York City via the west coast. I wrote to *Purple Warp* editor Tom Hosier, quoting the Ramones,

> Hey daddy-o, I don't wanna go...but whether I wanna or not, I am...going to move to the evil city itself, nooyawk...as soon as I get back from the waste coast/yeah, I leave to L.A. tomorrow...in a pale grey Valiant...I'm going to see the Ramones and my fave rave band in the whole wide world the Flamin Groovies at the Roxy Aug 11 and 12...I was in NYC for a week or so apt-hunting and found one on east ninth street in the el dumpo region of the village. There exist in said apt large cockroaches and other bugs, but otherwise, I LIKE IT. I will be living with

two demented pals. I am the only normal person I know anyway. I am a nice normal one year past teenage girl and my favorite band is the Flamin Groovies. I idolize Cyril Jordan and know all the Groovies songs off by heart.

Well, that LA trip the next day did not happen, because Bradley, the driver of the grey Valiant apparently got arrested for urinating on a police officer. The next morning here's me and James all packed and ready to head East, er, West, and our driver is in the klink, possibly for a month or more. James blew a fuse, and then stormed off to make some phone calls. He managed to rustle up local gal Tracey Lacy who could be persuaded by James to do just about anything. Just like that, Tracey was driving me and James to our new pad in New York in her convertible Karmann Ghia.

So here I was now, not knowing what I was getting into, and not knowing which end up was up on a drumstick, in with this snap-happy trio with a name, and a selection of photos, and zero experience, or musical ability for that matter. Lux handed me a brand new pair of sticks and pronounced me the world's greatest drummer. Let's go. Just like that. No audition, no test run, no lessons, no suggestions of what to play or how fast.

Meanwhile, Pam had come in with James and me at the Ninth Street pad – Three's Company, lower east side version: one Lebanese photographer with a humongous pet python (which ended up escaping its cage, slithering out the window into the night) and a vast collection of photo-print silk shirts and Cuban heel shoes (and an incredible sense of humour), teeny tiny, long-haired and gorgeous Pam (who we nicknamed Pam Balam – Blam- for the Groovies tune!) who missed Michigan more than I missed Ohio at the time, and me with the drumsticks and the bad perm. We were all flying by the seat of our collective pants, starting from scratch in the Snake Pit. Pam and I got jobs as lunch-time waitresses at Brew Burger (shades of Hamburger Patti), a job that obliged us to wear horrible Danskin leotards and steer-head medallions. Those creepy waitress outfits were as far as I would ever go with 'stage wear'. During that first year, I was oblivious to the fact that the band was in need of an image re-do. If anything, Bryan was the fashion icon, what with the Veronica Lake hair, the mod ties and the polka dots – it was all about his obsession with the Rolling Stones, and Brian Jones in particular (hence the moniker). I'd follow with the Stones fixation by giving myself a well-honed mop top as well.

The Cramps got rehearsal space uptown and (of course) immediately got James to take some band photos. Ivy's pride and joy was her clear Lucite Dan Armstrong guitar, just like the one Keith Richards and Cyril Jordan had, rare as sin and equally cool. Bryan played his trademark polka-dot Flying V, hand detailed with round white price-stickers. It may have been a knock-off, but it didn't matter. Bryan was capable of creating the most insane snarls and shrieks out of that crazy deal. He also had a gift for moving his cigarette around his mouth with his lips and shooting it out at some poor kid in the audience. It was bizarre and terrifying but you couldn't help but be riveted. He seemed to be constructed entirely of sinew, not an ounce of excess on his frame. That tough look from all concerned was real. Believe me, at the time, it wasn't all nice audiences and fun-loving appreciative types who 'got it'. There was a lot of crap to deal with. The band got something of a reputation for being hardasses, which was why Amos Poe cast the Cramps as thugs in his film *The Foreigner*.

I remember the first hint of theatrical get-ups for the group. Photographer/dancer Anya Phillips (RIP) wanted to take some studio snaps of the Cramps. She set up lights and umbrellas and then ran off, returning with some sort of rubber shirt with bones on it, dangling from a wire hanger. 'Put this on,' she said to me. 'Uh, no,' I said. She tried to encourage me to squeeze into the goofy get-up, but nothing in the world could get me to cooperate. I may be wrong, but I think Anya was the one who first put latex and chicken bones into the Cramps itinerary. I think *no-wavester* Lydia Lunch ended up taking that rubber-and-bones creation to heart and building some kind of look around it. Some time after my departure, I recall being stunned by the transformation the Cramps had made, when they took on some kind of bondage–drag identity with the make-up and high heels and all, a heavy-handed nod to the Dolls at their glitziest. That first year, Bryan held sway at a record store called Musical Maze and did some foot-massaging as a sideline. Lux worked at MM early on, too. When Bryan had first joined, and Pam was banging their gong, they would blast away in the basement of the store. Lux must have quit or had his hours shortened, as he would come downtown and we'd check out the record stores and junk stores, me running three steps to each of his long strides down the sidewalks. We'd do the flyering for shows, taping handbills to walk/don't walk signs and tacking them up at the record shops. At one point, Gregg Turner at Back Door Man appointed me the East Coast Promo Gal for Zero records and it was my job to get the singles into the shops. Same with Ohio bands Pere Ubu and Devo. So we added a bit of schlepping to the record hunt jaunts. Like the Avon lady, only different. It felt like a bizarre world episode of *Ozzie and Harriet*, and why not, Lux was obsessed by Ricky Nelson. It was kind of weird. He loved Ricky so much, he thought he resembled him. Beautiful.

Early on I remember waiting for the down-town Lexington Avenue train with Lux. I guess I was missing home, and told him I'd been writing to my friends back home and that maybe I should go back. He took me by the shoulders, looked me straight in the eyes, and told me YOU'RE A CRAMP NOW! YOU CAN'T GO BACK. There was a phone call home, bawling to mom, and another with my brother threatening to come and get me and bring me back. It never happened, though, and my proclamation to Nikki that I could never live in New York would fade. The band began rehearsing in earnest. I say rehearsing because there never was any practising. From day one, it was, 'We're a band, we have to make flyers and play shows.' I thought this was how it was done. Since nobody really knew how to play, it was pointless trying to cover any songs that anybody would know faithfully. So, as the recipe has come undone over the years, the idea was doing original versions of gnarly, attitudinal old obscuros, things that Ivy could deliver a dangerous guitar line on, that Bryan could fuzz-blast away to, that I could pound around, that Lux could verbalise over with his well-oiled vocal chords and seasoned imagination, stoked by hours of late night *Creature Features* on TV.

The first set of 'originals' became the first set of greatest hits for year one of the Cramps. You know the songs. 'Don't Eat Stuff off the Sidewalk', 'Sunglasses after Dark', 'Teenage Werewolf', 'Human Fly', 'Rockin Bones', 'Love Me', 'What's Behind the Mask', 'I Can't Hardly Stand It', 'TV Set'. I turned twenty-one in October. Ivy gave me a beautiful pair of hand-painted Japanese slippers and a lovely old oriental musical jewellery box with pretty geisha girls who went round and round when you wound it up. Lux gave me sealed copies of the Sonics *Boom* and *Here Are the Sonics*, fresh out of the crazy old record shop across from the Strand Book Store. We'd been gazing at those

Miriam Linna

albums in the shop a week before and *I never thought I'd have anything but the beaters back at the Snake Pit*. The Cramps debut was slated for the day after Halloween – 1 November 1976 at CBGB's opening for old pal and boss (next time for that story) Stiv Bator's new band the Dead Boys. During the eight months that followed, this first incarnation of the Cramps would play forty-some shows, most of them at Max's Kansas City and CBGB.

When we weren't playing, we were rehearsing, and when we weren't rehearsing, we were out watching bands. Initially it was all about the Ramones and the Dictators, and my admiration for them would never fade. The one drum 'lesson' I ever got was from Tommy Ramone, who showed me how to hold the sticks 'like this'. In spring of 1977, Richard Robinson, the revered producer of the Flamin' Groovies *Teenage Head* album, paid to take the Cramps into Bell Sound, recording eight tracks. This was stunning to me. Not in my wildest dreams could I believe that the guy who recorded my favourite band wanted to record us. I honestly felt that I was on *Candid Camera*, that this was all a dream or a hilarious hoax that was being played on me.

New York was a very different place in those days. The city was nearly bankrupt, some unknown psychopath dubbed the Son of Sam was shooting disco people every couple of months, and there were no yuppies or rich kids anywhere in sight. Everybody was a scrapper. Cheap rent, quarter coffee and hard work in some capacity. The Cramps were now opening for the Ramones, getting a dollop of attention from the press. At one point, Hilly Kristal, the owner of CBGB, was messing with the idea of having local bands cover Rolling Stones songs (great idea!) and everybody was making dibs on tunes. I remember blowing through 'Off the Hook' a few times, anticipating recording it, but the whole project fell through. Around the same time, we were messing with the Troggs' 'Night of the Long Grass'. That still is a personal favourite. God bless Reg Presley and all he stands for, crop circles and all. Somebody get Reg on Coast to Coast AM, please! That spring, my Ohio pal Peter Laughner came to visit at the apartment above a hardware store on 12th Street and First Avenue that I was by then sharing with Miss Lydia Lunch and nutty Cleveland import Bradley Field, who was fresh out of jail in Ohio. (The pair would go on to bang a gong as Teenage Jesus and the Jerks.) Peter arrived with Lester Bangs and Richard Lloyd in tow, and we hung around listening to records and a demo Richard had just cut, solo, finally taking a cab to pick up photographer Stephanie Chernikowski. It was a perfect late spring day, the windows were down and the taxi was going fast. I remember it clearly, as it was the last time I would see Peter. He phoned just before his death in June. I'll never forget the call, in the middle of the night. Lydia, Bradley and I had been invited to some kind of fancy-shmancy party and I'd fallen asleep in the living room. They'd tried to wake me up, but I was so sleepy, I told them I'd meet up with them later. The ringing phone woke me up hours later. In retrospect, it was already a call from the other side. We talked about good things happening in New York, about the Groovies fan club, and his writing, and music plans back in Ohio, about coming to New York to visit again. Of my many heroes at the time, he ranked at the very top. I learned of his passing days after the fact, when Lydia and I ran into Lester on the Bowery. LB was upset that we were out having a good time, 'considering'. I had no clue what he was talking about. When he told me, I was shattered. This was unbelievable to me, it was not supposed to happen. Impossible!

Meanwhile, the Cramps were slated to play their first three-night weekend stint at CBGB, hosting a bunch of Canadian combos. For two

weeks leading to that weekender, I was numb, haunted day and night by memories of my long-gone friend, without a doubt the most influential person in my short life at that time. I remembered the last phone call, turning it over and over in my head. Harsh. That's a word we'd use all the time back then. That's HARSH. Well, this was as harsh as it gets. Things got wildly complicated with friends and room-mates. By this time, Lydia and Bradley and I had moved to Warren Street in lower Man-hattan, to an abandoned, and certifiably haunted old basement shop with no hot water. This was also where the Cramps took to rehearsing. My state of mind was not good. I left Warren Street in July, having found a sixth-floor walk-up on 5th Street. For the first time in NYC, I had my own place. The three-day Canadian weekend at CBGB culminated in an impromptu housewarming at my new pad, with

all the Canuck bands, the Cramps and a houseful of friends blasting records way into the night. After weeks of sadness and confusion, there had been some relief in pounding the tubs and yapping with friends. The Canadians, especially the band Teenage Head, were nuts about the Groovies and were insanely impressed that we had recorded with grand, exalted pooh-bah Richard Robinson.

Three days later, on Wednesday night, lightning hit a Con Edison power station, and then another, plunging all five boroughs of New York City into total darkness. The city went berserk for twenty-five hours running in what was dubbed the Great Blackout of 1977. I was downtown when the lights went out, with bashing and crashing from all directions, and cop cars and ambulances shrieking up and down the avenues all night long. By dawn, huge sections of the city were burned, looted, trashed. Like

Miriam Linna

Pompeii, without the lava. Within hours, I would feel pretty much the same way, kind of like I'd been torched in a mouldy burlap bag and left to smoulder in a dumpster in the South Bronx.

....

You know, back in 1973 when my sister and I got back home to Ohio from England, we went to work at an automotive plant making hoods for Mack trucks. Enormous fibreglass parts would roll out of hot ovens on rail tracks and we'd grind and sand for eight hours a day, sweating in goggles, masks, earplugs, protective gear, four women to a frame, hood after hood, day in, day out. I considered it a necessary hazing. A life experience. One of those deals that doesn't kill you, but makes you stronger. My first year in New York was a necessary hazing, too, a full-time, full-on occupation that just happened to be filled with loud music and sweaty people, day in and day out – at least the earplugs were optional. Not entirely a bad thing, not by any means. And for someone who shot out of the hopper at full-tilt, I had a relatively soft landing, thanks to fellow Groovies fans Trixie A. Balm and Shawn Brighton, who showed up at my door the proverbial morning after with a hell of a pep talk and plans for, what else, a band. I'm eternally grateful to them for their timing. But I'm also thankful for the days to Lux and Ivy and Bryan. That first year shot me into an overdrive that I've yet to come down from. Before the snow would blow at the end of 1977, I would be bashing away with Nervus Rex (before their power pop alliance with Chinn and Chapman), having met my better half and instant sweetheart Billy Miller (at a record fair, natch), and would soon start a job with music biz honcho (Buddah bigwig – FLAMINGO!!!) Marty Thau at his new label, Red Star Records. Some time before the Cramps left New York, Lux and Bryan came to see the Zantees (who I'd joined straight out of Nervus Rex) at Hurrah's, and to say goodbye. I was so happy to see them there, and remember standing on the stairs, halfway up, halfway down. It was only Lux and Bryan, and the three of us kind of just stared at each other. I felt real bad. I had that hollow break-up feeling in my throat. It was the last time I would see Bryan, and I know he heard me choke on hard tears when I hugged him goodbye and shook his ring-covered hand. I remembered that hard-bitten goodbye when he too fell off the masthead, a year and a half later. I got messages from him over the years, 'Bryan says hi!' 'Bryan asked about you!' 'Bryan sends his love!' I never saw him again. I didn't see Lux or Ivy again until 2003. It was at the Warsaw in Brooklyn. I went to say happy birthday to Ivy, as she'd hit the big five-o, a big one for the ladies. A time to celebrate with everybody you've ever known. On leaving, I said goodbye to Lux on the long flight of stairs from the dressing room. I stared at him the same way as I had that night with Bryan at Hurrah's, that feel-bad choking goodbye that has to carry weight, because there are no plans ever to meet again.

kicksville66.blogspot.com

MATT THORNE
Gigolos Get Lonely Too
Prince: His Protégées, Side-projects and Their Influence
(Part One 1978–84)

There are four main strands to Prince's music – first, the official releases from his 1978 debut *For You* to 2009's *Lotusflow3r/MPLSoUND*, including the studio albums and singles but also myriad remixes and maxi-albums, often with as many as six or seven variations on the original track; second, the unreleased songs which have kept several bootleg labels afloat for decades, now so multitudinous that labels can put out twenty CD sets, or 43-hour MP3 collections and still not exhaust the circulating material; third, the live recordings: two official releases – the *One Nite Alone* box set and 2008's *Indigo Nights* – and literally thousands of bootleg recordings, including several versions of the same show in differing fidelity; and fourth, the songs he has given to other artists and protégées, from Sue Ann Carwell in 1978 to Bria Valente's *Elixer* earlier this year.

As with Prince's own releases, the records that his protégées and friends (and in Mayte's case, wife) have put out over the last thirty years have been of variable quality: some are considered classics of their kind (much of the output of The Time, Madhouse, The Family, Jill Jones and Sheila E), others have split opinion (Mayte's very '90s *Child of the Sun* or Ingrid Chavez's poetic *May 19 1992*) and a few (such as Carmen Electra's debut) are regarded as complete disasters. But just as almost every Prince track, even the bad ones, has something of interest, so any album or song that he has major involvement with is worth seeking out. It also seems significant to a deeper understanding of Prince's creative nature that he's continued to pursue this side of his career in the face of record company doubts and mass public indifference.

This strand of Prince's music is driven by two major motivations: Prince's delight in hiding from public view, something he suggested in an early interview was proof of his modesty, and his workaholic nature – the fact that, for all his interest in sports and movies, ballet and fashion, he enjoys being in a studio or on stage over anything else. But it's more than a straightforward desire to release as much as possible. It goes beyond the recording studio and into his life. In fact, it isn't stretching things too far to see 'Vanity', 'Apollonia' and 'Sister Fate' as Prince's characters, part of the novel he sings about trying (and failing) to write in the unreleased 'Moonbeam Levels'. Others have suggested it makes more sense to see them as Prince's alter egos, the name 'Vanity' believed to have been inspired by the physical similarity between Denise Matthews and Prince.

Prince's collaboration with soul singer Sue Ann Carwell wasn't released, but it was the start of several important trends that would play a significant part in his subsequent work with protégées. His 'Idolmaker' instinct: Prince's

JLN 09

attraction to women who have proved their raw talent by winning contests;[1] his desire to write songs either from a female perspective or ones that would work when sung by a woman, and his willingness to share out his stockpile of songs, never fearing he might dry up. It was also the first time he attempted to give a protégée a new identity, suggesting Carwell rename herself Suzy Stone, although unlike Denise Matthews (Vanity) or Patricia Kotero (Apollonia), Carwell refused, reluctant to have her career co-opted in this way.

Prince and Carwell worked together on a small number of songs (conflicting reports suggest there were three, four or five), of which the most well known are 'Make It Through The Storm', the lyrics of which were written not by Prince but by his early collaborator Chris Moon, and 'Wouldn't You Love to Love Me'. Both songs would later be released, the former three years later as the B-side of Carwell's single 'Let Me Let You Rock Me' (without Prince's music), and the latter not until 1987, when Prince would give it to Taja Sevelle.[2] Demo versions of the tracks (including one on Prince's very first home session) reveal them to be in the *For You* mode, reminding the listener that by nineteen Prince was a fully mature talent. It would take him a while to regress to the point where he could write a song like Vanity 6's 'Wet Dream'.

In the summer of 1979 Prince asked his management to organise studio time and took his band of the era – guitarist Dez Dickerson, bassist Andre Cymone, keyboardists Gayle Chapman and Matt Fink and drummer Bobby Z – to Boulder, Colorado, to work on his first planned side-project, a New Wave band named the Rebels. Unlike later side-projects such as Vanity 6 or The Time (or indeed Prince's own early albums, which he recorded mostly alone) this was a fully collaborative project. There are conflicting stories about whether the band was going to do the music with someone else providing the public image or if they'd be involved in the promotion as well. Bobby Z has suggested that the band was intended to be like Milli Vanilli or The Monkees, but Dez Dickerson told me this was never clarified, and that they were still talking about the photo shoot when everyone got distracted by the swift progression of Prince's career.

Although the nine Rebels songs are cherished by collectors, the album was never released. But unlike many of Prince's abandoned or unreleased side-projects, this is a finished project, and as such, essential to understanding Prince's early development. While the record was clearly an exploratory enterprise and produced in a relatively speedy eleven days, this doesn't mean Prince took it any less seriously, as he completed his own second album in a month. Dickerson remembers Prince taking painstaking effort over the project, whole days given up to getting the tracking and over-dubbing right.

'You', which Prince later renamed 'U' and revisited twice (recording an unreleased demo in 1987 before giving the song to Paula Abdul for her 1991 *Spellbound* album) is a simple track: Prince gives a woman a list of things he likes about her. Even on the Rebels version you can hear the seeds of Prince's own later take on techno (although it's definitely rock) that he'd display on tracks like 'Loose' from the 1994 album *Come* or 'The Human Body' from 1996's *Emancipation*, but by 1987 (one year *before* 'techno' was properly defined as a genre), it sounds as if it's come straight out of Detroit. When Abdul does it in 1991, she retains Prince's spoken sections from the 1987 version, but the techno-stomp is toned down, and the central sense of unblinking devotion loses something of its manic quality.

Another Rebels song that refused to die is 'If I Love You Tonight'. As well as the Rebels version, there are two Prince demos of the song from 1987 in wide circulation, and it was later covered by both Mica Paris and Mayte, who recorded two versions on her 1995 *Child of the Sun*, one in English and the other in Spanish. The Rebels version is sung by Gayle Chapman, a variation on Kris Kristofferson's 'Help Me Make It Through The Night' from a seemingly suicidal woman prepared to hand over her gun to a one-night stand. Prince's versions, unusually, are the weakest of the six recordings, a strange blend of the slightly syrupy style he would adopt in the early '90s on tracks like 'Graffiti Bridge' and the more pared-down 'Sign o' the Times' with its one-man bass, keyboard and drum machine approach. Mica Paris injects a bit of south London grit into her version, but by the time Mayte covers it, the song's been transformed from a despondent suicidal blues into a full-on (and good) sunny house track.

'Hard to Get' is the most New Wave song, seemingly written under the inspiration of The Cars *Candy-O* album, released a month before the Rebels went into the studio and no doubt still on Prince's turntable at this time. (Dickerson, a huge fan of the band, remembers playing Cars riffs in rehearsal and was surprised to hear Prince has recently started covering 'Let's Go' in concert.) Although musically appealing, it's a generic rock song about a girl who won't have sex. The Cars' influence is even stronger on a second version of the track, recorded in 1981 during the *Controversy* sessions. It recently emerged that Prince included a snippet of the song on a sampler tape of thirty tracks offered for other artists to record seemingly sometime in the late '80s, so it clearly remained high in his estimation for several years.

It is disappointing that the record wasn't released in 1979, since, just as his recordings as Madhouse reveal Prince the jazz musician, the rock underpinnings of several of Prince's Rebels songs reveal Prince the New Waver but also

Prince the rockabilly, pre-dating the style of *Controversy* and the much later *Chaos & Disorder*, and displaying a side of his work that still remains under-represented in his main catalogue. It is also the only album Prince has been involved in where he really is just one of the band rather than merely trying to give this impression; although he would draw inspiration from many collaborators in the future, from now on he would always remain in command.

Some critics have seen Prince's protégées and side-projects as outlets for different sides of his music that won't fit his mainstream releases, but this seems inaccurate. Better instead to see them as spurs to further production, ways of pushing himself to produce still more, or a laboratory for experiments likely to find their way into his own albums, and equally as likely to inspire worthwhile music as the record company's request for a new album. With the Rebels, Dickerson believes there may have been some concern from management about keeping the focus on Prince's burgeoning career, but later side-projects and band slotted in easily alongside Prince's own releases, and as Dickerson points out, Prince would look forward to moving from his own projects to albums where he remained incognito as the average person might look forward to a holiday.

Instead of the Rebels, then, Prince's most significant early side-project was the first, eponymous, album by The Time. The six-track album features Prince in deep disguise, eschewing a song-writing credit and coproducing under the pseudonym Jamie Starr. Although The Time would evolve into a band with a very clear identity, the project initially grew out of jokes and silliness, Lisa Coleman told me. She was living with Prince at the time, and her contribution to the album was seemingly greater than has previously been acknowledged. 'My room was upstairs,' she explained, 'so he would call me down, "Lisa, would you help me do this string part? What about these lyrics? Can you finish this verse?" He involved me, I punched him in while he was playing the drums, whatever it was.'

She wasn't there on the night they decided to make Morris Day the front-man, but remembers him as a cute freckle-faced boy with a big 'fro who would run and get them hamburgers, a left-handed drummer who loved to jam. One version of the story of The Time's genesis is that Morris Day was offered the band as compensation for giving Prince the song 'Partyup', although Lisa says she wasn't there the night this decision was made and Dickerson can neither confirm or deny the rumour. Lisa says Prince never doubted that Morris would rise to the challenge, although she felt, 'The guy had had a huge responsibility thrust upon him and what seemed like fun and games at first became a big deal.' But he soon got into it, especially once he'd established his uniform: Stacy Adams shoes and a leopard-print jacket. Prince also made use of his live band at the time and Matt Fink remembers playing the synthesiser solo on 'The Stick'.

As well as being an artistic success, this is one of Prince's most commercially popular side-projects, initially outselling his own *Dirty Mind*. *Dirty Mind* is arguably the better of the two records, but *The Time* feels more sophisticated, the lengthy nine- and ten-minute songs reminiscent of 'DMSR', 'Automatic' and 'Something in the Water (Does Not Compute)'. The pleasure of this album is the looseness of the jams. While a tighter song like 'Girl' pales when compared to 'Free' or 'Scandalous', long, lyrically simple tracks like 'Get It Up' (which would gain particular power when played live, Morris's slinky vocals sounding wonderfully sleazy-smooth) or 'Cool' work well, encouraging the listener to settle into a groove before shocking them to attention with a weird synth squiggle.

Vanity 6, Prince's first female-fronted side-project, was closer to Dirty Prince. The band started out as the Hookers, and very nearly had a lead singer named 'Vagina', but Vanity 6 were always a pop band, and the first song Prince wrote for the project, 'Make-Up' has an almost childlike innocence. For all his later play with male and female identity, nothing in his oeuvre seems quite as odd (or delicious) as the idea of Prince going into the studio and play-acting this song. A clear influence on Chicago house (it's a toss-up whether this track or 'Little Red Corvette' was behind Frankie Knuckles's 'Baby Wants to Ride'), the song describes a woman putting on make-up, smoking a cigarette and lounging in a camisole as she waits for her lover to call.

'Wet Dream', the other song that Prince demoed for The Hookers, has a salacious title but aside from the labial double-entendre in the first line ('my lips start shaking') and a mild sexual analogy ('deliver the dam to the river') in the second verse, is a relatively innocuous lust song about a woman's interest in a seemingly unobtainable man, a theme Prince would return to obsessively when writing songs for female protégées.

What gives Prince's earliest work much of its charm is his tireless subservience before unkind, promiscuous or uninterested women, and it seems surprising but sweet that when writing his first songs for women to sing he didn't take on the persona of the unavailable lover, but imagined instead a sister to his poor sexually frustrated brothers. As the lyric describes the woman's jealousy when she sees the object of her affection taking another girl to the soda shop for ice cream, it doesn't sound much like a song for a 'hooker' to sing. And from the description of money changing hands in the song in return for fulfilment of fantasy, it seems this 'hooker' may have fallen for a gigolo.

It took over a year for the Hookers to metamorphose into Vanity 6. During that period Warner Brothers put out Prince's fourth album, *Controversy*, and the first record by The Time, and Prince went back on the road (supported by The Time) for a five-month 48-date US tour. Meeting a new woman often seems to inspire new bursts of creativity or changes in direction for Prince – and in a break during the *Controversy* tour he met Denise Matthews at a backstage party (an event he'd later dramatise in *Purple Rain*) and decided to make her the front woman for his girl group project.

Vanity 6's most famous song, 'Nasty Girl,' may be less well known than Prince's greatest hits, but it's among the most influential songs Prince has written. It's easy to trace a line from Madonna – who in her earliest incarnation could've been a fourth member of the band – to Janet Jackson, whose 1986 song 'Nasty' (produced by two former members of The Time) reverses the gender from 'nasty girls' to 'nasty boys' to Britney Spears, who claimed that the track 'Boys' from her 2001 album *Britney* had 'a kinda Prince feel to it', but actually lifts directly from 'Nasty Girl' (the song is produced by the Neptunes, and its remixed version, 'Boys (The Co-Ed Remix)', features vocals from Pharrell, a producer and rapper and die-hard Prince fanatic). Britney's 'Let's turn this dancefloor into our own little nasty world' and repeated invocations to 'get nasty' are clear Xeroxes of Vanity's 'my own little nasty world' and 'dance nasty girls'.

The video for 'Drive Me Wild' begins with Susan in bed in striped pyjamas and clutching a teddy (a look later borrowed by Britney for a *Rolling Stone* cover) before Brenda and Vanity emerge from the dry ice looking like zombie hookers and drag her out of her bedroom and into a waiting Cadillac. The creepy '80s porn feel of the video is emphasised by the strange guests at the party: a fat white-haired man in cardboard crown, red cape and rude-boy T-shirt; a man in a Richard Nixon mask juggling cassettes and various men who've mislaid their trousers or shirts. Brenda, in dog collar and chain, punches a greasy-haired dude in shades who's been coming on to her, before the whole video is revealed to be Susan's peculiar dream.

'Drive Me Wild' is another invocation to a lover, but sweet-yet-strange Susan is a less demanding sexual partner than Brenda or Vanity, closer to Prince in her willingness to please (although she lacks his sexual confidence or experience: in the lyric, she compares herself to a car, telephone, radio and baby doll and implies she's still a virgin). What's most appealing about the song is its simplicity, and in the extended version at least, the possibility that Prince might spin out this basic track forever. The moments of Prince's music that give me greatest pleasure are when he stretches these jams to almost ludicrous extremes (e.g. the over 50-minutes-long 'Billy', inspired by a character in *Purple Rain*, or the hour-long original version of 'Soul Psychodelicide') where you get a sense of Prince proving his youth, energy and exuberance by matching himself against machines. It's this side of Prince that seemingly influenced the bedroom-bound musicians of Detroit, and it has been argued that Prince played as important a role in influencing techno as the more commonly name-checked Kraftwerk. If this is true, then perhaps Prince's greatest contribution to this style and sound was in combining sexuality with technology.

With his Linn drums and synths taking care of the backing, Prince didn't even need band mates, although by now day-long rehearsal sessions were a regular part of how Prince drilled his fellow musicians. Lisa remembers, 'You never knew what it was. He'd say, "Groove in A. Everybody groove B flat." It was an exercise in finding the cogs, especially with funk music where there's syncopation, so we weren't playing on top of each other, we were experts at getting in synch, two guitar players, two keyboard players. Prince would call for certain people to drop out or come back in. "Lisa, what have you got?" "Let's see, I got this." What chords, things like that. It was an exercise, band yoga, relay racing. We became Olympic musicians, it was great.'

While working on the Vanity 6 album, Prince had also been preparing The Time's second album, released a fortnight later. While the first album cover showed the whole band, Morris Day stands alone on *What Time Is It?* checking his watch in front of a wall covered with clocks. The record has more character than its predecessor, and although it is structured similarly, with three long dance tracks and three shorter songs, the lyrics are sharper and less generic, the concept now clearly in focus. It would be the hits from the third Time album that would fix the band in the public consciousness, but this is just as good. Prince's association with the band was now well established, as they'd supported him on his *Controversy* tour, but once again he kept his involvement hidden, with only the coproduction credit for 'The Starr Company' – the anonymous Jamie Starr's[3] new enterprise, also responsible for the Vanity 6 record – hinting at Prince's involvement.

Dickerson says that as with 'Cool' on the first album, Prince gave him the title 'Wild and Loose' and he came up with the words, here a milder lyric Prince sexed up. The lyric has some superficial similarities with the later 'Hot Thing'. Both songs are about a man picking up a young, sexually free woman and taking her to a party. In 'Hot Thing', she's 'barely 21'; in 'Wild and Loose' her 'body's saying 21' but her face '17'. In 'Hot Thing' Prince tells the girl to give her folks a call because she's going to the Crystal Ball; in 'Wild and Loose', Morris gives his girl the porno-creepy instruction to tell her mother she won't be home because they have plans for her. The disturbing sense that this groupie is going to be roasted by all the members of The Time is intensified by a mid-section breakdown where multiple male and female voices bring to life the kind of after-party R. Kelly would appreciate, but countered by the fact that the groupie's played by Vanity, who's surely more than a match for Morris.

While Dickerson was shocked to hear how Prince had altered his lyric, he was even more surprised to hear the second track on the album, as its title – '777-9311' was his phone number, recalling that he was called by 'every bozo with a telephone and a cheesy sense of humour'. Although the song's a throwaway about Morris trying to get a woman's digits, it was the album's biggest hit. 'Onedayi'mgonnabesomebody' is similarly disposable, a short itchy funk song about making it big.

Nine-minute dance track 'The Walk' is a dry run for the more famous 'The Bird', introducing a new dance style to First Avenue and ending with a hilarious exchange between Day and Vanity, as he persuades her to take off her skin-tight jeans and change into the lingerie he keeps in his car's glovebox (none of his girls wear gloves), only to be surprised by the size of the butt she reveals when acquiescing to his request.

The silly party mood of the first two-thirds of the album is abandoned for the last two ballads, 'Gigolos Get Lonely Too' and 'I Don't Wanna Leave You', which would have sat well on any of the first four Prince albums. 'Gigolos Get Lonely Too' is the better song, a lament from a lady-killer who wants to make love without taking off his clothes. The other ballad, 'I Don't Wanna Leave You' is another Prince song about an impossible woman, and another frustrated lover prepared to put up with anything to keep the relationship going.

Prince took Vanity 6 and The Time on tour as support when promoting *1999*, seemingly now happy to reveal himself as puppet-master. For the era, this is a relatively well-documented tour, with a number of high-quality soundboard and video recordings in circulation, and although only a handful include the opening sets, it's possible to get a good sense of the revue quality of these dates. The live versions of Vanity 6's songs don't differ that significantly from the record, but the more shocking lyrics lose some of their power when thrown away onstage. It's unclear whether this is due to vocal weakness or a deliberate tactic, but it seems telling that when introducing 'Nasty Girl' live in Minneapolis, Vanity has to psyche herself: 'Listen, Minneapolis, in order for me to keep up with my reputation, I want you to tell me, "Vanity is nasty . . ."'[4]

Although it's now common for Prince to play up to five hours a night, his *1999* performance was little more than an hour, just twenty minutes longer than The Time's average set, and it seems Prince was being genuine when describing his fear of being upstaged by his support act. Playing the best tracks from their first two albums, Monte Moir and Jimmy Jam's electro keyboards sound incredible, and there's a truly manic unhinged energy to their audience-pleasing chicanery. 'Gigolo's Get Lonely Too' is a live highlight, spun out to twice its recorded length with a Morris Day soliloquy about his diamonds, 'baggies' (baggy trousers), and afore-mentioned Stacy Adams as he invites a woman on stage for a glass of wine. During this tour a screenwriter was on the bus with them, noting down details for what would later become *Purple Rain* (although the project would change writer before reaching the screen.) There was also friction between the various camps and

Lisa remembers there being no doubt as to who was in charge. 'There were three buses. Vanity 6 had a bus, we had a bus, and The Time had a bus. Our bus had a video-machine on it, and we stopped at a truck stop and the video machine was gone. Me and Dez went onto Vanity 6's bus and Prince was on the bus watching something with Vanity. And we said, "Hey, that's from our bus," and he said, "They're all my buses." Oh . . . right . . . but that really hurt us and we had to do the walk of shame back to our bus.'

Almost two years would pass between the second Time album and Prince's next full-length project with a protégée, Sheila E's *The Glamorous Life* (1984). In the meantime, Prince worked on tracks for the third album by The Time, *Ice Cream Castles*, released a month after Sheila E's record; reconfigured the line-up of both his backing back the Revolution and The Time, axing Terry Lewis and Jimmy Jam; recorded (and abandoned) half a second Vanity 6 record; completed the *Purple Rain* movie and soundtrack, alongside several songs that wouldn't make it onto the released version of the album; recorded two songs for *Around the World in a Day*, recorded a number of B-sides as good as anything on his albums, including 'Erotic City', his first collaboration with Sheila E; recorded an early version of an album for a new girl band called Apollonia 6 and, perhaps most significantly, had his biggest success to date with 'When Doves Cry', the first single from *Purple Rain*.

As with previous protégées, Prince presented Sheila E with songs that he'd already recorded, allowing her to replace his scratch vocal and then building up most songs around her percussion. Prince often experiments with techniques and styles in his side-projects that don't reach full fruition in his own work until several years later and the first Sheila E album has less in common with the very mainstream

('Darling Nikki' aside) rock record he'd just completed than their later collaborations on *Sign O' The Times* and *Lovesexy*.

'The Belle of St. Mark' is another unrequited lust song, describing Sheila's love for a teenage Parisian. 'Strawberry Shortcake' is an instrumental with Prince's backmasked lyrics buried deep in the mix. 'Noon Rendezvous' has Sheila looking forward to a lunchtime assignation with a possibly older (or, at least more experienced) lover. The crepuscular pace seems inappropriate for a song about a daytime sex-session, and the lyrics are awkwardly phrased, but the biggest problem is that this is a 'Purple Rain'-style epic condensed into four minutes. Prince's own first live version of the song, recorded at a rehearsal for his 1984 First Avenue birthday show, runs to fifteen minutes and transforms the track into one of his most awesomely desolate recordings.

Alongside Prince's version of 'Noon Rendezvous', the only track on the album that seems worth considering as an important part of Prince's (as opposed to Sheila E's) oeuvre, is the nine-minute title track, 'The Glamorous Life', which gives the album its overall concept and helped fix Sheila E's pop personality (as well as giving her a showcase for her percussion skills, particularly when played live). The album's conceit was that it was an aural movie rather than a mere record, and, along with 'Oliver's House' this is the album's most obvious story-song. It has some interesting lyrical parallels with Madonna's 'Material Girl', released the following year, which takes the opposite perspective from Sheila's insistence that money only pays the rent and it's love that is forever.

The Time's third album, *Ice Cream Castles*, released a month later, features the two songs for which the band are now best known, 'Jungle Love' and 'The Bird' (they perform both in *Purple Rain*), but the first single was 'Ice Cream Castles', in which Morris Day drops his usual 'bring me a mirror' schtik to sing about falling in love with a white woman.

Nothing else on side one of *Ice Cream Castles* is as powerful. 'My Drawers' is another tedious Prince song about underwear (not his worst: that honour goes to the unreleased 'Drawers Burnin'', one of the few Prince songs I'd be happy never to hear again) while 'Chili Sauce', like the New Power Generation's much later 'Mashed Potato Girl', is a silly skit set in a restaurant (Prince considers a restaurant the funniest location in the world, although he usually makes the same joke: a man buying a restaurant just to sack the staff), and hard to listen to now after twenty years of this filler on rap albums.

But it's the three songs on side two that make this The Time's most commercially and artistically successful album. 'Jungle Love', a simple party song with its infectious 'oh-wee-oh-wee-oh' call-out, remains in the band's set to this day. More evidence of Prince's love of muddling concepts come with 'If The Kid Can't Make You Come', in which Morris voices a character named 'The Kid' who seems to have no connection with Prince's character of the same name in *Purple Rain*. Among the most explicit of The Time's seduction songs, it has a long central passage where Morris removes his date's bra, admires her breasts, and makes her promise never to breastfeed before his date, played by Sharon Hughes (an actress best known for parading around in Vanity 6-style underwear in the 1983 'women-in-prison' exploitation movie *Chained Heat*), announces that it's 'titty time'. 'The Bird' is a celebration of yet another imaginary dance craze, and the best yet, where you can dance how you like as long as you flap your arms in the air. Prince isn't the only Minneapolis musician to write a song about a bird-based dance-craze, as before his rise the city was best known for the Trashmen and their immortal 'Surfin' Bird', recently given a new lease of life by *Family Guy*. But for all his love of party-time, Prince's musical experimentation with side-projects was about to get more serious, and the events surrounding his next project, the Family, would ultimately change the direction of his music, and the course of his career, forever.

Interview with Wendy & Lisa

Hidden within Henson studios in LA and guarded by a giant Kermit the Frog, is 'The Treehouse', a music-lover's haven where Wendy Melvoin and Lisa Coleman score hit US TV shows including *Heroes, Nurse Jackie* and the forthcoming *Virtuality*. The walls are lined with framed covers of classic rock magazines, underscoring the musical erudition these two women have built up during their time in the industry. Lisa Coleman, a warm, funny and irreverent spirit with a knowing laugh and a laid-back, philosophical outlook, joined Prince on the *Dirty Mind* tour at nineteen, moving into his house and contributing to side projects such as The Time (and, much later, Apollonia 6), as well as inspiring Prince to write songs such as 'Little Red Corvette' and the unreleased 'Strange Way of Saying I Love You'. With her equable nature and deep musical knowledge (she introduced Prince to everything from Paul Hindemith to Bill Evans's *Symbiosis*), it's clear Prince was lucky to have her around as a foil during the most adventurous period of his career. Wendy Melvoin, a sharp, funny and deeply charismatic straight-talker, contributed to *1999* and later replaced guitarist Dez Dickerson when Prince's band became the Revolution and had just as big an impact, her ideas and presence an essential part of what made his mid-'80s music and shows so compelling.

The Revolution were arguably Prince's best-loved and most enduring band, with whom he recorded three of his most highly regarded albums, *Purple Rain, Around the World in a Day* and *Parade*, as well as five albums' worth of material that included many songs that have reached bootleggers and have been referred to as the *Dream Factory, Crystal Ball* or *Roadhouse Garden* albums, but which Wendy and Lisa say were recordings either intended for *Sign o' the Times* or other projects that remained inchoate. After their time in the Revolution, Wendy and Lisa released three albums as 'Wendy & Lisa' (all of which are worth seeking out), a fascinating concept album about grief under the alias 'Girl Bros' (the name change heralding a new sophistication in their lyrics and sound) and now a new record, *White Flags of Winter Chimneys*, initially released as a download before getting a physical release in CD and vinyl form. It is their greatest record to date, a dense and bewitchingly elegant song-suite that rivals anything they recorded as part of the Revolution.

It's a richly allusive record, referencing everyone from Joni Mitchell (the title nods to a lyric from Mitchell's *Hejira*, a source from which Prince also once found a title) to the MC5, continuing from some of the themes from their *Girl Bros* album, but with a new musical complexity borne from their soundtrack work. 'When people hear the new record they're a little confused because it goes so far away from the funk roots people expect from us,' Wendy told me, 'but we wanted to get out of the formula and experiment with words and soundscapes.' What about the MC5 reference? 'That was funny. I kept envisioning that scene in *Say Anything* where John Cusack goes up to the chick's house and he's got the boom-box on his shoulder and he's playing Peter Gabriel and tried to reverse it, so "I'm a chick, I'm a younger, I'm more bad ass, I'm a young fucking Patti Smith" and I'm going to a woman or a man's house and instead of playing that, I was fucking playing the MC5 and I wanted this person to come out in the middle of the night and get in my car and have at it. The MC5 are iconic, and saying their name out loud was that much more bitchin'.'

But there also seems a softer influence to some of the tracks on the album. 'Balloon', for example, sounds like The Beatles. 'I guess it's because I'm using the twelve-string,' Wendy says, 'that's gotta be it.' 'No,' says Lisa, 'it's this sound,' and she hums a Beatles-esque melody. 'But that's more Bacharach than the Beatles,' Wendy protests. Lisa turns to me and smiles. 'Well, then you must be wrong,' she says, before taking pity on me. 'No, people have said that, even before that guitar part. I don't know why that is other than we grew up listening to the Beatles.'

'Prince hated the Beatles,' Wendy tells me. This is something I've always wanted to know. Although Prince has played 'Come Together' and 'The Long and Winding Road' in concert recently and once indicated in an email chatroom that 'When You Were Mine' was influenced by listening to John Lennon, when asked if *Around the World in a Day* had a Beatles influence, he initially denied it. 'My take on it,' she says, 'is that he hated the Beatles not for the music but for something else. Maybe because of the iconic look of them, or there was something about them that didn't ring true for him and his rock stardom. But I always knew that if he listened to 'Let It Be' and 'Dig A Pony' he'd change his mind. I know the guy's taste. And 'Polythene Pam', if he just sat down and listened to that stuff, he'd get it. But he thinks of 'I Wanna Hold Your Hand' or 'Strawberry Fields Forever' and thinks they're too popular and he becomes competitive.'

I ask Wendy and Lisa if their relationship in the studio has changed during the twenty-five years they've worked together professionally.

'No,' says Wendy, 'it's always the perfect storm. We usually fight before we get to the release, because we're really stressed and we don't know what we're exactly going to do.' They fight over who's driving the car, but never over the music. 'No, we both love what the other does,' says Lisa. 'We push each other's buttons. I'll grab her guitar and bass and I'm so bad.' Wendy laughs. 'You should see me do the same thing with the keyboards.' 'Yeah,' says Lisa, 'and I'm like, "Get off my keyboards, I'll show you how it's done."'

The song 'Invisible' on the new album references their musical past. 'In the spirit of full disclosure, the verses are sung as if Prince were singing them and saying, "You weren't anything unless you were next to me." And then when the chorus comes it's like the emancipation of us. So, yeah, it's a little bit of a self-pity party,' she jokes. Lisa, however, is keen to emphasise how emotions in songs come out as part of the creative process and should never be seen as definitive statements. 'Ripped from the headlines,' she says with a laugh, a refrain she'll repeat in good humour whenever I make a too-literal interpretation.

On the subject of definitive statements, Wendy and Lisa point out also that the dialogue from the beginning of 'Computer Blue' etched on to every Prince fan's brain ('Wendy?' 'Yes, Lisa.' ' Is the water warm enough?' 'Yes, Lisa.' 'Shall we begin?' 'Yes Lisa.') were just some lines on a piece of paper handed to them by Prince and dispatched in five minutes with no real thought to any 'weird psychosexual lesbian thing'. I mention to them that I've noticed baths play a large part in the lyrics of early Prince songs like 'Extra Loveable' and 'Purple Music.' 'It's funny about bathtubs,' says Wendy, asking Lisa, 'was it the *1999* or *Purple Rain* tour when the bathtub fell on him?' Lisa is pained by the memory, the empathy she still feels towards the man she once spent so much time with but who has become more distant in recent years shining through. 'He'd been really mean to someone that day and it was sad because he knew it was karma. He was laying on the ground because the bathtub wasn't tacked down and he fell out. He was scared and we were worried he might be broken.' 'Yeah,' Wendy agrees, '"The bathtub rules me." It was like frickin' *Equus*, only with bathtubs.'

....

Notes

1 The talent-show side to popular music is something that has always interested Prince. Carwell gained a rep from playing talent shows around Minneapolis; Tamar appeared on *Starr Time*; Sheena Easton came to fame through Esther Rantzen's TV show *The Big Time*; Maya McClean, one half of his backing dancers The Twinz, was a contestant on *Australian Idol*. And Prince himself began by performing piano pieces at school talent shows. Ironically, when Prince appeared on *American Idol* in 2006, he was subjected to criticism from Simon Cowell for playing two songs from then-current album *3121* and departing rather than doing a duet with a contestant. If Cowell had bothered to listen to the whole album, he would've realised from 'Beautiful, Loved and Blessed', the duet with Tamar, that Prince has an ambivalent attitude to these latest TV talent shows, which he believes are less about demonstrating talent, and more about coveting fame. At the same time he was performing, those of us who had signed up to his website received an email with a line from 1 Corinthians 10:14: 'Therefore my brothers, have nothing to do with the worship of idols.'

2 Although Sevelle is one of Prince's least-remembered protégées, having released one self-titled album on Prince's Paisley Park label, she is one of the most industrious, currently writing self-published novels, managing rappers, inventing new kitchen appliances sold on home shopping channel QVC (seriously) and running Urban Farming, a Detroit-based charity that plants food on unused land and gives it to the homeless, supported by Atlantic Records and Prince to this day.

3 Although Prince appears to give the game away in the lyrics to 'DMSR', a track on his *1999* album later that year, where in a verse not printed in the lyric booklet he appears to take ownership of all his side-projects singing in quick succession 'Jamie Starr's a Thief', 'It's time to fix your clock' (a response, of course, to The Time's 'What Time Is It?') and 'Vanity 6 is so sweet', not owning up to the alias seems, for a while at least, to have been of considerable importance. In his only interview to promote *1999*, with the *LA Times*'s Robert Hilburn, he had three points to make: 'One, my real name is Prince. Two, I'm not gay. And three, I'm not Jamie Starr.' The controversy lasted until at least the following year, when Debbie Miller addressed the subject in her third *Rolling Stone* article about Prince and/or his protégées. In the article she interrogates Morris Day and Steve Fargnoli about Jamie Starr, both of whom insist he's real, before Sue Ann Carwell gives the game away: 'Prince is Jamie Starr'.

4 Just how nasty Vanity would get is revealed in Motley Crue songwriter and bassist Nikki Sixx's 2007 book *The Heroin Diaries: A Year in the Life of a Shattered Rock Star*. The book includes Sixx's memories of his relationship with Vanity, who now calls herself Evangelist Denise Matthews, which begin: 'We saw Vanity on MTV, and when Pete said, "Dude, that's Prince's old girl," I said, "Excellent – he's got a tiny dick." The office rang Vanity and arranged for us to meet. She opened the door naked, with her eyes going around in her head. Somehow I had a feeling that we might just hit it off.' The book also includes Evangelist Denise Matthews's thoughts about her former persona: 'I don't answer to Vanity. I would much rather be a fish stuck in a pond with a starving shark than take on such a foul name of nothingness.'

Matt Thorne

ELISA AMBROGIO
Up Cedar Hill

The most interesting person I knew when I was seven was my dad. He could get the paper flat and symmetrical on the *Mad* magazine back cover fold-in and he had a great job. He traveled around Connecticut photographing car damage, writing claim file summaries and response letters, and researching suspected fraud. He was an Auto Insurance Claim Representative. When my father worked on the weekend he would bring me along and we would work as a team, like Starsky and Hutch. First we would hit the site of the accident and see if it gibed with the insured's claim. My father would pace and squint at curbs. 'Do you see tire tracks there?' he'd ask me and I would crouch and squint at the curb, looking for any sign of tread. He'd shoot rolls of film, and let me take pictures too. Most were isolated shots of automobile damage: smashed tail lights, tire tracks on curbs, and cracked windshields, but there are some of us. There I am looking at a bent fender, there's my dad walking away from a buckled pinto hood. I am too young to focus the lens, so he is often blurry or too distant. In focus he has freckles, he is skinny. He is wearing a big suit from J. C. Penney's, no tie. His hair is a thick brown tear-drop bang falling over his forehead and even in the blurry shots he has an air of authority, his long black wool coat flaring behind him like a cape.

Through our conversations on the road and on the job experience, I learned that being an Auto Claim Representative is not an easy job. Claimants didn't fill out required paperwork. It was some kind of bureaucratic tap-dance to have your gas receipts reimbursed. The home office in Chicago assigned too many files to each Representative. They expected you to get every claim filed, but then, the goddamn thing was, if you didn't dot every i and cross every t, your supervisor was going to make a federal case out of it. You could save the company five million bucks and they won't even give you a fifty-cent raise. The thing is if you make your file-closing goal for the month, they just give you more files the next month and tell you you were on the promotion track so you work like an idiot. That's how they get you. I came to understand that an Auto Claim Representative was expected to be a journalist, a lawyer, a detective and a professional photographer, and god help him if he didn't close out his files under cost. Sure, I would think, it wasn't an easy job, but what could be more exciting? We would bump along the highway, rolling down the windows, stopping for McDonald's and my dad would say, see we're on the clock, the company's payin' for this one, and he'd tuck the receipt into his wallet. There seemed no better job than that of Auto Insurance Claims Representative.

After a couple of years my parents got a divorce and my father got promoted from a claim representative to a claim adjuster. It was disappointing to not drive around investigating on the weekends, but my father seemed to think the weekends would be improved by this. Previously, when we weren't investigating on the weekends, we were relaxing by watching boxing and football until individually we were either asleep or getting into the bleach under the bathroom counter and destroying the very expensive porcelain doll from Sicily given to us by our great grandmother, or pulling apart the last hardpack of Merit Light 100s and ripping the tobacco from the filter and grinding it into the rug, or setting a pot on fire trying to make hot chocolate from ex·lax. Though I had not known my father to be a man lured by the petting zoo or the craft fair, once we started spending whole weekends alone he began to seek out adventures for us. Now there were new rolls of weekend photographs. My father standing in damp New England hay, next to a blurry goat. I am yanking the steering wheel of an immobile metal car on a track. I am next to old stuff and people, quilts, acorn squash, local creeps, 4-H club ribbon ceremonies. I am sniveling after getting off my first roller coaster, the Thunderbolt. I have pink bead and feather 'barrettes' (roach clips) in my hair. My father is wearing a Burger King crown. I am going down the world's biggest slide on a piece of burlap. I have a signed 'Handbook to Shirley Temple Collectibles 1985–6' by the author and editor, made out to me. I remember my long involved talk with this woman in a damp Kiwanis Brothers sponsored tent, and I remember my father by my side. Nodding. Offering to pay for the book.

The only weekend adventure I refused was my father's desire to go climb the mountain by my grandparents' house. The mountain was more of a steep rock hill, covered in moss and birch trees and bordered by an old folk's home, a rock-blasting quarry and a fancy old cemetery called Cedar Hill. You could climb it and get to the other end of Hartford. My dad told me he and his friends would hike up the mountain and sneak into the old cemetery at night. In the winter they'd put baked potatoes in the pockets of their winter coats and ice-skate there by the tombs and leafless trees. In the summer they'd swim in the pond like there weren't a bunch of dead people everywhere. I liked playing pretend as Indiana Jones and my father suggested that Indiana would probably not make a big deal out of a cemetery. Especially when it wasn't scary at all, and was mostly like a park. Especially in broad daylight. I remained uninterested.

That summer my dad got laid off from the insurance company. He was home all day, living in the apartment over my grandparents, blasting *Synchronicity* on the stereo before dinner. He would spend the morning on the phone. 'No, a BS, not a Master's. No I don't have a JD. OK, thanks a lot, let me know.' He would hang out with me all day after that. Sometimes we would finger-paint on huge rolls of butcher paper, or just watch TV. At first it was like having my best friend around all the time. Then one day I was watching the pinball countdown on *Sesame Street* and loudly yelling along to it when my best friend said, 'Damn it Elisa, I can't concentrate, go outside.' In the early morning he would play Emerson Lake and Palmer's 'Lucky Man', or Blind Faith's 'Can't Find my Way Home'. Then he took to getting up later than me and playing the entire cassette of Frank Zappa's *Hot Rats* start to finish and then James Taylor's 'Fire and Rain' a few times in a row.

One week that August my dad was home, it rained every single daylight hour. There were piles of smashed cigarettes piled in the living room ashtray. They were not hardpack Merit Light 100s, but Basic Full Flavor. My dad was

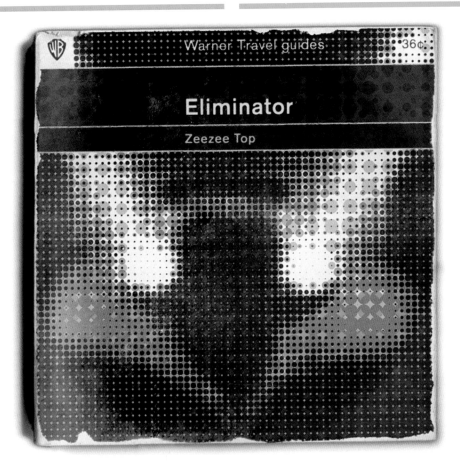

on the couch with a heating pad because he threw his back out. I played Tom Jones's 'Delilah' over and over on my record player until my father asked me to stop. I was messing around with lemon-scented dish-washing liquid in the kitchen sink because I thought my dad was just smoking in the living room and would not catch me. Before I even knew he was in the room he slapped the yellow bottle out of my hand and it skidded across the room. He was bright red and said, 'DON'T WASTE that!' He had never lost his temper with me before, and I started crying.

He sat down at the kitchen table. The rain had let up and the sun was coming in through the kitchen window on to my sticky lemon-scented dish-liquid hands and I didn't move; I thought about how I should probably call one of those child abuse hotlines on him and how sad it was that I was not an orphan living in a mansion like Annie. My dad got up and said, 'Well, I am going to pack a lunch.' I was still snuffling and making sure he knew how sad and mad I felt and how awful he was, but my curiosity was peaked. For what? He was going to take a hike up the mountain for fun, and he would leave me with my grandparents if I didn't want to come.

It was a clear fall day and I carried our packed lunch in my backpack. We climbed through the front part of the woods to a path through the brush. The mountain led up past a Korean church and the old folk's home. The mountain wasn't as scary as I thought. We took a break on a rock and unpacked tuna sandwiches. You could see my grandparents' house from the rocks. I took a picture. I brought two plastic Cabbage Patch doll figurines and some Smurfs. I set them down on a rock and took a picture of them as though they were full-size people, with the little houses behind them. My dad said, 'You smell like lemons, you idiot' and put his hand on my head.

We kept hiking and made our way from the old folk's home side of the mountain to the edge of the quarry. When the quarry would blast sides of the mountain away it would shake the copper and hurricane glass lamp which hung above my grandparents' dining room table. As we walked along the quarry edge my dad told me he and his friends used to like to come up here and drink and he thought people probably still did. There was a white spray-painted 'led zepplin' and 'class of '83' on the rocks. My father lowered his voice and said that people stopped coming up here for a little while after some drunk teenagers fell into the quarry. Drinking beer. Horsing around by the edge. He heard the police found their open beers after the neighbors heard screaming and called in. The neighbors said the canyon of the quarry made their screams echo through the neighborhood. Their beers were still cold when the cops got there. 'The canyon made their screams echo,' he said, 'and now some people say if you're quiet, you can still hear their screams echoing.' He stopped walking. 'Did you hear something?'

My dad had a long history of trying to scare the hell out of me, handed down from his own parents' amusement at terrifying him. Sometimes casual, and sometimes almost Machiavellian in their intricacy, my grandparents and my father plotted out elaborate pranks against each other. When he was a young boy, my grandparents delighted in telling my father that one day he would be a 'big shot' working in the city and forget all about them. They would be homeless, ask him for a dime on the street, and he would spit in their faces. This would always make my little father cry, which my grandparents found very cute. My grandmother would see my grandfather asleep in his chair and put her ice-cold fingers against his neck, causing him to jump awake and yelp, and causing the rest of the room to laugh at his discomfort. My grandfather purchased a novelty box with a tiny mouse puppet in it made of real fur. He enlisted my father to pretend he had purchased a pet, and then opened the box for my grandmother, wiggling his finger frantically. My grandmother ran and hid in the closet, screaming the whole time. Forty years later she had a mild stroke and she attributed it to the mouse box.

My father started small with me, but worked his way up. He would hide behind a door and jump out. He would play Jethro Tull's *Aqualung*, which would send me into fits of tears and horror. He would cue up Van Halen's *1984* to the section right before David Lee Roth would say, 'might as well JUMP!' and then turn it up to ten and press play to wake me up for kindergarten. One time I drew on a 5-dollar bill and he told me that it was a federal offense to draw on money and he was going to have to call the police, and he picked up the phone. I buried the bill in the backyard and hid in the basement for two hours. Here I took his talk of the echoing beer screams of teenagers with a grain of salt.

We climbed. Now there was a path. The path had long lumps of dirt and fallen oak leaves on either side. A leaf pile is one of the best things, and I was not going to pass all these leaf piles without jumping in them. My dad told me there were worms in there. Slugs. Beehives. Then he said, 'Lise, I didn't want to tell you this, but we're in the cemetery now. You don't want to jump in those piles. That's where they bury the people who can't afford to be buried at Cedar Hill.' My father's face looked serious. I kept kicking a pile casually, but began to survey the lumps. He told me he didn't mention the path before because then I wouldn't want to come hiking. The dirt piles were wide enough for human bodies, long enough too. I moved into the center of the path. I asked him who might not have the money to be buried at Cedar Hill. My dad said, 'Orphans, poor people, maybe the old folks from the home.' With the mounds of dirt and leaves, wide and long beside us, we walked toward the cemetery. I thought about the orphans. I thought about the people I had known that had died. Only my great grandmother. And the *Thriller* video. I pictured them buried there under those mounds of dirt by the path. Then I pictured the orphans I knew of. Annie, Anne of Green Gables, Pollyanna and Oliver Twist. Most of them were poor. I pictured them under the mounds of dirt with closed eyes. I wanted to cry, but I just acted cool. I had never been on a hike before. Maybe this is what hikes were like.

After a bend in the path we were at the gates of Cedar Hill Cemetery. Cedar Hill had little trees like dogwood and ginko, but it was also filled with white birch and maple and solemn funereal pines. It was a very quiet place. It did not seem like a park like my father had said. There were no swings or drinking fountains. There were headstones, statues of angels and small white houses. My father explained they were filled with dead people and called mausoleums. He wanted to show me the one J.

P. Morgan was buried in. I used to spend a lot of time watching TV game shows with my grandmother, and *The Gong Show* had a funny, slighty risqué judge named Jaye P. Morgan. She also was a celebrity clue-giver on the *$10,000 Pyramid*. My father was making it a point to tell me an old rich man with a bank was also buried there, but I just understood that to be her father or something. I was sad she died.

The tomb was like all the other tombs: white and fancy, made of marble, beaded up with rain and streaked with moss. My dad said, inside the coffins are on shelves, like books. My dad said that Morgan had the tomb designed to look like his idea of the Ark of the Covenant. I knew what that was from *Raiders of the Lost Ark*, and this little house was unimpressive. My dad was peeking in the window of the tomb. Then my father screamed. He said, 'Lise, it looks like one of the graves, like the top of the casket is opened! That mosuleum is locked, it would have had to have been done from the inside.' Yeah, right. 'No really!' I was too short to see in, so my father lifted me up. Then I knew he was serious. My father had a very bad back. I had only been picked up my father three times in my life, my great grandmother's funeral, the time when grandfather won the state lotto, and this time. He wasn't kidding! The marble slat on the top coffin was completely lifted off and askew. From the correct angle you could have seen into the coffin. My father put me down.

It was damp. I felt like I was going to pee. Stones were grey and white and I was surrounded by orphan corpses and the marble tomb of zombie Jaye P. Morgan and her banking father. I thought of her, with closed eyes covered in white opal eyeshadow and mascara, doing the side-to-side arm dance of *Thriller* against the lid of her coffin. Buried alive in black sequins, scraping to get out! We did not dwell at the quarry cliff or by the dirt mounds, we made our way down the mountain fast and quiet, like soldiers. Snuffling, crying, running soldiers wiping their noses and chewing on the sleeve of their turtlenecks. Soldiers who yelled, 'Elisa, my back, don't go so fast.'

Near the bottom of the mountain my dad took a seat on a flat rock and lit a cigarette. I asked about the orphans first, how their parents died, how they died. He looked irritated. 'Lise, there were not any orphans, I told you I was making that up 'cause you were driving me nuts getting into the leaves. I'm sorry I said that. What I can't believe is that the coffin was open. Huh. Must have been grave-robbers or something. That was weird.' I told him if he thought I was dead he should make sure and wait a week before he buried me, and that I didn't want to die, and that he should make sure he has enough money that I wouldn't have to be buried in a lump on the path. He tried to tell me I wasn't going to die, and that there were no orphans, he just didn't want me to jump in the dirt, and that he was perfectly sure that there was a logical explanation for the coffin and that he shouldn't have said anything. Jesus, he wished he never said anything at all.

He told me even if I did die, there is something called reincarnation and it means you come back alive in a different form. The only word I knew that made sense with that word was Carnation, the brand of the chocolate and vanilla powder packs I put in my milk. My understanding was something like: our bodies die and turn to a light instant breakfast dust, then reform into a new thing and come back to earth. I said I never wanted to be buried in the ground, or in a marble house. My father explained cremation, and this word also reminded me of instant breakfast. I stopped crying. My dad lit another cigarette, knocking the ash into his hand. I thought of my body, flicked away like that. My father said, 'All right, you went up the mountain, you survived. It wasn't so bad.' I sucked up snot and cried a little bit. 'We're OK.' He said, 'All right, I'll tell you a joke, a grown up joke. Ahh, forget it, it might be too racy for you.' I stopped sucking snot and shook my head, no, I was sure it was not too racy for me. 'OK, so, this cab driver in New York City, he cleans out his cab, vacuums it, the whole nine yards, the cab has never looked so nice, right? Then he takes it out on Fifth Avenue. He picks up this lady from France. She doesn't speak any English. So the cab driver goes, "You want to go to Bloomingdales?" and the French lady says, "Oui! Oui!!" So then, he goes, "Not in my cab lady, I just cleaned this thing!"' I laughed so hard I started crying again, and kept trying to recapture the joke by saying WeeWEE for the rest of the walk on the mountain.

The clouds had moved and the sunset was bright. The light on the stop sign at the top of my grandparents' street reflected in a circle on the ground. Pink-colored sky was mirrored in car fenders and windows. I skipped the sidewalk cracks and with the sun at our backs, my father and I cast gargantuan shadows on the cement, stretching far out before us. I decided, if I died, my dad should know that I wanted to be cremated AND reincarnated, and he should throw my ashes off of the Thunderbolt Roller Coaster at the peak of the first big drop. He promised. He said, you're not going to die for a long time so when you get older, promise me you'll never get a job in insurance. I promised.

PICCADILLY RECORDS
EST 1978

www.piccadillyrecords.com
53 oldham street
manchester
M1 1JR

ANDY MILLER
Est-ce est-ce si bon?
Gainsbourg in the Culture Bunker

Je défendrai le sable d'Israël,
Les villes d'Israël, le pays d'Israël . . .
Tous les Goliaths venus des pyramides,
Reculeront devant l'étoile de David.
Serge Gainsbourg, 'Le Sable et le Soldat', 1967

It all feels so silly being an artist when the Israeli
army are sending tanks into Gaza. It seems such
a whimsical occupation. What did you do in the
war, daddy? Oh, I expressed my deep melancholy.
Yeah, right. Fuck off!
Robert Wyatt, interview, 2009

Take me to the moon,
It's safe and I want to lie down.
The Teardrop Explodes, 'The Culture Bunker', 1981

By early 1967, the French singer and songwriter Serge Gainsbourg had been a professional performer for nearly a decade. At 38, he had not quite perfected his image of himself – it would take the worldwide infamy of 'Je t'aime . . . moi non plus' two years later to achieve that – but he was never short of a paying date. In later life, he would be celebrated for his heroic drinking, womanising and serial Gitane-smoking, but during the '60s Gainsbourg seemed addicted only to work. His output as a *chansonnier*, pop star, producer, actor and writer-for-hire was so prolific – so profligate – it is still being catalogued forty years later.

In January, Gainsbourg co-starred with *nouvelle vague* pin-up Anna Karina in the television film *Anna*, a pop musical written in collaboration with Michel Colombier, a landmark colour TV broadcast and successful spin-off LP. During the course of the year, he and Colombier would produce three further film scores – *Toutes Folles de Lui*, *Si j'étais un espion* and *L'Horizon* – and Gainsbourg would also provide incidental music for obscurities like *L'une et l'autre* and *L'inconnu de Shangidor*. He appeared in the TV series *Vidocq* and – naturally – contributed a number to that too, the Dylanesque '*Chanson du forçat*'. While Britain and the USA baked in the summer of love, Gainsbourg prepared for and filmed a sub-stantial role in director Jacques Poitrenaud's *Ce Sacré Grand-père*; he also made several other on-screen appearances, most notably as the Marquis de Sade in Abel Gance's three-part historical television extravaganza *Valmy*.

Elsewhere, in his role as cultural mischief-maker, Gainsbourg attempted to remount one of his greatest *coups de foudre*. In 1965, the barely disguised piss-take '*Poupée de cire, poupée de son*' had won the Eurovision Song Contest on behalf of Luxembourg and become a major hit all over Europe for its singer, the *yé-yé* poppet France Gall. Now the tiny but very rich nation of Monaco had hired Gainsbourg to repeat the trick for them. On 8 April the winsome Minouche Barelli took to the stage of the Hofburg Imperial Palace in Vienna to deliver a new Gainsbourg composition entitled 'Boum Badaboum'. To deafening orchestral accompaniment, Barelli clip-clops her way through a lyric which equates the singer's burgeoning sexual awakening with imminent global nuclear apocalypse: 'When I've tried everything – *Boum boum!* – I can leave without regret – *Badaboum!*' (At this juncture, disbelieving readers may find a visit to YouTube useful.) The judging panels preferred the rather less bombastic UK entry, 'Puppet on a String' by Sandie Shaw[i], and 'Boum Badaboum' finished in fifth place. But, in a popular phrase of the era, what a way to go.

Gainsbourg released only one EP under his

own name in the course of 1967, *Mr Gainsbourg*, which featured four tracks with Anglo-American titles – 'Comic Strip', 'Torrey Canyon', 'Chatterton' and 'Hold-Up' – in the style of contemporary English beat music (several songs were attempted with Yardbirds producer Georgio Gomelsky). To some extent, the EP was a knowing genre exercise like his previous successful forays into jazz and African music. However, Gainsbourg enjoyed the experience of recording in London with British session musicians; soon it would be his preferred way of working.

Meanwhile, Gainsbourg the hitmaker turned out new songs for acts as diverse as France Gall ('Teenie Weenie Boppie'), Stone ('Buffalo Bill'), Dominique Walter ('Les Petits Boudins'), Claude François ('Hip Hip Hip Hurrah') and, most significantly, Brigitte Bardot. His liaison with the divine BB seemed to inspire Gainsbourg to new heights of avant-garde pop genius: 'Harley Davidson', 'Bonnie and Clyde', 'Contact' and the first – suppressed – version of 'Je t'aime . . . moi non plus' remain some of his greatest records. By the year's end he would be filming *Le Show Bardot* for French TV and conducting an open and passionate affair with its star.

Although 1967 was arguably Gainsbourg's most successful and productive period to date, in many ways it was just another working year. Let others grow their hair and kick off their shoes; for Gainsbourg there was always the next record, the next song, the next film. One of his sillier contributions to BB's TV special offered '*La bise aux hippies*' – a kiss-off to the hippies, the new youth cult which had rapidly become synonymous with the laid-back mood of the times. But for Gainsbourg there was always more work to do, whatever and wherever that work happened to be. And why not? As the title of another song for Dominique Walter had it, '*Je suis capable de n'importe quoi*' – I am capable of absolutely anything.

It was Gainsbourg's fierce work-ethic and even fiercer self-belief that resulted in the most uncharacteristic composition of that year, perhaps of his career. On the eve of the Six Day War, he was approached by a cultural attaché from the Israeli embassy in Paris. Would Monsieur Gainsbourg like to do his bit for his spiritual homeland? The army was in need of a new march, something stirring for the troops to sing at this difficult moment. (It was around this time that Harpo Marx bequeathed his famous harp to the nation of Israel.) Gainsbourg accepted the commission.

The song he produced was entitled '*Le Sable et le Soldat*' – 'The Sand and the Soldier'. Its rousing partisan lyric was intended to be translated into Hebrew:

All the Goliaths coming from the pyramids will recoil from the Star of David.

A basic recording of the song, with droning organ accompaniment, was dispatched to Tel Aviv and that, as far as the composer was concerned, was that – job done, business concluded.

For reasons unknown, '*Le Sable et le Soldat*' was never put into action and Gainsbourg's demo gathered dust in the vaults of Kol Israel radio until the early twenty-first century, when it was rediscovered by a fan and posted on the internet. 'I will defend the sand of Israel,' sings Gainsbourg, '. . . die for the sand of Israel, the land of Israel, the children of Israel.' To the modern listener, there is something genuinely startling about it. In its own way, the song is more unsettling than well-thumbed infamies like 'Lemon Incest' or '*Je t'aime . . . moi non plus*'. The man who was born Lucien Ginsburg to immigrant Jewish parents, who as a boy was made to wear the hated yellow star, never set foot on Israeli soil and usually referred to Russia as his 'spiritual homeland'. But here he is, apparently offering to lay down his life in the service of the Jewish state. He sounds disarmingly sincere. Officially, the song remains

Andy Miller

unreleased but one can find it easily on the web, where it is often accompanied by highly politicised blogarrhoea or co-opted as unambiguous propaganda.

We are still not used to musicians addressing us directly on matters of politics, or of taking sides in wars, though plenty have done – Robert Wyatt, for example, articulates a pro-Palestinian stance in keeping with a public, leftist world view. But Gainsbourg and Wyatt albums coexist peacefully on neighbouring shelves in my record collection (literally side by side; I only noticed it while writing this sentence). I don't have to choose one or the other. All sides meet in the culture bunker.

Serge Gainsbourg had no reason to think that a demo recording made as a private donation would enter the global public domain many years after his death, in a manner that in 1967 would have seemed pure sci-fi. His words, which we mistakenly take as addressed directly to us, were supposed to be rendered in Hebrew, chanted by soldiers, unrecorded, carried on the winds of the Golan Heights and blown away. If we prefer, we can remind ourselves that this was a commission, just one of a number of projects or opportunities from a madcap, chaotic year. Or we can offer a final absolution to ourselves and the artist and simply say: it's only a song.

But still, the question remains. 'I will defend the sand of Israel . . . die for the sand of Israel.' Would it be worse if Gainsbourg really meant this? Or if he didn't mean a word?

II: 1974

In his modest Left Bank house at 5 rue Verneuil, Gainsbourg was becalmed; as Sylvie Simmons notes in her biography, *A Fistful of Gitanes*, 1974 was chiefly notable for 'a remarkable absence of Serge'. *Après le déluge, moi . . .*

In contrast to the manic activity of 1967, Gainsbourg's output for 1974 amounted to just one single for his wife Jane Birkin and an appearance in the movie *Les Diablesses*. He masterminded a pornographic photo shoot for *Lui* magazine, with Jane in handcuffs and little else. He played with his little daughter, Charlotte, who was three years old that summer. Otherwise, as Paris quietly marked the thirtieth anniversary of liberation from the Nazis, Gainsbourg stayed at home and wondered what he should do next.

His previous LP, the playful, scatalogical *Vu de l'extérieur* (1973) had been acclaimed by the French press as a triumph, but it had not been a hit. On the album, the epic orchestral sound which Jean-Claude Vannier had concocted for *Histoire de Melody Nelson* (1971) was exchanged for Alan Hawkshaw's small group arrangements, mostly for piano, bass guitar and drums. In musical terms, these were perhaps the least ambitious settings of Gainsbourg's career, but the comparatively plain backdrop placed renewed emphasis on lyrics and delivery, an inimitable flow of puns, alliteration and innuendo.

Professionally, he was still enjoying the success of 'Je t'aime . . . moi non plus', five years after it had topped the charts, caused international scandal and earned censure from the Pope. Gainsbourg was working on a script for the film he hoped would be his directorial debut, also called *Je t'aime . . .*[2] But the ongoing notoriety of his biggest success also put Gainsbourg at a creative disadvantage. The ambivalence of its title would come to epitomise a new duality in his work; a moment of truth – *je t'aime* – contradicted in a shrug of denial – *moi non plus*. As time wore on, he would feel obliged to build every project around some new scandal, some fresh affront to public decency or bourgeois morality. In itself, this was not difficult to achieve; the bourgeoisie was easily outraged and Gainsbourg was brilliant at it. The difficulty lay in making a record good enough (*je t'aime*) to justify the brou-haha which inevitably accompanied it (*moi non plus*).

It is often assumed that *Rock Around the Bunker*, the album dreamt up by Gainsbourg in the summer of 1974, is a debacle along exactly these lines, the incorrigible shock merchant's 'Nazi LP'. It is generally regarded as gratuitously offensive and musically pedestrian, at best. In Britain and the USA especially, it seems baffling that the artist who produced the sumptuous, sampled and adored *Histoire de Melody Nelson* could so swiftly issue a follow-up which appears to be little more than a series of bad jokes, badly told. As one of the LP's daredevil puns has it, *Est-ce est-ce si bon?* The answer is usually an emphatic '*non*'.

In fact, critics and biographers usually deal with *Rock Around the Bunker* by trying to ignore it. Gainsbourg's posthumous critical reputation picks up again with *L'Homme à tête de chou* (1976) and the justly iconoclastic reggae 'Marseilleses' (*Aux armes et caetera*, 1979). On those rare occasions the album is written about, it is alongside long-playing 'disasters' such as *Everybody's Rockin'* or *Self Portrait* or *Metal Machine Music* – necessary aberrations in a brilliant career, legend-enhancing in their own way. Otherwise, *Rock Around the Bunker* is a staple of heritage music mag pieces about rock's occasional flirtations with fascism, a footnote to Bowie's 'Nazi salute' or Eric Clapton's public pronouncements on immigration and stout defence of Enoch Powell. But it deserves a better fate.

By the mid-'70s, rock music was old enough to have a past; for the first time, nostalgia swirled into pop's milkshake. Glam rock was tinsel and spandex, but it was also a return to the three-chord dogma of 'traditional' rock'n'roll. In turn, a wave of souped-up, retro rock'n'roll groups started to appear on the charts: Showaddywaddy, Shakin' Stevens and the Sunsets, the Rubettes – 'Sugar Baby Love' by the Rubettes was a huge hit during the summer of 1974, selling over two million copies in France alone. In England, there were stirrings of a Teddy Boy revival. Self-pro-

claimed futurists like Roxy Music remade and remodelled the iconography of post-war America into something that was both new and 'new'. *American Graffiti* and *That'll Be the Day* were in the cinemas; *Happy Days* debuted on American TV in January 1974. Even the 'rock'n'roll future', as epitomised by Bruce Springsteen, was a backward-looking package of '50s and '60s greatest hits. In Britain, this combination of introspection and retrospection was captured most perfectly in the theme song to the era's defining sit-com, *Whatever Happened to the Likely Lads?* (itself a revival of an earlier hit sit-com):

> Oh, what happened to you? Whatever happened to me?
> What became of the people we used to be?
> Tomorrow's almost over, today went by so fast.
> It's the only thing to look forward to: the past.[3]

There was also the phenomenon of 'Nazi chic'. The influence of Visconti's *The Night Porter* (released in France on 3 April 1974) or Fosse's *Cabaret* (September 1972) proved to be widespread and long-lasting. 'The Liza Minnelli look in *Cabaret* had a huge impact on punk, if you think of Siouxsie Sioux,' Neil Tennant has said. 'It was part of pop culture, it wasn't just musical theatre or musical film.' An aura of Weimar decadence could be found in everything from Roxy Music to *The Rocky Horror Picture Show*. David Bowie, meanwhile, the original 'homo superior', was presenting himself as a kind of Isherwood *manqué* in Oxford bags and making statements to the press such as 'Adolf Hitler was one of the first rock stars . . . he staged a country' (1974) and 'Britain could benefit from a Fascist leader' (1976). Which would be all good fun – raiding the dressing-up box – were it not for a revival in actual fascism which was taking place across Europe at the same time. Jean-Marie Le Pen's enduringly popular Front National had formed in France in 1972; by 1974 the British National Front had as many as 20,000 members and had managed to come third in three parliamentary by-elections.

Rock Around the Bunker, then, was conceived in an atmosphere of anything-goes revivalism. In a bunker on the Left Bank, with the Rubettes on the radio, Rampling and Bogarde on the silver screen, the far right on the rise and memories of occupation in the air, Gainsbourg formulated a response which was both profoundly sincere and scornfully facetious. *Rock Around the Bunker* yoked together two rival revivals – rock'n'roll and Nazism – and treated both with the contempt they deserved.

Let me be precise: heard cold, *Rock Around the Bunker* is not a great LP. I understand why many listeners prefer the grand design of *Histoire de Melody Nelson* to the concrete drabness of *Rock Around the Bunker*. *Histoire de Melody Nelson* swoops and soars; *Rock Around the Bunker*, on the other hand, is ersatz, wimpy rock'n'roll, '50s-style, played with soul-sapping expertise by top British session men. At times it sounds like a listless Showaddywaddy with chirpy Dave Bartram replaced by a singer who can't sing, making enigmatic jokes in French about Hitler and the gas chambers (and those are the good bits). For those looking to be offended, there is plenty to offend. But in what it says about its author and in how we listen to it today, *Rock Around the Bunker* is, I believe, Gainsbourg's most consistent, compelling and relevant work.

The LP tells the story of the rise and fall of the Third Reich in roughly chronological order. To the non-French speaker, Gainsbourg's barrage of puns, jokes and allusions can be mystifying (if you download this LP out of curiosity, keep a dictionary handy), but the *sound* of his words is plain: quick-fire, repetitive, percussive. Side 1 takes us from decadent Berlin in the early '30s ('Nazi Rock'), via Hitler's intensifying lunacy ('*J'Entends des voix off*'), to the chimneys of the concentration camps (a mordant rendition of 'Smoke Gets in Your Eyes'). So far, so kitsch.

Side 2 offers a more complex picture. '*Zig zig avec toi*' might be more correctly heard as '*Sieg sieg avec toi*'; '*zig zig*' is a euphemism for sex; and we also think of Ziggy Stardust[4]:

> *Zig zig avec toi, et lorsque ton corps zigzague,*
> *Zig zig, toi et moi, Zig zig, hmm quel émoi,*
> *Zig zig, oui je t'aime, j'aime ton petit corps bleme,*
> *Zig zig, toi et moi, Zig zig, hmm quel émoi.*

In other words, this is a song which draws a line between fascism and sex and rock'n'roll, '70s-style, climaxing in Gainsbourg's droll request – '*Tout le monde danse!*' ('Chain Lightning' from Steely Dan's 1975 album *Katy Lied* also deals with the seductiveness of mob rule but in far more elliptical, and musically tasteful, style.) '*Est-ce est-ce si bon?*' follows, another dubious pun parade. And then we come to 'Yellow Star'.

For some 'Yellow Star' is the weakest point of *Rock Around the Bunker*, a failed get-out-of-jail-free card; by invoking his own Jewishness in such a convenient and glib manner, Gainsbourg is trying to pre-empt any and all criticism of the album's subject matter. But this is nonsense. On 'Yellow Star', in marked contrast to '*Le sable et le soldat*', Gainsbourg is fully, brilliantly engaged with the problem he has set himself. In three short verses, he sketches his emotion as a child who was forced to wear the 'curious hieroglyph'. The ambiguity he felt then – 'perhaps it says sheriff or marshal or big chief' – is matched by his blunt assessment of what the star means to him now, what it continues to mean for all Jews:

Je porte la yellow star,
Difficile pour un juif,
La loi du struggle for life.

(The song has a parallel in a famous Gainsbourg story from the same time. After the success of '*Je t'aime . . .*', Gainsbourg commissioned Cartier to make him a facsimile yellow star made of platinum. It was both an exorcism and a gesture of magnificent disdain for both his past and present; as a Jew, he would always be wearing a metaphorical star, but at least it would be garish and expensive and on his terms.)

The album closes with 'Rock Around the Bunker' and 'SS in Uruguay'. The former ends with an explosion, the wreckage of culture itself at the end of the war. Meanwhile, down in South America, a former SS officer wears a straw hat, sips his papaya juice through a straw and commands a small 'rabble' of loyal supporters. '*Pour moi pas questionne de payer l'additionne*' – For me, no question of paying the bill. The comeback – the revival – is only a matter of time.

Rock Around the Bunker was recorded in London in late 1974 and released in France the following year.

Appropriately, it bombed.

III: 2009

These days, Serge Gainsbourg's place in the culture bunker is assured. Here are five things you already knew about him.

• *Histoire de Melody Nelson* is Serge Gainsbourg's best LP.
• In 1985, he released a hit single and video with his 13-year-old daughter, Charlotte, called 'Lemon Incest'.
• Towards the end of his life he appeared on a TV chat show and informed a stunned

Whitney Houston, 'I want to fuck her.'
• When Gainsbourg died, his funeral brought Paris to a standstill.
• Beck really likes him.

In 2009, we know all we need to know about an artist's great recordings: *Pet Sounds*, *Revolver*, *Astral* bloody *Weeks*. Magazines and newspapers chronicle the making of this or that famous record, again. DVD documentaries tinker with the master tapes of such 'classics' as *Bat Out of Hell* and *Rio* by Duran Duran. Earnest scribes have written entire books about single LPs – why, I have written one myself (*The Kinks Are the Village Green Preservation Society*; please note the pedantically correct title). Sometimes it can be hard to hear an album like, say, *Blonde on Blonde* for all the critical noise and chatter around it. Did I know Kris Kristofferson was the studio janitor? That Dylan kept the Nashville cats waiting until four in the morning? I did actually.[5]

This has created the novel situation where, in the hyper-annotated twenty-first century, great artists are in danger of being erased from their best work. The Beatles music needs the new context of a Vegas show or a video game because the traditional platforms of radio, TV and magazines – of sitting and listening to records then checking what Nick Kent thinks – are all clapped out. Conversely, if you wish to be reminded of what made John Lennon or Brian Wilson or Van Morrison remarkable in the first place, you will need to look in some unlikely places.

For example, there is something properly thrilling about hearing John and Yoko's *Some Time in New York City* for the first time, precisely because it is considered an unmitigated, irreversible disaster; no one is ever going to produce a version of Rock Band where you get to be the drummer in Elephant's

Memory. The lyrics are frequently risible, both in their political naivety and their McGonagall-like grasp of rhyme and scansion (e.g. 'They gave you coffee | They gave you tea | They gave you everything but equality.' – and they printed them on the front cover!) But because the album has been dismissed and ignored for forty years, it has resisted cultural assimilation, and the bits which work – 'New York City', 'John Sinclair', 'We're All Water' – sound scathing and difficult and loud and new. They sound like John Lennon in a way 'Give Peace a Chance',

say, no longer does. They sound like rock'n'roll.

I am not saying *Some Time in New York City* is a better LP than *Imagine*; it isn't.[6] Nor am I suggesting the Dylan neophyte ignores *Blonde on Blonde* and heads straight for *Empire Burlesque*.[7] But the type of Gainsbourg listener who worships *Histoire de Melody Nelson* and dismisses *Rock Around the Bunker* is in danger of not really understanding either. Which would be a shame. In the words of Neil Young, who has made more than his fair share of inscrutable albums, it's all one song.

It may be difficult to accept that *Histoire de Melody Nelson* and *Rock Around the Bunker* – and for that matter Gainsbourg's later albums – are founded on the same sonic principle. In many of Gainsbourg's records the musical setting and the words never quite gel with one another. In the case of *Histoire de Melody Nelson*, a non-French speaker need not be too concerned about this; Gainsbourg's vocals are murmured, suggestive, and the music is both baroque and a colossal groove, which is precisely why the LP rose to prominence amongst 'crate-diggers' in the breakbeat-happy era of the early '90s and has remained popular ever since. But on *Rock Around the Bunker*, the lyrics are central both to the concept and the sound of the LP – the groove, such as it is, emerges from Gainsbourg's tongue-twisting delivery of the words rather than the purposefully antiseptic musical backing, and the feeling those words evoke is not intended to be one of eroticism or ennui. It is a nasty itch, a filthy joke.

'He used to grumble, "Why aren't there any covers of my songs in England or America?"' Jane Birkin told Sylvie Simmons. 'But people would say that you can't translate things that have two meanings, if not three; it put them off.' A literal translation of *Rock Around the Bunker* loses not just the jokes but also the intensity, both of what Gainsbourg is saying and how he is choosing to say it. The LP's power lies in that precise combination of style and substance. In this regard, it is significantly more punk rock than Siouxsie's swastika armband or the superficially similar 'Belsen Was a Gas' from the Sex Pistols. At heart, it is an act of appropriation and confrontation similar to 'No Future'/'God Save the Queen' or Nico's '*Das Lied der Deutschen*' or Gainsbourg's own later '*Aux armes et caetera*' (all of which provoked death threats or riots when performed in public), national anthems dished up as hate mail.

In later years, Gainsbourg performed little from *Rock Around the Bunker* and when he did the material was usually recast in the style of punk rock. It is certainly more fun to listen to and makes more sense to the modern ear than the slickness of the original, partly because we are used to hearing these kinds of lyrics attached to that kind of sound. But again, something is lost in translation.

The original *Rock Around the Bunker* is hilarious and brilliant in the way it skewers the era in which it was made. It is also tasteless, dumb and ugly. If such a thing is possible in pop – or any art – it offers a perfect aesthetic response to the Holocaust. It is also its author's most truthful acknowledgement of his Jewishness, without self-pity or telling the gentiles what they want to hear. You might not enjoy listening to it but who cares? Gainsbourg's heart did not lie in Israel but in his own calling as an artist and his skills as an artisan. He always found a way out of the bunker. Let's call it a triumph of the will – Serge would surely approve.

But did he mean it?
Moi non plus . . .

....

Notes

1 Ironically, 'Puppet on a String' might well be considered a gormless rewrite of '*Poupée de cire, poupée de son*'.
2 The finished movie, starring Jane Birkin and Joe Dallesandro, was released in late 1975.
3 Issued as a single 'Whatever Happened to You' in late 1973 and credited to Highly Likely.
4 Pre-dating Bowie's controversial 'Nazi salute' by two years.
5 Someone urgently needs to outlaw the phrase 'thin wild mercury music'.
6 *Some Time in New York City* is, however, a better album than anything Lennon recorded subsequently.
7 Further ex-cathedra recommendations for listeners who enjoy a challenge: *Love You* by the Beach Boys, *Watertown* by Frank Sinatra, *Soap Opera* by the Kinks, *The Hardest Way to Make an Easy Living* by the Streets, *Trans* by Neil Young. But not *Landing on Water*. That really is shit.

Andy Miller

Talking to me last year about OffOnOff, a noise–jazz supergroup featuring members of Dutch punk collective the Ex and Italian math-rock trio Zu alongside Norwegian free-jazz drummer Paal Nilssen-Love, Joakim Haugland, who releases their music on the Smalltown Superjazzz label, commented that the band have 'more in common with Black Flag than Albert Ayler'.

Whether or not it stands up to musical analysis, the description is a smart one. Not only does it draw attention to the band members' disparate musical backgrounds – ranging from anarcho-punk squats to Trondheim University's music department – it suggests parallels between two very different areas of extreme music: the hardcore movement, born out of youthful, suburban alienation in Reagan-era America, and the fiercely ecstatic, revolutionary free jazz of '60s New York. Such parallels inform much of the roster of Haugland's Oslo-based label, which currently includes Original Silence (featuring Sonic Youth's Thurston Moore), No Wave-inspired Japanese indie rockers Nisennenmondai and free-jazz legend Joe McPhee, but they are also becoming more common to the way many of us talk about music now, re-drawing maps of underground music that is, with hindsight, more fluid than we first thought.

When I first listened to Red Square's *Thirty Three*, a CD compilation of a series of tape recordings from the mid-'70s released in 2008, it was likely that I would come up with some similar juxtapositions to describe it to my contemporaries: it's from Essex, 1976, I might say, but it sounds like Chris Corsano, Lee Ranaldo, Mats Gustafsson; like Ultralyd, or *The Hard EP* by Zs; like it could be on Load or Smalltown Superjazzz. They never had a record out, just a few cassettes, I might enthuse. Proper DIY.

In doing so, I am not only trying to put the CD into a noise-geek context. I'm also relishing the incongruity of the album, splashing around in cross-currents of influence and reference, enjoying figuring out where it would have sat in relation to other, more established music of its era – alongside the more simple pleasure of digging up some new, exciting sounds from an ostensibly unpromising geographic location; a location that I, too, am familiar with. The current reissue culture has its naysayers, decrying the slew of releases from the past as fostering nothing but nostalgia and classicism, but equally, the more musical marginalia that is rediscovered and re-presented, the more adept we become at deciphering not only where music comes from, but where it went, writing independent, often intensely personal histories that subvert those linear narratives of rock's back pages we're all a little too familiar with.

The ten tracks on *Thirty Three* would sound new even if they hadn't just been remastered

Frances Morgan

and re-released. For a start, they sound uncompromisingly loud, with a momentum and urgency that confronts the listener like an imminent stampede. On the extracts from 1976 cassette release *Paramusic*, angular electric guitar lines, precipitous and surly, lay chaotic foundations for rasping woodwind and frenetic drums to chase one another around. Pauses are few and solos almost non-existent: guitar and sax, or bass clarinet, occasionally come together in shifting harmonies like a punk take on Terry Riley. Low-end, atonal riffs kick in, closer to King Crimson or Black Sabbath than the era's touchstone for improvised electric guitar, Derek Bailey, although his presence can be felt in the wide intervals, the scribbles of noise and feedback. Cymbal crashes pile up like debris; clatters of unlikely percussion amid rolling, fluid full-kit playing. There's a scrawl of violin. It's loose, unself-conscious, psychedelic music, with the kind of gonzo charge of the British noise that followed in the 1990s and that on first hearing seems to have little to do with jazz, at least not technically. Phil Todd's Ashtray Navigations springs to mind, as does Mick Flower and Neil Campbell's Vibracathedral Orchestra: both sprawling and prolific outfits that strip all the careful refinement from minimalism and improv to expose a raw, ecstatic DIY transcendental music. In the storming urgency of 'Circuity 3' I also hear contemporary sax-led noise bands such as the aforementioned Zu and Scandinavian power trio the Thing, who rejoice in the instrument's noisiest possibilities.

And then there was the name. The connection of British free jazz, improv and contemporary classical music with the radical Left before, during and after the time of *Thirty Three* is well documented; the audible results, to modern ears, can sound varied, from Cornelius Cardew's attempts to find common ground with industrial workers via revolutionary song, to the communal, complex avant-rock of Henry Cow. Where did this band's anarchic sound fit in with the austerity and dogmatism that their name implied? At least on the evidence here, they seemed to address the oppositional stance of the era on a less verbal, more visceral level: a precursor to punk's explosion of anger. The noise leaves little space for debates or discussions or toeing any party line. I wanted to know where it had come from.

Jon Seagroatt, Ian Staples and Roger Telford began playing together as Red Square in Southend-on-Sea, Essex. Southend is an estuary town set in the Thames Gateway, more on mud than on sea, and the view out across the bay is punctuated with the chimneys of a power station. Its days as a desirable seaside resort can still be seen in the Victorian and Georgian buildings along the seafront, and in the fire-damaged remains of the pier, which was once the world's longest. As Essex rapidly redeveloped after the Second World War, with new towns built to accommodate the inhabitants of a bomb-ravaged East End, Southend expanded too, with offices, shopping centres and housing more of a priority than rapidly declining tourism.

Unlike many British coastal towns, Southend has never been gentrified: people don't own second homes here, or pay huge sums for a beach hut, although some do have static caravans over on Canvey Island and small boats moored in the mud. A department of the University of Essex, an establishment whose Colchester campus was one of the UK's most active during the student protests of 1968, opened there just a few years ago, and a small art-rock scene fronted by The Horrors, Ipso Facto and These New Puritans made minor ripples in the music press, but, like much of the surrounding county, Southend is perceived mostly as somewhere to escape from: a down-at-heel satellite town. Yet the relative isolation and the perceived featurelessness of these London hinterlands can breed strong musical communities as virulently as they can spawn boredom or intolerance. It is possible to map the utopian ideals of Essex's new-town builders on to a displaced city's working population and its children, and come up with a psychogeography of musical opposition, from Crass's Epping commune to the illegal raves of the acid house era.

Trevor Taylor, on whose Chelmsford-based FMR label *Thirty-Three* was released, tells me that in the '70s it was possible to play 'seven nights a week, just playing in an area of two miles in Southend . . . I got out a map and found fifty places I used to play, just in that small area'. The members of Red Square recall a similarly prolific scene, although over the years they've relocated west, all three now settled in or around Cropredy, a picturesque Oxfordshire village known for its yearly folk festival.

It is here that I meet Jon Seagroatt, Ian Staples and Roger Telford. We talk in Roger's back garden, while Jon gives occasional technical assistance over the phone to his wife, Bobbie Watson, who is rehearsing with Comus at his studio nearby. Bobbie is one of the original vocalists of Comus, and the acid-folk band are practising for a performance at the Equinox Festival in London a few weeks hence, at which Jon will be performing: since Comus reformed in 2008 he has taken the place of original member Rob Young on bongos and flute. It seems a long way from furious improv sessions and the flat glare of the Thames Estuary, and from the Queen's Hotel, where Red Square performed on a regular basis.

The Queen's was a large, Victorian hotel overlooking Westcliff, just outside Southend's main centre and along the road from Cliffs Pavilion, a home for more well-known entertainers. Used as a music venue for a brief period after its demise as a hotel, the three members of Red Square agree that by the time they took up a residency there, it was 'semi-derelict'. 'There was music going on all over the place, so you might just as well find someone playing folk guitar,' says drummer Roger Telford. 'It was in that interregnum between the time when it stopped being what it was and became a building site. It was just an open place, really. You sort of said, "Can we play here?" And they'd say, "OK, there's a room up there in the corner." And I walked into this room and it was lovely: it had an octagonal bay in the corner – windows all the way round – and I thought, that's the place to set a drum-kit up!'

'We built up a reasonable sized audience,' says Ian, the guitarist responsible for Red Square's squalling riffs. 'When I say reasonable-sized I mean thirty-five, maybe forty on a good night. But for that kind of music, at that time . . . we did it weekly and they came every week.'

Although it was fully improvised, Red Square's music did not fit comfortably alongside much of the British improv of the period, which frequently used more contemplative, restrained instrumentation and technique to explore the boundaries of music-making, a practice probably most fully realised by Eddie Prevost, John Tilbury and Keith Rowe's AMM. In its raucous spirit, and in Telford's storming drums, it had more in common with free jazz, yet with two players schooled mainly in the outer edges of rock and pop music. But while rock music had embraced sonic and structural experimentation in the '60s, by the mid-'70s much of this had become derailed into the over-complexity and stuffiness of progressive rock. Perhaps the reference points are to be found further afield: the directness and groove of the Red Square recordings I've heard are reminiscent of Krautrock band Faust's alchemisation of rock and avant-garde techniques into something exhilarating and abrasive, and not in the least academic.

A story emerges of three quite different paths into music. 'I was playing in the '60s down at the Middle Earth club with Ginger Johnson's African Drummers,' Ian tells me. 'But I can trace that whole interest in improvised music back to being about three years old and banging a piano key and just really loving the sound. I've always been interested in sound as much as how music is constructed, and I like the idea of creating music that surprises me as well.

'I used to play in a folk band in the Isle Of Man in about 1968, which would now be described as "new folk", because we were using feedback on electric guitars and screwdrivers on strings,' he adds later, disclosing that it went under the name of Henry's Head Band. 'Before I met Jonny I was experimenting with multi-track taping and stuff like that – putting a microphone outside the window and recording all the street noises and overlaying it and multitracking it.'

Jon Seagroatt's interest in experimental music, and his route to the sax and clarinet, seems to have sprung from an early exposure to Soft Machine, whose experimental, improvisational take on pop music must have opened many a young mind to more out-there sounds. 'I grew out of that into things like the Art Ensemble of Chicago and Terry Riley, and then those records that Trevor had of twentieth-century percussion.'

Percussionist and director of the FMR label Trevor Taylor is, the three agree, an important part of the story, as both an instigator of live music-making and someone through whom connections were made. 'He was behind a lot of things that were happening in Southend, and the fact that there was improvised music and modern music being played in Southend. He was a big influence at the time,' says Roger.

Jon added, 'He organised this festival which was astonishing: it was a combination of the interests that Trevor had – he covered both bases, interestingly; he was a fabulous jazz drummer and he was also a fabulous percussionist. When I got to know Trevor I used to borrow loads of his records. He was the only person who had those records of contemporary music.'

It was Taylor who put Roger Telford in touch with his band mates, after Roger had noticed Jon at one of Southend Art School's regular improv nights – 'he was about 17 at the time, wandering backwards and forwards playing the tenor, and I thought, he sounds interesting.' How did Roger's drumming, clearly influenced by free players such as Elvin Jones and Milford Graves, fit into the mix? 'I had come from a straight jazz background – I'd heard of Soft Machine, but never heard them,' says the drummer. However, when asked about the first time the trio played together, he says, 'It worked fine because I was able to not play time – which was such a relief. It was nice not to have to do it. I wanted to hear what the drums could do.'

What drummers did you admire at the time?

'Well, there was [Tony] Oxley, and I'd seen Paul Lytton play as well, then of course I was listening to all those American people. I'd been at the great drum festival where Sonny Murray was booed off the stage. I was there, not booing. Then I read an article in *Jazz Monthly*, in 1967, which was comparing Tony Williams, Milford Graves and various other people; it was really interesting, and I thought, that sounds like what I want to do. It was all about polyrhythms, and playing round the beat . . .'

'I'm curious – did you actually know what they sounded like?' Jon asks.

'No. I had a friend who was a saxophone player and he had some of these records – he had [Archie Shepp's] *Four For Trane* –'

'You see, that's something that used to happen,' says Jon. 'It's really good that Rog brought that up because it does take you right back there. I remember rushing out to get *Melody Maker*, going through it and reading reviews and imagining what the music was going to sound like. I'd forgotten about doing that. I've always been interested in how much the text creates music, in a way.'

When asked whether Red Square set out deliberately to antagonise their audiences – by playing in unlikely venues such as folk clubs, or just through sheer volume and intensity – Jon and Roger's 'No' is met with a 'Yes, to some extent' by Ian. The guitarist is more keen than his band mates to cast Red Square as sonic aggressors, noisenik precursors of punk: 'We had quite an attitude,' he says rather proudly. 'We had the attitude of a modern-day metal band, in a way, and as improvisers, that was a bit frowned upon. We were quite confrontational . . .'

Listening to 'Nakamichi 5' where the guitar shreds amid rapid-fire beats and guttural sax, along with tales of the Red Square PA system ('Two enormous speakers, which are now in Bristol – there's a gang of young DJs who still use the original Red Square speakers') that accompanied the band to their gigs, it's not hard to imagine a confrontational attitude alongside the sound. What, or who, were the band confronting?

Given their presence on the organising committee of 'Music for Socialism' – a 1976 festival orginated by Henry Cow, with whom Red Square performed the same year in Lindisfarne Hall, Southend – it's possible to place the band in the tradition of politicised experimental music of the time. Yet the relationship between ideology and sound was not, and is not, a straightforward one. Improvisers are by and large drawn to the political Left, but, as Jon muses thirty years on, the politics and music are 'not necessarily bedfellows, are they?' Meanwhile, Ian laughs as he tells the story of a gig at a Right To Work march in London, organised by his then flatmate, a member of the Socialist Worker Party – 'and of course they were expecting a dance band! We played for about five minutes, and the whole place started booing. The organisers walked on stage and said, "We think you'd better leave out the back door!" I left my guitar on stage up against an amplifier feeding back at full volume . . .'

Jon and Roger are quick to qualify: 'They'd come to the end of a march and they wanted a good bop, and someone had got them an improvising band, which was a ridiculous thing to do. I don't blame those people or think they're bigoted or backwards for doing that.'

For those of my generation, born after punk, growing up amid the gradual toppling of Communist governments throughout Europe, rightly suspicious of party politics and surrounded by symbols separated from their meaning, the commitment of a previous generation to revolutionary ideals is something it can be hard to think ourselves into. It is a stumbling block that holds, even as identity politics and community-building figure highly in our experiences of modern-day punk, noise and DIY scenes. Did it really seem a possibility at the time, that making free music would have an impact on society? Or was the relationship more indirect, a shared political rhetoric just one factor that held an artistic community together?

Roger: 'We thought that there would be an opportunity to do that sort of music and people would be open to it. And I think the '80s closed that down.'

'Did we actually think it was going to change the world?' Jon asks. 'I'm trying to remember back. I was incredibly idealistic, as one should be at that age.'

Ian: 'I remember thinking that people would be interested, in the same way that people responded to Jimi Hendrix and Pink Floyd, because to some extent what we were doing was a continuation down those roads, and when popular music didn't carry on in that direction, I remember us talking about it and being somewhat surprised and disappointed' – although, he says, 'when the punk thing happened we all paid a lot of attention to that.'

'Suddenly music had come alive again,' Roger agrees. 'Although it was being played by people of sixteen and seventeen who could hardly play. It had a lot of life. So I threw myself into that – I played with some punk bands.'

Do they still feel a connection between music and politics?

'I think so,' says Roger. 'But then I'm not sure whether I can feel a disconnection between anything I do and politics, so who knows whether it's true or not – whether it's possible to play this music without being political?' Ian, meanwhile, cites a more personal ideology: 'I have a few acres of land, it's all organic and it's a wildlife reserve, and I live on boats, and my living comes from painting and playing.'

The act of revisiting their '70s material has provided an impetus for the band to play again, twenty-five years after last working as a trio. As the music on *Thirty Three* works well on modern ears, so has Red Square's new live presence found a receptive audience. 'It was remarkable how much better the response was to anything we had done before,' says Jon of a recent gig in Oxford. 'It was almost like things had caught up with us. The majority of times, people didn't entirely enjoy what we did, in the early days.'

If memories can be untrustworthy, music at first seems less so. Yet one of the chapters I find most interesting in Red Square's history is the most recent one of revisiting and re-presenting, not least because of Jon Seagroatt's interest in the recording and production processes and electronic music. Currently listening to the decaying tape pieces of William Basinski and the hauntological electronica of the Ghost Box label, his awareness of the ambiguity of the recorded document, especially with regard to improvised music, is acute: 'Once you record something, it does alter everything,' he says. 'Once you can play it again and again, you anticipate pieces, which is bizarre because you're almost retro-fitting composition, in a way. We post-pattern it.'

He explains, 'I did all the re-engineering but we all selected [the album material]. We debated for a while the idea of putting some kind of context in it. Because of the idea that a recording is an artefact that's separate from the production of music itself, we did kick around the idea of maybe using audio signifiers from the '70s, bringing those in, but we didn't in the end.

'I thought it might be interesting to experiment. But again it's the problem with all freedom. Where do you stop? What do you take? How do you include it? Do you then do something to the original Red Square music?'

In the end, the band settled for choosing and remastering ten tracks from reel-to-reel tapes (the 'Nakamichi' tracks seem to be named simply after the tape stock), a process which Jon documents in detail on the band's Myspace blog. 'Generally, when we rehearsed, we would plonk a couple of mikes down in the room where we were playing, and press record,' he writes. 'Sometimes one of the mikes might be on a chair, or on the mantelpiece. We tended not to have enough room to set up for a text-book stereo recording, and I'm not even sure that we knew what one of those was at the time!'

That the recording sounds as natural, analogue and present as it does – neither overly cleaned up, nor noticeably archival – owes a lot to a sensitive mastering job that seeks to retain the presence of the original tapes but add clarity lacking in the originals. It's the kind of warm, punchy but clear sound many bands seek today; a kind of constructed directness that goes hand in hand with advances in studio technology that allow for better and better simulations of analogue atmosphere. Soundwise, *Thirty Three* achieves a happy liminality between old and new, a strangely evocative quality which is, of course, one of the newest things about it.

The time and place that it evokes is one that remains, for the most part, as hidden now as it was then. Back in Southend, the Queen's Hotel site is now home to a quiet, low-rise housing development, built in the last few decades. The shopping street leading away from it is typical of coastal suburbia: two martial arts shops, a couple of faded department stores, and charity shops at regular intervals. A Slovak restaurant and two Portuguese cafes, newer additions. The Cliffs Pavilion is still standing, host to Blur's 2009 Glastonbury warm-up show and a musical featuring the songs of Take That. A community noticeboard outside the flats invites residents to get involved in the Southend Timeline website – 'to settle arguments or just share memories'.

Later, I check the site and, of course, there is no mention of Southend's alternative past: spontaneous music festivals, improv clubs, art squats and industrial organisers all conspicuous by their absence. Locally, it's left to southendpunk.com to fly the archival flag for Red Sqaure. 'They used to just play in this room making as much noise as possible,' remembers one forum member, 'and anyone who felt like it could go along and watch them'.

Frances Morgan

DAN FRANKLIN
Extremely Loud and Incredibly Fast
Napalm Death and the Possibility of Life's Destruction

It was a big day for Napalm Death. John Peel's producer, John Walters, had called drummer Mick Harris at his parents' house in Birmingham to ask the question every up-and-coming band wanted to hear: whether the band could come down to London to do a session. They knew that Peel had been going crazy for their debut album *Scum*, and holding the DJ in no little reverence, they agreed. Too excited to be nervous they looked forward to a Sunday afternoon in the BBC's Maida Vale studio, and the prospect of a free meal.

The teenage band – as ever – had to converge on Birmingham from disparate points: bassist Shane Embury came from home in Ironbridge near Telford, Shropshire, and stayed overnight at Harris's house. Bill Steer's parents dropped him off in the morning (they still wouldn't let the guitarist travel on his own by train from the Wirral). They piled into the rented van and picked up vocalist Lee Dorrian in Coventry before heading towards their destiny.

Long-suffering Peel Sessions producer Dale Griffin was aghast. Harris had gamely presented him with the twelve-song set list that the band wanted to perform in their twenty minutes in studio 3, beaming from ear to ear, the hyperactive little shite as ever. But this was not the way things ran, Griffin explained: bands had twenty minutes divided into four slots: A, B, C and D. Yes, a band could get away with five,

maybe six songs if they squeezed two into one slot, but twelve was out of the question. Harris had to repeat to yet another sound engineer how Napalm worked: that it would only take a few minutes – their songs didn't last long. Griffin was perplexed as much as exasperated, but soon relented and stood open-mouthed as the band blazed through their set in one take. Music had taken some very strange paths since he had co-founded Mott the Hoople in 1969, but this was something else.

Dorrian and Harris took their positions to overlay the vocals, credited on *Scum* for 'lead growls' and 'Caveman screams and growls' respectively. Once they started Griffin had to be fast to stop them in their tracks: half-laughing and half-crying he ran out and brought back avant-garde punk vocalist Danielle Dax who had been recording in the adjacent studio. They started again, before Dax exclaimed, 'You can't sing like that! You'll damage your vocal chords, boys!'

Napalm Death's first Peel session, recorded on 13 September 1987, is the most extreme recording by one of the most extreme bands Britain has ever produced. Because it was for Peel, they made it special.

The shock-and-awe ferocity of its execution is remarkable even now, when hundreds and hundreds of bands since have tried to supplant them. It's at once a terrifying, hilarious and totally life-affirming encapsulation of their

Dan Franklin

determination to push and push and push the boundaries of rock music; its sheer physicality and visceral, shit-kicking energy attests to a sort of human triumph. Precision and control, calamity and chaos are poised on a knife-edge. Napalm Death arrived that day with a bass guitar, a pair of drumsticks and Mick Harris's trusted Pearl drum pedal (used since his first gig on drums with a band called Martian Brain Squeeze) which he regarded superstitiously as the only one capable of letting him unleash the supersonic beats which made Napalm Death legend. Force of a hurricane, fast as lightning: the art of 'blasting'.

The first three-track section of the session holds within it all of Napalm's mercurial madness. 'The Kill' starts straightforwardly enough with a searing guitar tone and a three note up-and-down riff before the snare fill kicks it into warp speed: a white noise, sheet-metal firestorm overlaid with screaming, syncopated vocal ravages. It lasts less than twenty seconds: musical conventions of rhythm and melody are seemingly destroyed. 'Prison Without Walls' is slightly slower, which by any other standard is very fast, but without being flat-out it lurches drunkenly around the beat, Dorrian sounding like he's sending himself up. But the wayward delivery is abruptly counter-punched by 'Dead' (called here, sardonically, 'Dead, pt 1'), two seconds that razes the opening section to the ground.

Throughout the session, the traditional order of instrumental prominence is upended: the drums dominate, given space to reverberate in the mix. Napalm's signature blast beats – Harris's super-tensed peppering of the ride cymbal and alternate striking of the crash – solidify to a terrifying wall of noise. 'Lucid Fairytale' even unveils the bass, hardly discernible as anything but buzzing, the distortion more prominent and potent than the melody it adorns; a subsonic abrasiveness that led Harris to dub this new musical form 'grindcore'. The session goes on in squalls and flurries, violently probing the boundaries of what constitutes the acceptable.

And then there's 'You Suffer': notorious for being barely over a second long; here again (concluding their little joke) called 'You Suffer Pt. 2'. Like a stinging blow it comes and passes, and the shock sinks in as it echoes out in the mix. It's as if one of the denizens of the cave has broken his shackles and dares to look out at the outside world which has hitherto only been reflected on the wall by firelight, and seeing the horror turns and barks one of the most vital questions of the twentieth century: 'You suffer . . . but why?'

....

Napalm Death's ferocious new form of music developed within a fecund ecosystem of tape-trading and one-upmanship within the punk and metal scenes of the mid-to-late '80s. Its DNA was threaded together by a small, close-knit community that crossed the Atlantic and had roots in Scandinavia. Napalm's debut album, *Scum*, captured a sound stretched in one direction by the velocity of punk and in another by the down-tuned heaviness of metal; it was the culmination of an arms race in which speed was the most sought-after weapon.

But grindcore's visceral intensity is also a product of its era: the years of Thatcherism which presented non-negotiable tenets of governance as opposed to a coherent ideology, pitting working men and women against each other in confrontations which scarred the country forever. Napalm Death is the sound of political thought disengaging from itself, and dissolving into nihilism.

Mick 'human tornado' Harris played his first gig on drums for Napalm Death on 18 January 1986, supporting anarchist 'crust punk' stalwarts Amebix. Joining vocalist and bassist Nik Bullen and guitarist Justin Broadrick, the floorboards of the Mermaid pub vibrated, bowing under the pressure of the blasts which were met with bemusement and derision. The pub in Birmingham's Stretford Road, in the poor Sparkhill area of the city, was the furnace of the hardcore punk scene in the Midlands.

Harris used to come and watch Napalm as part of hardcore all-dayers held from midday until late at weekends, convened by promoter Daz Russell. First witnessing the band in the summer of 1985 he saw a group in thrall to the fast, politicised hardcore punk of Chaos UK, Disorder and Discharge (harder, heavier and faster than the likes of the Sex Pistols, The Clash and The Buzzcocks) but also heavily inspired by the desolate, melodic coldness of Joy Division. That would change.

This little guy with the psychobilly haircut intrigued Bullen and Broadrick so much with his velocity that he replaced drummer and founder member Miles 'Rat' Ratledge in November 1985. In his bedroom at his parents' house Harris holed up with Broadrick, his Premier drum kit and a small amplifier, and began a process of pushing Napalm to its limits which lasted for the best part of five years. Harris loved to play fast and craved more speed, more energy, needing to stress the tensile limits of musicality. At the Mermaid he got locked into a week-by-week showdown with the drummer of Nottingham band (and fellow Peel favourites) Heresy, whose drummer Steve Charlesworth similarly felt the need for speed, but who was soon outgunned by Harris.

Two bands could be heard looming large in Napalm's new sound: Boston's Siege, whose six-song demo recording and three contributions to a classic 1985 hardcore compilation called *Cleanse the Bacteria* (re-released together in 1994 under the title *Drop Dead*) was thrashy and unwieldy hardcore, and the early crossover of Flint, Michigan's raw-throated Repulsion, whose demo of January 1986 *The Stench of Burning Death* (recorded as *Genocide*) roared

and grooved and blasted in tight arrangements rarely lasting longer than two minutes. The demo set the tape-trading underground alight, and Napalm soon lifted the opening riff of the title track to play as an introduction to the live and session versions of *Scum*'s 'Deceiver'.

In a one-bedroom flat further east in the midlands, in Nottingham, Digby Pearson had dropped out of studying medicine to focus on putting out bands that attacked and inflicted noise on the society around them. He called his label Earache Records. Slightly older than the teenage Napalm, in his early twenties, Pearson is a pivotal and controversial figure in the grindcore story. He saw his role as friend first, facilitator second and then as obsessive evangelist for the nascent hardcore punk and extreme metal scenes, pushing tapes of anarcho-punk bands at metal gigs and vice-versa.

He also exploited Thatcher's desire for a vibrant enterprise culture within a free-market Britain. He raised £1,000 (mainly selling off his own record collection) so he could be entitled to take advantage of the Enterprise Allowance Scheme. Unemployment had peaked at 3.2 million in 1985; once the government grew sick of counting the growing cost of benefits it made it less easy to qualify for unemployment benefit and then cooked the unemployment statistics, counting only those defined as 'unemployed and claiming benefit'. Unemployment promptly fell below three million in June 1987, and the allowance of £40 a week that Pearson collected was another way for the government to claim that more people were in work and self-employed. In fact Pearson did nothing with the money he was given and it was only the imminent end of the scheme after one year that galvanised him to start putting records out. And Harris kept telling him to come and see Napalm play: 'I'll be even faster next time, Dig. . .'

Napalm Death recorded the first twelve tracks of *Scum* in August 1986, using Rich Bitch studios in Birmingham, while taking advantage of its midnight to 8 a.m. 'evening rate' of half price. The recording cost a total of £120. The songs buzz with Broadrick's razor-sharp guitar tone, overdriven with an MXR distortion pedal provided by local thrash band Sacrilege. The opening of the album tingles and rings not unlike the opening of Robin Trower's 'Bridge of Sighs' before Bullen roars into the vortex: 'Multinational Corporations | Genocide of the Starving Nations'. It's at once mantra, decree, and condemnation.

He rails against the 'Forms of escapism | And entertainment' that 'disable thought' ('Caught . . . in a dream'), fed through a television screen, the 'Siege of Power' within the land and its inhabitants' minds, rendering them helpless; the 'fascist control' that has made its way into everyone's heads. The sentiments are typical of the anarchist punk mindset: rebels in search of a cause, railing against the system to satisfy their need to lash out against something – anything.

The songs shift gears from urgent mid-tempo, up to fast, and up again almost impossibly further, to very, very fast. Harris unleashes hell during 'Polluted Minds' (which even crams in a rare, dive-bombing guitar solo) and 'Sacrificed'. Somehow the songs become more agonised – 'Born On Your Knees', 'Human Garbage' – before one of the shortest songs ever written, 'You Suffer', completes the set. Increasingly from the start it feels like there is an overpowering force at work, a chaos that threatens to spill out and destroy the musical order. But this first half of the album is still recognisably hardcore, albeit bolstered with moments of incandescent speed and fury.

The recording was given to Pearson but even at that early stage he knew he wouldn't be able to successfully put it out with twenty minutes of music alone. But the emerging sound couldn't tolerate any impediment to its progress. It seemed to have taken on a life of its own: a wild animal straining at its leash and then dispatching any unwilling handlers.

Broadrick was tempted away from the Napalm guitar position to play drums with fast-rising and frequently touring group Head of David in October 1986. According to Harris, Bullen began to arrive to rehearsals extremely drunk, which for the largely sober drummer was simply not good enough. It was a manifestation of a deepening lack of interest in what Bullen perceived as Napalm's use of speed for speed's sake. He had been worn down and made way for new blood in March 1987. Harris's message to them both in the sleeve of the finished album is plain: 'Keep Your Heads Together'.

What became side two of *Scum* was recorded in May 1987, on a primitive 8-track, all the instruments miked up live in the studio. Under the aegis of Pearson, Harris had recruited Bill Steer on guitar. Steer had just left school. His main concern was the pioneering death metal band Carcass, formed with childhood friend and drummer Ken Owen and bassist/vocalist Jeff Walker. Their early lyrics dealt entirely with the destruction of the human body, wryly subverting the cartoon-like blood'n'guts imagery of the genre by rendering it in medicalised minutiae, making it more real than reality. They spawned their own subgenre: goregrind (or even better, hardcore). Steer always perceived his role in Napalm as a hired gun. Harris speaks highly of him today as the 'permanent stand-in' who was at the heart of the band.

Harris excitedly showed Steer the new riffs he had been coming up with on the two-string guitar he had tuned so he could play bar chords with one finger: condensed, simple, the bare components of music. Steer was a flair player, a devotee of classic rock who adhered to groove, but in Napalm he played it straight and took instruction. His dirty, muffled guitar churns up the bedrock of the second half of *Scum*, which begins with a song-as-question, 'Life?', and blizzards throughout, restless and insatiable.

New lyricist and bassist Jim Whiteley bluntly interrogates everything around him: 'Where is your success gained from? | What of the lives you've shat upon?' ('Success?'), 'When will you see? We'll never be free' ('Parasites'), 'Not your problem | Why should you care?' 'Stigmatized'), 'Is this the price we're gonna pay?' ('M.A.D.').

Rather than aim its sights at amorphous international corporations, it sarcastically baits those who would unquestioningly accept the status quo ('Uniformity | Conformity | How long can you hide the truth?' – 'Pseudo Youth') in a world where the fate of humanity itself is sealed and atomic genocide is assured. One question remains at the end of the record: will you 'accept the end?'

However, the lyrical content of Napalm Death is problematic, because language itself is destroyed in new vocalist Lee Dorrian's delivery of the songs. He was so fresh to the material he had one rehearsal the night before to learn it and went into the studio carrying sheets of newly scrawled lyrics he had worked on with Whiteley. He even had to be cued in during the recording, which contributed to its abrupt, ragged, near inhuman vocal emissions. If the symbolic order of the world is preserved by language, here it dissolves into incomprehensibility.

When he was nominated for the Turner Prize in 2006 artist Mark Titchner cited Napalm Death's creation of 'a language that ceases to function and ceases to be able to communicate in a normal way'. For him the album passes from having meaning and a message in the first half to something deeper that functions on a primal level: an emotional engagement that obviates clamouring systems of belief and operates by a new, indefinable set of rules. On the second half of *Scum*, the incomprehensible rushes in: a nuclear wind of the guttural and the unutterable.

Scum was released in July 1987, a month after

the Conservatives were re-elected with a majority of 102. The socialist and anarchist agenda of hardcore punk was wiped clean by Napalm Death's grindcore. In its sarcastic rebuttals to music and order itself (the second Peel session of March 1988 starts with a version of 'Multinational Corporations' so over the top it seems to mock the song's strident lyrical assurance) it behaves similarly to that other wild animal: free-market capitalism. It held a mirror up to Thatcher's stance against state interference in favour of individual freedom.

Napalm Death's debut emerged after some of the most pivotal years in recent British political and social history. The miners' strike, and particularly the battle at Orgreave coking plant near Rotherham on 18 June 1984, had pitted two Titans against one another. On one side, the President of the National Union of Mineworkers, Arthur Scargill, a radical Marxist who believed that capitalism produced contradictions only resolvable by a change in society:

> I hope that people do regard me as a dangerous man, in the respect of changing society. I'm certainly a danger and a threat to those who support the capitalist system. And I'm very proud to be a threat to the capitalist system and I hope – by being a threat – we're able to bring about a fundamental change in society and create a new order.'

The Marxist view of Thatcherism was that it was an ideological campaign, tailored for and by the rich and powerful capitalists, to lord itself over the wretched and underprivileged working man.

On the other side was Thatcher, a prime minister who perceived the Marxists' belief in state ownership to be a form of enslavement: 'the corrosive and corrupting effects of socialism.' The victim of this clash of ideals was the working class, divided between the police

Dan Franklin

and miners at flashpoints such as Orgreave – torn apart from within. Napalm Death blazed through this harrying of the British social and political landscape. Their sonic assault whipped up the ashes in its wake.

Ironically, in their wilful destruction of ideology, their breaking of systems of understanding, the way in which they engineered their own futures, Napalm Death might have been proudly perceived by Thatcher as the independent offspring of her preferred form of capitalism. But their second album took the capitalist journey one step further, to its logical conclusion: self-destruction.

....

In his study of the development of Institutions in the western world during the eighteenth century, *Discipline and Punish*, Michel Foucault posits the notion of the 'docile' body: 'A body is docile that may be subjected, used, transformed and improved.' As the eighteenth and nineteenth centuries progressed, institutions of power utilised disciplines to exert the subtle coercions which worked the body not just en masse, but individually, 'which made possible the meticulous control of the operations of the body, which assured the constant subjection of its forces and imposed upon them a relationship of docility-utility'.

These disciplines constitute a form of domination so efficacious because unlike enslavement – which merely appropriates the body – it creates an 'elegance' of discipline 'at the formation of a relation that in the mechanism itself makes it more obedient as it becomes more useful, and conversely'. The human body becomes a microcosm, a 'political anatomy' and a 'mechanics of power': 'Discipline increases the forces of the body (in economic terms of utility) and diminishes these same forces (in political terms of obedience).' Foucault believed the factory provided the principal space and machinery for this subjugation. And so did Napalm Death.

When Thatcher denounced the enslavement and overbearing power of the unions she advocated an individualism that disguised this same power relationship. In the original transcript of her 'no such thing as society' interview with *Woman's Own* she delineated this flow of power in the form of responsibility:

> Who is society? There is no such thing. There are individual men and women and there are families and no government can do anything except through people and people look to themselves first. It is our duty to look after ourselves and then also to help look after our neighbour and life is a reciprocal business and people have got the entitlements too much in mind without the obligations, because there is no such thing as an entitlement unless someone has first met an obligation.

And so in Thatcher's vision, the disciplining of the docile body of the citizen, and its economy of obligation and entitlement, masquerades as empathy.

Napalm Death's second album, *From Enslavement to Obliteration*, released in October 1988, cuts to the heart of this political thought, as the 'political anatomy' of the individual rages against and breaks free of the system only to dissolve in a psychosocial and sexual meltdown. It is a deeply introverted, solipsistic record that at first seems to wrestle with the anarchist punk basics: the ignorance of racism ('Unchallenged Hate'), drugs as a means of escaping your own confused identity ('Sometimes'), and the traps of the hardcore scene's idealism ('Think for a Minute', 'Practice What You Preach').

At its heart though are two diatribes: one against the body's unquestioning allegiance to capitalist rapaciousness in the relatively groovy, though still rampant, 'Mentally Murdered'

('The will to succeed | Overpowers the will to resist'), and the other more surprisingly against the (unionised) workforce in the title track which starts steady and builds speed, allowing for chopped up, Carcass-like chord progressions, before the breakneck lyrical barrage: 'Committed to a life of slavery | In the factories our own hands have built'.

But, more crucially, the album warns that rejection of these manacles of the mind, or any system of belief, often results in the reversion to more primitive, destructive thought processes and a recapitulation of negative actions towards others. A sexual power-play is portrayed which lampoons the sexism of heavy rock that makes '"idols" of assholes', '"raunchy", "hunky" machismo-type fools' where 'capitalism, racism, sexism' are the foundations of 'Cock-Rock Idealism' ('Cock-Rock Alienation'). Female subjugation is portrayed as part of the economy of military-industrial domination: 'Female subservience | To impervious male domination | Male subservience | To the countries [*sic*] defence' ('It's a M.A.N's World').

Dan Franklin

It goes still further. Dorrian, aware he is in essence still a Coventry lad, dares to turn the spotlight glare on himself and his complicity in the cattle market on 'Inconceivable' and 'Social Sterility': 'Must inebriate my senses | Into a state of delirium, | Before I turn to the meat rack | For my penial selection'.

'Uncertainty Blurs the Vision' proposes a (qualified) way to escape: to live 'Unbound from an existence | Of fear and pain' is possible only through the 'External freedom' that 'Must evolve from liberation within.'

But this seems to be impossible. Dorrian disengages, shattering his self-image in the grotesque and violent upheaval of 'Display to Me'. He takes the part of someone begging to be consumed, senses stretched, peaking on the verge of insanity:

Chew on my flesh
With perverted lust,
Display to me
The depth of your compassion.

As you excrete
My digested corpse,
Into the shit-pan,
– My place of rest.

The album is a traumatic journey towards inexorable self-annihilation, bellowing at modern Britain's greed and moral ruin, and ending with 'The Curse' (originally released as an EP included with early vinyl copies of *From Enslavement to Obliteration* in 1988, its tracks later added to the CD edition), an industrial dirge devoid of humanity.

The two album covers brilliantly depict this schism. *Scum*'s cover art focuses on the external world, a starving African family stood upon a pile of skulls strewn with corporate logos, presided over by suited puppet masters as the rancid angel of death spreads its wings over the scene. But *From Enslavement to Obliteration* has at its centre an individual whose expression is the very definition of anguish: teeth clenched, eyes clamped shut, gripping his face with his hands, surrounded by scenes of starvation, imprisonment, pornography, the factory and the wasteland.

....

Carcass's debut album, *Reek of Putrefaction*, resisted the 'mighty challenge' of *From Enslavement to Obliteration* to become one of John Peel's albums of the year for 1988 in the *Observer*. He described it as a 'wonderful year' for British hardcore: 'I like the idea of defining for yourself an area of operation as apparently limited as hardcore and then finding room for innovation within that area.' Peel endorsed the scene with fervour: he got ten sessions out of five of the first ten bands on Earache's roster, including Unseen Terror from which Shane Embury joined Napalm on bass for the recording of *From Enslavement to Obliteration*. Outside of the Earache roster there was Ipswich's similarly brutal Extreme Noise Terror, with whom Harris had played for a year. During the Brit Awards Peel held up grindcore records in the Rough Trade store, and he snuck in the back of venues such as the Garage in Nottingham where Pearson studiously avoided him, intimidated by the man who'd taught him so much, preserving their relationship instead on an almost telepathic level.

But it got far bigger than that. In the November 1988 edition of the *NME* Steven Wells, whose own iconoclastic ranting found like-minded intent in Napalm, heralded the band as the 'grave digger' of rock'n'roll: the logical end-point in a musical development from Jerry Lee Lewis to the Sex Pistols. Then in 1989 BBC's *Arena* series showed a documentary called 'Heavy Metal' which featured the band. They seemed to bypass the hierarchy of the heavy music scene and mainline into a much wider area of consciousness. The person on the street knew who they were, this band stretching rock music to its very limits.

One particularly surreal appearance was on children's musical education programme 'What's that Noise?!', presented by Craig Charles, who had been known to attend Napalm gigs with Vic Reeves in tow. After a performance of 'You Suffer' in an episode also featuring Cliff Richard and astronomer Patrick Moore, Charles assails the group. A doe-eyed Dorrian explains 'You Suffer' by dismissing it, telling the presenter it's three or four years old, after which Charles quips: 'What sort of songs are you doing now? Longer songs . . . ?'

But his affection for the band is clearly immense, quoting to them from a vinyl copy of *From Enslavement to Obliteration* he's clutching the first few lines from opening track 'Evolved As One'. Then there's the crucial question: 'That's real deep lyrics, but you can't hear them. Why?'

Dorrian struggles to describe how the words are 'running around' in his head, that the loudness and aggression, the extreme number of beats and riffs, means he is forced to adopt his ultra-harsh approach. He presents the viewer with the possibility that rather than a deliberate, radical negation of language, he actually has no other option. His vocal style, which helped signal a sea-change in extreme metal vocalists – from Cannibal Corpse to Anal Cunt – is a product of necessity rather than invention. Harris, a ball of nervous energy, butts in with a hulking platitude: 'It's an aggressive style of music.' Steer takes control with a measured explanation, which verges on impatience, of the necessity of a lyric sheet: 'We don't pretend that anyone can actually understand them when we're playing.'

Charles is satisfied and introduces their next song as Steer looks to his right with a smirk: 'Well look: they're rootin', they're tootin', they're electrocutin'. I mean, this is music for young lovers. Step aside Kylie Minogue. Turn up the TV, plug in your pacemaker. Don't get out of breath. Ladies and gentlemen . . . NAPALM DEATH!' A toxic yellow warning flashes on screen as choppy, strobe-like editing begins: 'Parent Hazard Warning'. The band scorch through 'From Enslavement to Obliteration' and the nation's children return to Andy Crane and Ed the Duck in the BBC's 'Broom Cupboard' never the same again.

·········

The gnomes stand contentedly at the edge of the Harrises' pond as Napalm Death look out over the garden from their drummer's bedroom window, beyond the fence the housing estates of King's Norton. A strong breeze eases a colourful ball across the surface of the dun water and the washing flaps on the line against a slate-grey sky.

Crowded on Harris's bed they look every inch the defiant youngsters they are as Dorrian and Steer take the lead trying to explain the band, interspersed with performance footage of them at the height of their fame as part of 'Heavy Metal' director Helen Gallacher's spin-off documentary 'Thrashed to Death'.

Their attempts to explain themselves pale in comparison to the glimpses of their frenzied live performances during the film's second half. The first focuses on Slayer, the Californian thrash act who set the high water mark for heaviness three years before them. But by 1989 Slayer had released *South of Heaven*, which moved on and slowed down from 1986's thrash genre-defining *Reign in Blood*.

As his roadies erect a mocked-up church stage-set behind him, likeable, smiley bassist and vocalist Tom Araya smugly explains how it can't get any more extreme than Slayer: 'The hardcore kids are the ones who are thrash. They like the fast stuff right. *Reign in Blood*: they

Dan Franklin

consider that *the* thrash album, the ultimate in thrash. How much further can you take that? If you took it any further it would be stupidly fast and it wouldn't make any sense . . . We feel like we've set the standard for a thrash album – ten songs, twenty-eight minutes long – an album in twenty-eight minutes, that's the ultimate in thrash. We've got a song that's like a minute and a half that has three verses, two choruses and two guitar leads and it's all in a minute and a half. That's like we've set the standard. And we don't wanna outdo ourselves and go overboard. Because then you're crossing the line between metal, or thrash metal, and punk.'

He's oblivious to the meltdown of Napalm that follows him in the film: how punk is metal is punk, how you can be so fast that time itself is warped. He's unaware of the birth of grindcore, to the album of fifty-four songs in just over an hour Earache put out when it combined *From Enslavement to Obliteration* and *Scum* into one devastating CD edition, to emphasise that no, *this* is the last word in extremity.

....

But the extremity of Napalm Death meant they could not last forever, at least in this incarnation. They burned brightly and faded fast. The breaking-point came during their summer tour of Japan in 1989, that country that has always embraced the outer reaches of music. Harris had already been ejected from Extreme Noise Terror that summer as well because of his wearing temperament, and Napalm was itself sundered into two camps: Harris and Embury, and Steer and Dorrian. Steer ultimately felt more comfortable in Carcass, but Dorrian had been angered when only his royalty cheque, which he had been slow to cash in, was cancelled to cover the whole band's tour losses. At the last gig he dared to repeat to the crowd a famous question: 'Ever feel like you've been cheated?' Dorrian and Steer left after they returned to England.

So Steer concentrated on Carcass, a band that delivered a masterpiece of the metal genre in *Heartwork* in 1993, and has recently reformed to headline the festivals that did not exist in their heyday and capture the glory of a considerable legacy that grew exponentially after they broke up in 1995. But he also stripped away the layers of extremity to the essential vintage blues boom playing of ongoing power trio Firebird.

Dorrian also engaged with the ur-spirit of classic heavy rock from the late '60s and early '70s, slowing down and channelling a more melancholy, decadent emotion into Cathedral, a pioneering band within the funereal doom genre. In 1989 he started Rise Above Records by also taking advantage of the Enterprise Allowance Scheme: a label which remains a repository of 'Heavy Music for Heavy Minds'.

Harris persevered with Napalm, helping assemble another line-up, before leaving the band many consider him to embody in 1991. He even re-interpreted the feral un-musicality of the group with saxophonist John Zorn's overtly avant-garde and hyper-musical rendering of grindcore in the Painkiller project. A three-hour improvisation session in bassist Bill Laswell's Brooklyn Greenpoint studio produced their first release, the *Guts of a Virgin* EP, which was later seized and destroyed by UK customs under the Obscene Publications Act because of the art-work that interpreted the title too literally for their liking.

Harris then left drumming almost altogether to explore the realm of bass, forsaking the speed and treble of Napalm for over fifteen years in the project he calls Scorn, which has continued his steadfast indifference to trends while at the same time presaging both Breaks and the Dubstep movement (both categorisations he abhors). He continues to push the envelope, taking the 'bass mantra' to near psychedelic levels.

Only Embury remains in today's Napalm Death. He steadfastly persisted with the band through its '90s nadir, which saw the release of a series of watered-down albums. It took being dropped by Earache at the turn of the millennium for the band to recapture its piss'n'vinegar with *Enemy of the Music Business*. The irony was not lost on Pearson.

In fact, grindcore roared back to life in these years, benefitting from sleek, pulverising production: Pig Destroyer's *Terrifyer* and Nasum's *Human 2.0* set new standards. With twenty years gone since the heyday of Napalm, Pearson can now savour the band's legacy. Earache recently put out Insect Warfare's *World Extermination*, an album which blatantly idolises *From Enslavement to Obliteration*. It is a spectacular piece of hero-worship, from its unyielding sonic attack to the monolithic cooling towers on its back cover, reminiscent of the Ratcliffe-on-Soar power station by the train line on the way into Nottingham.

Napalm Death were not the most extreme band in the world: with numerous experimental noise acts in existence there will always be those who seek to make increasingly unlistenable sounds. But within the parameters of rock, Napalm Death were revolutionary. They blackened the sky with stark warnings about the fragility of the individual, the perils of freedom and the futility of human existence. Of the bands that benefited from the Peel era they stand proudly alongside the more eulogised Joy Division and The Fall. And in terms of the true essence of punk, as contrarian music dedicated to smashing the world order, not because they were the first but because they were the most radical, they are Britain's greatest-ever punk band.

Dan Franklin

LAVINIA GREENLAW
Silent Disco

She's dancing to a song you can't hear,
to inner signals rather than noise.
They give such pure direction,
for once there is an only way.
She's not listening. Something's arising:
a thought that has to be kept moving,
a place in herself that was once so full.
You think you know her by that gesture,
the flick and twist of her hand as it lifts
to catch at her nape as her head tips sideways
but this is routine – a move perfected
while she was waiting, long and quietly,
for someone to let her in.
There followed the summer of dancing
out in the dark beyond the last houses
among the sneaking holly and dogwood
in a breezeblock creosote pre-fab temple,
by day a world of jumble and cordial,
by night a heaven of line and ring.
The look on her face is filling the room.
Someone else would describe it as joyful
only to you it is space she is taking
and you will never have seen her so clearly,
so within, she forgets herself as seen.
She is pure direction, she is line and ring.

MARK FISHER
Why Don't Groups Split Up Any More?

Why don't groups split up any more? This immediately begs another couple of questions: why is it a problem if they don't? Who demands that groups split up, and what is at stake in this demand? And what we are talking about here – let's be clear – is *our* groups: not the 'mainstream time-servers who can be expected to trundle around the nostalgia circuit forever, but those who come out of a culture – post punk – which was supposed to be intolerant of tired reiteration and careerism'. Here they are: The Fall, Sonic Youth. Another year, another record. Persistence, consolidation, becoming an institution: wasn't this everything that post punk's scorched-earth modernism disdained? And the problem isn't confined to the groups who have stayed together, because even those that did break up return. Fill in your own example here – but you would be hard pressed to come up with anything more grotesque than the return of the grandaddys of the post punks, returning as grandads: the Stooges, strutting back onstage in their sixties, geriatric teenagers singing 'Last Year I Was Twenty-one'. In the age of Web 2.0, nothing goes away, everything comes back – if not in the flesh, then as a YouTube clip.

The expectation that groups split up belongs to what in retrospect seems like the speeded-up popular culture of the '60s and '70s. A pattern was established that was followed as much by Throbbing Gristle as by the Beatles. A group would make a name for themselves, release their landmark records and then disintegrate, usually in the space of less than a decade. (But whereas the Beatles never came back, Throbbing Gristle, of course, did.) For those of us whose perception of pop temporality was formed by this accelerated '60s and '70s culture, there's something *disappointing* about the dogged persistence of a group, even – or perhaps especially – if we are fans. In the early stages of fan enthralment, each release is treated like a new religious artefact: reconfiguring our perception of the group and – since our experience is partly filtered through the artistic vision of the band – changing our relationship to the world too. Yet this rapt intensity is not sustainable indefinitely; after a while, particularly if there are no great reinventions, it's hard for libidinal fatigue not to set in. This can't be blamed solely on the fickleness of fans – in fact, the problem with so much 'alternative' rock culture is the opposite one. Fans are too indulgent of their idols. There is a kind of unspoken complicity between fan and group, the result of which is usually a lowering of expectations. At a certain point, fidelity becomes betrayal – keeping faith or carrying on constitutes a repudiation of the very thing that the group stood for in the first place.

The story of the last thirty years – of what the philosopher Alain Badiou has, in the context of politics, called the 'Restoration' – has been precisely one of lowered expectations. The restoration of power and privilege and the retreat of the great emancipatory political projects has led to what I have called 'capitalist realism': a dreary sense that horizons are limited, that nothing much can be expected, that – in Margaret Thatcher's immortal words – there is no alternative. The neoliberal lockdown that enforced capitalist realism began to take power around 1980,and its early effects on – and dissemination via – British pop culture are nowhere more carefully traced than in Dave Rimmer's *Like Punk Never Happened*. Rimmer's book was published in 1985, the ominous year in which the miners' strike was defeated and Live Aid convened, creating a new pop space whose global reach anticipated the near-total dominion of capital that would come into effect when the Berlin Wall fell four years later. Read now, *Like Punk Never Happened* looks like a partly celebratory, partly bewildered, partly aghast glimpse into the Restoration as it began to coalesce. Although Rimmer was shaped by the New Pop – as a journalist for *Smash Hits* he was right at its centre – it is clear that his attitudes were still informed by post punk. The New Pop that Rimmer talks about – not the reflexive wit of August Darnell, Martin Fry or Phil Oakey, but the dull gloss of their progeny, Culture Club and Duran Duran – was itself a kind of airlock between post punk and the Restoration, a de-contamination chamber in which post punk was transformed into a series of stylistic gestures, before being ultimately erased altogether (only to return, thirty years later, as pastiche and spectre). At the start of *Like Punk Never Happened*, Rimmer imagines a young punk in 1977 being shown the future by a fortune-teller:

> The stark, monochrome surrounds of the Roxy fade away into a distant hum as you are suddenly drawn into a procession of nightmare scenes: pop stars dripping with

pearls and swilling champagne, pop stars counting their money in long black limousines, pop stars bowing humbly to Prince Charles and chatting amiably to Terry Wogan on prime time television, pop stars – many of them familiar faces from the very club in which you are standing, transfixed – flying on Concorde and buying mansions around the world, *just like Elton John or Rod Stewart.*

What's interesting, now, is how naive, how quaint this looks. The anxiety about pop stars being reabsorbed into the entertainment establishment belongs to a time when it still seemed plausible to imagine a space outside capital's communicative matrix. But the expectation that groups should split up belongs to that older world, a world, that is to say, where capitalist realism is not yet totally dominant. It is predicated on the notion that pop (and/or rock) can definitively be separated out from two other models of popular music. First, there is the entertainment model (which Rimmer is on hand to see his New Poppers fall back into): the singer as celebrity, a souped-up supper-club crooner. Then there is the proletarian model of the musician as worker: the classic example being the raddled old bluesman, scratching out a living on the road, resigned to a hard-bitten realism that abjures all celebrity or superficiality. On the one hand, business and fame and on the other, craftsmanship and subsistence. The expectation that groups should split up arises from the idea that they are neither businessmen nor workers but artists, and that, when artists have exhausted their inspiration, they should retire from the stage. *Like Punk Never Happened* documents the collapse of post punk will-to-art into capitalist realism.

Yet the (re)embrace of entertainment, of pop as surface and froth, was itself part of the logic of post punk. Post punk was at the heart of the neoliberal reaction and the struggle against it. The post punk scene – and this included, evidently, the music press as much as the musicians and the fans – was a zone where the culture wars that had been fought since the early twentieth century – the struggles over the political function of art fought between the likes of Lukacs, Benjamin and Adorno – could be re-staged in a new terrain. It's no accident that it was in this context that the dispute between 'rockism' and 'popism' originated. For post punk was self-consciously, sometimes earnestly, about the very meaning and significance of rock music and popular culture. So an act like the Pop Group could move from the febrile hyper-aestheticism of their first LP, Y (in which a rock pre-deconstructed by dub would claim kinship with the highest of high art: Baudelaire, Cage, Artaud), to agit-prop militancy (in which the group's implication in multinational capital, the status of their records as commodities and entertainment, became the source of a stern Maoist autocritique which could only lead to them splitting up). The idea that politics and art could meet in pop was by no means unique to the Pop Group, or to post punk (and, as Mark Stewart has emphasised to me when I have interviewed him, the name 'Pop Group' was not at all ironic: they really wanted to be successful, to be 'an explosion in the heart of commodity'.) Post punk was, rather, the moment when a certain logic in popular music *culminated*. Post punk did not repudiate early '70s prog and art rock for their high-minded aspirations so much as it aimed to succeed in making popular art where they had supposedly failed.

The return to entertainment was in some respects prepared by the critique of 'rockism' that post punk itself had initiated. In some ways, post punk can be identified with this critique, its various stages of development correlated with different versions of the attack on 'rockism'. First, there was punk's symbolic parricide of the dinosaurs of rock, attacked precisely for their stale persistence, for carrying on long after the inspiration had waned (although it's worth noting – and here again we can see the contrast between those accelerated times and now – that the whole of the Stones's career up until the mid-'60s comprised a period somewhat shorter than the time since Sonic Youth released *Daydream Nation*). Then there was the immanent critique of punk *rock* itself, the idea that the rock form was itself fundamentally reactionary, and was to be dismantled and reassembled using elements of noise, disco, funk, dub. The contact with disco and dub led to a second critique of rockism. Here, rockism became associated not with a particular *form* but with a particular *mode of production*: so-called 'real' instruments – guitar, bass, drums, vocals. The fetishisation of this mode of production constituted something like rock's 'metaphysics of presence', its privileging of the embodied, natural body over the synthetic instruments of the disco or the disembodied voice of the dubbed singer. Rock illegitimately claimed that its mode of production granted meaning and depth, but these could equally well be found in the genres that rock fans had dismissed as disposable trash. But this shaded into another kind of position altogether, one that was more in tune with the Restoration. For this critique, it was the emphasis on depth and significance *rather than pleasure* that was the hallmark of rockism. Here we had a position that is a combination of consumer nihilism and cultural studies relativism: canonical judgements of any kind are to be rejected, and we are to look to the listener, rather than the producer, as the source of value. Instead of the aggrandising claim that pop is capable of delivering everything that rock can, this is a 'democratisation' that is under-mining and deflationary: all culture, it suggests, is as empty and depthless as pop was held to be. From this perspective, it is the very claim to be superior to 'mere entertainment' that is what is 'oppressive' about rockism.

If one route out of post-punk was the embrace of pleasure and entertainment, another was the repudiation of art in the name of work. When Mark E. Smith scrawled 'Unsuitable for Romantics' on the cover of The Fall's *Hex Enduction Hour*, the slogan was both a warning and a provocation: a blast from Smith's pulp modernist naturalism blasting against the prissy sentimentalism of the very New Pop that Rimmer was documenting. But in the gruelling three decades since then (remember that The Fall have now being going ten years longer than Elvis's entire music career lasted), The Fall have gradually but implacably undermined rock's romanticism in quite a different way. Smith no longer locates the proletarian along with the visionary; rather, he embodies an increasingly dour pragmatism. For some time it has looked as if The Fall has been a job for Smith, a job like any other job. The demons and goblins that drove Smith on have for a long time been in abeyance, and, in the lack of any palpable sense that Smith *needs* to make more records, we're left with the inescapable impression that he's only doing it because he can't do anything else. And we're only buying the records, if we still are, out of loyalty, nostalgia, habit. At the same time, The Fall have become institutionalised, respectable, indulged in a way that The Fall of the '70s would have sneered at. Part of the problem of course is that The Fall, like the other post-punk old-stagers, are not being put under any pressure by younger groups; the stalling of innovation in experimental rock has proved an alibi for the inertia of both the group and its fans. To gauge the kind of slackening rate of innovation (and of antagonism) that's involved here, it is worth performing a similar thought experiment to the Rimmer's. Imagine now, not that we have a '77 punk being given a preview of '85 New Pop, but that we have a fan of The Fall

from 1982 being shown 2009 in a crystal ball. What would they think when confronted with the fact that, *twenty-seven years later*, The Fall are still plugging on, with a sound that is a thin replica of the one that they established all those years ago? Or that their young rivals in experimental rock – groups comprising individuals not even born in 1982 – would be making music that was at least as antiquated, as rooted in post-punk signifiers and sonic traits, as that of The Fall? There is more at stake here than the old story of radicality lapsing into complacency, because there is nothing new in the contemporary scene to contrast with the complacency of the former radicals.

But if The Fall aren't being harried by young pretenders, then neither is there any 'establishment' which they are troubling or upsetting. What they stand for is one form of what Dan Fox calls 'avant-conservatism'. Here, the 'avant' does not signify formal innovation, but precisely represents a relationship to a projected 'mainstream' to which they are held to be an alternative. But this is now a question of niche marketing more than anything else: a 'cult' group like The Fall now has a guaranteed status, a fixed position in the print and broadcast media ecology. We don't expect The Fall to go away (they can't split up – as has been clear for more than twenty years, The Fall are Smith plus whatever group he happens to be working with). At the same time, we don't expect them to ever make a record again that will compete with *Hex Enduction Hour* and *Grotesque*. We haven't expected that for some time – and the price of The Fall's surviving is nothing less than our giving up these expectations.

But is survival worth this price? A group can pastiche itself, can offer modulations on a settled formula, indefinitely; but it seems that it can exist in a state of permanent revolution only for a short time. In an incendiary review of Thurston Moore and Byron Coley's *No Wave* in *The Wire*,

Mark Fisher

Ray Brassier totally rejected this trade-off:

> 30 years on and the short-lived musical catalepsy christened 'No Wave' still stands as a sobering reminder of a realm of possibility that rock has had to abjure in order to perpetuate itself. Although regularly lumped in with 'post-punk' . . . No Wave was in fact more or less exactly contemporaneous with punk; yet the distance between Teenage Jesus and the Clash in 1977 is the same as that between Webern and Vaughan Williams in 1927. Just as the cold but coruscating nihilism exhibited by Teenage Jesus and The Contortions relegated punk to music hall oafishness, the clinical asperity embodied by Mars and DNA withered the residual romanticism of post-punk, rendering much of it pre-emptively redundant. Better for beat music to have expired in the terminal throes of Mars's 'N. N. End' than to have limped on ignominiously into the persistent vegetative state known as 'independent rock'. Routinely patronized as an unpalatable and ultimately sterile exercise in petulant extremism, or derided as a symptom of 'formal exhaustion' . . . No Wave's intractable negation of R&R tradition pointed to uncharted territories that continue to haunt a terminally atrophied rock culture now, 30 years of interminably recycled cliché later.

Better for beat music to have expired in the terminal throes of Mars's 'N. N. End' than to have limped on ignominiously into the persistent vegetative state known as 'independent rock'. There was no need for rock to have survived. If it was a case of 'that or die', why not choose death? The No Wave groups, like the Birthday Party, The Pop Group and The Fall up to 1983, were all impelled by the conviction that the only way in which rock could continue to justify its existence was by perpetually reinventing itself; they were driven by a sense that it wasn't acceptable for them to resemble anything pre-existing, even themselves: never settle, never repeat yourself, never give the audience what they want – these were the unwritten maxims inducing them into further convulsions. It's easy to forget now, after Smith and Cave's Sunday-supplement canonisation, how divisive this music was, how it engendered revulsion and denunciation as much as adoration, how it shattered any *sensus communis*. Perhaps this process reached its termination with something like Swans – a group who, up until 1984, maintained a ferocious fidelity to No Wave's austere interdiction against reiterating the past. Swans literally prolonged rock's dead end into an inhumanly distended, super-tense grind, astonishing and unprecedented in its brutal starkness. After this, it seemed, there could only be reconstruction: once he'd scoured rock clean of all excrescence and ornament on an LP like *Cop*, Swans' Mike Gira started to re-incorporate elements of musicality until he had, to all intents and purposes, reinvented himself as a folkish singer-songwriter. It was at the point at which Swans started to retreat from punitive minimalism that so-called experimental rock began to return to the '60s. The most obvious example here would be the Jesus and Mary Chain, who rehabilitated reference points from then – The Byrds, the Beach Boys – that post punk had up until then regarded as the problem. (And it's not a coincidence that the moment that The Fall started faltering was marked by a Stooges' citation: the hijacking of the 'I Wanna Be Your Dog' bassline in Wonderful And Frightening World's 'Elves'.) Instead of projecting itself forward, the rump of post-punk started to subside into a flattened-out, ahistorical temporality, gradually declining from modernism into postmodernism. This retrenchment partly took the form of a widening of taste, an

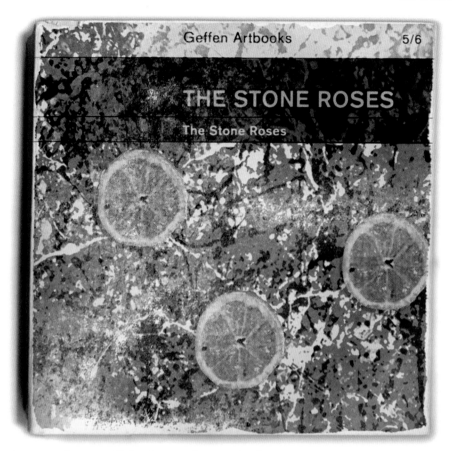

THE STONE ROSES

The Stone Roses

Huw Gwilliam

abandonment of post punk's intolerance. At an event celebrating the publication of Simon Reynolds's *Totally Wired* held at the Roundhouse in London in 2009, the Slits' Viv Albertine and Scritti's Tom Morley displayed an attitude towards the strictures and the strictness of the (post) punk period that stopped just short of outright hostility. Every aspect of your life was under scrutiny, Albertine complained, your clothes, your sexuality, what you said . . . But this refusal of 'well-roundedness' and 'proper histor- ical perspective' was almost certainly crucial to the power of post-punk music. When tracks by the Slits and early Scritti were played through the Roundhouse's PA, the music's crystalline ascesis, its lucid abrasion, showed that dogmatism can deliver intensity whereas laissez- faire well-roundedness produces precisely the bleary retrospection of postmodern rock. You couldn't admit to liking Neil Young, someone said: but that not being allowed to admit liking things, arbitrarily closing down aspects of the past even – no, especially – if they were 'good', was crucial to the drive to make something new. Nietzsche argues that a certain level of stupidity is essential for any strong culture. The powerful artist must be capable of a kind of willed ignorance, an arbitrary narrowing down of perspective. In an apparent paradox, Nietzsche shows that only those cultures that lack historical awareness can make history. An excess of historical awareness makes cultures behave like spectators rather than producers, and, after 1985, alternative rock began to enter its own 'retrospectatorial' mode.

Ever since rock entered its dotage, there is a new (anti-Nietzschean) model for the rock musician, alongside that of the entertainer and the worker: the curator. This is essentially the role that Sonic Youth fill for an alternative scene that is 'alternative' only in its structrual position, not by virtue of any of its formal properties. Sonic Youth, so deeply embedded in the art world, constitute another version of Fox's 'avant-conservatism'. Sonic Youth came to the fore precisely at the moment when post-punk experimentalism was on the wane. In presupposing the 'unlivability' of No Wave, Sonic Youth's sheer existence – as a stable post-No Wave rock group, in which No Wave's experiments were partly retrenched, partly absorbed into a new college rock – asserted a resurgent reality principle: this is what you need to do to survive. It was Sonic Youth, more than anybody else, who made it acceptable to like Neil Young and the other rockers that punk had abjected; it was they who built the bridges back to the '60s that punk and post-punk had incinerated. Postmodern good sense insists that this is a good thing, that the rejection of Young and other rockers of the '60s and '70s was harsh and unfair, and that it was long past time that punk and postpunk's distorted, negative judgement of the past was corrected and overcome. But the past can look after itself; it is the future that will suffer if the new does not engage in a violent struggle with the old. Sonic Youth's continuing ascendance is symptomatic of a situation where the word 'alternative' has been entirely co-opted by the rock/youth model of rebellion, but where none of these synonyms – rebellion/youth/ alternative –

are anything but marketing tags devoid of content. The problem is that, on the one hand, Sonic Youth derive their cachet from belonging to a rock culture which is inextricably wedded to the equation of youth with the new (look at their name!), while, on the other hand, they are neither young nor the producers of anything new: as even their admirers will admit Sonic Youth, like The Fall, have effectively pastiched themselves for the last two decades.

Sonic Youth's precise function for Restoration culture is to be a hypervisible simulation of an alternative *within* the mainstream: here they are on *Later With Jools Holland*; here they are doing compilations for Starbucks; here they are, the darlings of the broadsheet press, their records not exactly guaranteed a good review, but always automatically accorded event status. In what way is the so-called mainstream perturbed by any of this? In what way, in the decentred era of web 2.0, is this *not* the mainstream? That is why the citation of Sonic Youth in the alt.teen film *Juno* provides such a depressingly accurate picture of certain impasses in US alternative rock culture. In *Juno*, a supposedly smart alt.teen becomes pregnant and gives up her child to baby-crazed professional, whose husband – a failed rocker now miserably writing advertising jingles – turns her on to Sonic Youth. The fact that Juno – who is into Patti Smith and the Stooges – has mysteriously not heard of Sonic Youth is the key to their fantasy positioning. When she falls out with the husband, Juno says that she 'bought another Sonic Youth CD and it's just noise' – at this point, everyone's happy: SY are name-checked in an indie–mainstream commodity, but posited as something that is ultimately *too extreme*.

In his unfocused but provocative book *Secular Devotion: Afro-Latin Music and Imperial Jazz*, Timothy Brennan provocatively argues that the youth-rock-rebellion matrix is a Trojan horse for capitalist globalisation.

There is no globalisation without the idea of

youth, which is the group whose friendliness to the new gives it the power to issue calling-cards to foreign capital or provide openings for next year's documentaries on the next wave of twenty-something entrepreneurs. Their experimentalism and novelty, which supposedly comes from having thought less along the rutted paths of their elders, can be moved by inches to the concept of entrepreneurship . . . The well-known colonial contest between civilisations where capitalist technologies and dynamism on the one hand are pitted against traditional religious or rural life on the other is here recast in a macro-contest between youth and age. As the managerial specialists would have it, capitalism is for youth. Capitalism *is* youth.

Brennan goes on to argue that 'a resistance to designer radicalism can often take the form of *preservation* . . . a lot of youth rebel (paradoxically) by adopting their parents' tastes – or rather by taking the unexpected view that music from the '60s and '70s is more worth listening to. It is very little commented on how many young people immerse themselves in standbys from the '70s – Led Zeppelin, Neil Young, and the most obvious case, the Rolling Stones'. But, what Brennan is missing is that this kind of (albeit disavowed) preservation is the very form that 'designer radicalism' takes. The Restoration has shown that postmodern capitalism is increasingly *incapable* of generating cultural novelty, only its simulation. And the young, weighed upon by an excessive historical awareness, end up preserving the forms of the past, less as an act of rebellion, than as an expression of impotence and exhaustion. What the last decade in particular has established is that there is no necessary link between 'youth' and the 'new' or 'radical'. By failing to 'kill their idols' - in fact by doing just the opposite, by continuing to buy their records, by attending the ironically named All Tomorrows Parties festivals, it is the young who allow the likes of Sonic Youth and The Fall to carry on

occupying the structural position of the 'alternative'. It is important to stress that this is not a generational flaw so much as a cultural pathology, one effect of the flattening of cultural time in capitalist realism. But we should give up the idea that the young can offer either hope or novelty: walled off from history but embedded into a world that is saturated with the past, teenagers and those in their twenties have only known retrospection. They are the victims of the failure of the future, not its cause. It could well be that the model of violent generational change (as opposed to preservation) is part of the mythology of capitalism; and it is certainly long past time to reject the premium that capitalism puts on youth. But perhaps we need a model of cultural change in which preservation and the rejection of the past are not opposed to one another – the modernist poetics of T. S. Eliot (in 'Tradition and the Individual Talent') or Harold Bloom (in *The Anxiety of Influence*) offer such models: the new asserts itself against the old and established by struggling against it, but the very act of struggle is also a kind of preservation. What we certainly need is a new model of adulthood – it ought to be possible for musicians to grow older without either lapsing into a respectable maturity, or playing the role of perpetual adolescent (à la Jagger or Iggy).

The most important revolts in the counter-culture are always internal to the avant-garde; it is precisely the complacent occupation of a position allegedly 'alternative' to the mainstream that punk and post punk mobilised itself against. Hence the significance of Johnny Rotten's 'I hate Pink Floyd' T-shirt, the supreme punk gesture, and all the more powerful if – as has been suggested – Lydon once liked and respected Pink Floyd. It seems to me that if such a gesture were to be made now, the T-shirts that should be mutilated would be those of The Fall and Sonic Youth.

Party Time with David Mancuso and the Loft

Like a soup or a bicycle or Wikipedia, the Loft is an amalgamation of parts that are weak in isolation, but joyful, revelatory and powerful when joined together. The first ingredient is the desire of a group of friends to want to get together and have some fun. The second element is the discovery of a room that has good acoustics and is comfortable for dancing, which means it should have rectangular dimensions, a reasonably high ceiling, a nice wooden floor and the possibility of privacy. The next building block is the sound system, which is most effective when it is simple, clean and warm, and when it isn't pushed more than a fraction above 100 decibels (so that people's ears don't become tired or even damaged). After that, the room should be decorated, with balloons and a mirror ball offering a cheap and timeless solution. And because the party might last a long time, and because some friends might be hungry, a healthy spread of food and drink should also be prepared. Finally – and this really is the last thing to get right, and can only follow once everything else is in place – the friends will need someone to bring along some dance records. After that, it's party time.

All of these parts were assembled at 647 Broadway, in the abandoned NoHo district of New York City, when David Mancuso hosted a Valentine's Day party in his loft in February 1970. That party, which soon became known as the Loft, wasn't so much a moment of inception, or the point from which all subsequent events can be traced, as a moment of synthesis in which a number of practices and experiences, some of which can be traced back to a much earlier period, came together in a new form. The children's home where David was taken straight after he was born suggested that families could be extended yet intimate, unified yet different, and precarious yet strong. Sister Alicia, who took care of David and put on a party with balloons and food and records whenever she got a chance, suggested the Loft from another time and space. The psychedelic guru Timothy Leary, who invited David to his house parties and popularised a philosophy around the psychedelic experience that would inform the way Mancuso selected records, was another resonant figure. Co-existing with Leary, the civil rights, the gay liberation, feminist and the anti-war movements of the '60s were manifest in the egalitarian, come-as-you-are ethos and rainbow coalition demographics of the Loft. And the Harlem rent parties of the 1920s, in which economically underprivileged African American tenants put on evening events to help fend off their landlords, established a template for putting on a private event that didn't require a liquor or cabaret licence (and could

Tim Lawrence

accordingly run all night because they lay beyond the control of New York's licensing authorities). These streams headed in a multiplicity of directions before meeting at 647 Broadway in February 1970.

The February party didn't have a name, but the homemade invitations carried the line 'Love Saves the Day'. A short three years after the release of 'Lucy In the Sky with Diamonds', the coded promise of acid-inspired things to come was easy to unpick for those in the know, although in this instance Beatles' gobbledygook was exchanged with a commitment to universal love. The invitations also reproduced an image of Salvador Dali's *The Persistence of Memory*, which now looks like another cryptogram, but didn't resemble one at the time because David hadn't yet had his latent childhood memories of Sister Alicia jogged into Technicolor revelation. Of course, the image of Dali's melting clocks wasn't simply random: David offering his guests the chance to escape the violence and oppression of everyday life, and the idea of entering into a different dimension of time, in which everyone could leave behind their socialised selves and dance until dawn, was intended. 'Once you walked into the Loft you were cut off from the outside world,' says David. 'You got into a timeless, mindless state. There was actually a clock in the back room but it only had one hand. It was made out of wood and after a short while it stopped working.'

When David's guests left the Valentine's Day party, they let him know that they wanted him to put on another one soon, and within a matter of months they had become a weekly affair. Inasmuch as anyone knew about the events – and few did because they were never advertised, being private house parties – they acquired a reputation for being ultra hip, in part because 647 Broadway was situated in the ex-manufacturing district of downtown New York where nobody but a handful of artists, composers, musicians, sculptors, video film-makers and dedicated bohemians had thought about living. They moved in because the district's abandoned warehouses offered a spectacular space in which to live, work and socialise, and the inconvenience of having to hide the kitchen, bedroom and bathroom from view (in order to avoid the punitive searches of the city's building inspectors) turned out to be an innovative way to free up space in order to do things that weren't related to cooking, sleeping and washing. Outside, the frisson of transgression was heightened by the fact that there was no street lighting to illuminate the cobbled streets, and because David didn't serve alcohol, he was able to keep his parties going until midday, and sometimes even later, long after the city's bars and discotheques had closed. 'Because I lived in a loft building, people started to say that they were going to the Loft,' remembers David. 'It's a given name and is sacred.'

From the beginning, David looked for ways to improve his sound system because he was convinced this would result in a more musical and intense dance-floor experience. He began to invest in audiophile technology and asked sound engineers to help him build gear, including tweeter arrays and bass reinforcements, which David would tweak during the course of the party, sending shivers down the spines of revellers. Yet by the time they came to dominate the increasingly popular discotheque scene of the '70s, David had concluded that such add-ons interfered unnecessarily with his audiophile set-up, and he had resorted to purchasing increasingly esoteric equipment, including Mark Levinson amplifiers and handcrafted Koetsu cartridges, which he combined with his Klipschorn speakers. 'I had the tweeters installed to put highs into records that were too muddy but they turned into a monster,' explains David. 'It was done out of ignorance. I wasn't aware of Class-A sound, where the sound is more open and everything comes out.'

Like the space, the legal set-up and the buffet, the sound system was introduced in order to assist the party dynamic, and as David relentlessly fine-tuned his set-up the dancing became more free-flowing and intense. 'You could be on the dance floor and the most beautiful woman that you had ever seen in your life would come and dance right on top of you,' says Frankie Knuckles, a regular at the Loft. 'Then the minute you turned around a man that looked just as good would do the same thing. Or you would be sandwiched between the two of them, or between two women, or between two men, and you would feel completely comfortable.' Facilitating a sonic trail that was generated by everyone in the room, David picked out long, twisting tracks such as Eddie Kendrick's 'Girl, You Need a Change of Mind' and War's 'City, Country, City'; gutsy, political songs like the 'Black-skinned Blue-eyed Boys' by the Equals and 'Brother's Gonna Work It Out' by Willie Hutch; uplifting, joyful anthems such as Dorothy Morrison's 'Rain' and MSFB's 'Love Is the Message'; and earthy, funky recordings such as James Brown's 'Give It Up or Turnit a Loose' and Manu Dibango's 'Soul Makossa'. Positive, emotional and trans-cendental, these and other songs touched the souls of dancers and helped forge a community.

The influence of the Loft spread far and wide. At the end of 1972 a Broadway regular set up a similarly structured party for an exclusive white gay clientele called the Tenth Floor, which in turn inspired the establishment of Flamingo, the most influential white gay venue of the '70s. Objecting to the elitist nature of Flamingo's so-called 'A-list' dancers, another Loft regular founded 12 West, which was intended to create a more democratic party environment for white gay men. As all of this was unfolding, another Loft regular, Nicky Siano, set up his own Loft-style venue called the Gallery where he mimicked David's invitation system, hired David's sound engineer, and also borrowed a fair chunk of David's dance crowd when the Broadway party closed for the summer of 1973. Richard Long and Mike Stone's SoHo Place along with Michael Brody's Reade Street also drew heavily on David's template. And when both of those parties were forced to close, Brody opened the Paradise Garage, which he positioned as an 'expanded version of the Loft', and invited Richard Long, considered by some to be New York's premier sound engineer, to build the sound system. Meanwhile Richard Williams, another Loft regular, moved to Chicago and opened a Loft-style venue called the Warehouse. Having grown up on the dance floor of the Loft, Larry Levan and Frankie Knuckles went on to become the legendary DJs at the Garage and the Warehouse, where they forged the contours of what would come to be called garage and house music. Other spinners such as Tony Humphries, François Kevorkian and David Morales look back on the Loft as an inspirational setting. The Loft, in other words, was an incubator.

Like any party host, David has had to face some unexpected hitches during his thirty-eight-year journey. In June 1974 he moved into 99 Prince Street after he was pressured into leaving his Broadway home, and ten years later he bought a promising building in Alphabet City, only to see the neighbourhood slide into a virtual civil war instead of receiving moneys promised for regeneration. By the time David was forced to leave a space he was subletting on Avenue B towards the end of the 1990s, things were beginning to look inescapably grim. But before he vacated that particular space, David received invitations to travel first to Japan and then to London. Initially reluctant to put on a party outside his home, David accepted both offers, and although he experienced some problems, he ended up returning both to Japan and to London in order to team up with other groups of friends who wanted to put on regular events. As he went about this work, David stuck to the principles that have driven him from day one: be faithful to your friends, find a good space for a party, seek out the best sound equipment available and say 'thank you' when you're invited into someone's home. In the process, David drew on the life-shaping experience of his orphan childhood to understand a profound philosophical lesson: homes can be built wherever you put down roots and build relationships. Returning again and again to Japan and London, David realised his own universal vision, which was previously constricted to New York, but has now captured the imagination of partygoers across the globe.

Shortly after making his first trips to Japan and London, David also hit upon a hall in the East Village that has become the new home of the Loft, and although the parties are now held on holidays rather than on a weekly basis, David is convinced the dance floor is as vibrant and energetic as ever. The fact that David doesn't live in the space is a little inconvenient in that he has to set up his sound system each time he plays, but even though he doesn't sleep in the hall, he's also more comfortable in his current space than any of his previous homes. 'It's in the heart of the East Village, which was where I always used to hang out,' he says. 'I might have lived on Broadway, but for the other five or six days I was in the East Village. This is where I've been hanging out since 1963. My roots are there. My life is connected to the area.' Forging new roots and connections, grandparents have started to dance with their grandchildren on the floor of the New York Loft.

Thanks to David's longevity and belated recognition as a seminal figure in the history of New York dance culture, it has become easy for partygoers to assume that the Loft has come to resemble a nostalgia trip for the halcyon days of the '70s and early '80s. Since February 1970, however, David has always played a mixture of old and new music, and he continues to mix it up in a similar way to this day. New faces in Japan and London might arrive expecting a trip down disco alley, but that's not what they get, because the party isn't a fossil-like impression of what it used to be. Throughout, David has remained committed to selecting records that encourage the party to grow as a musically radical yet never musically negative community. This sonic tapestry can sometimes sound strange to dancers who have become accustomed to a political climate in which communities are dismantled in favour of materialistic individualism and capitalist–nationalist wars, but the countercultural message is persuasive. 'After a while the positive vibe and universal attitude of the music was too much for me, but this moment of hesitation and insecurity only lasted for a few minutes,' commented a dancer after one party. 'Then all the barriers broke and I reached the other side. Like a child, I stopped caring about what other people might think and reached my essence, through dancing.'

Confronted by the tendency of partygoers to worship at his DJing feet, even though he has never considered himself a DJ and is resolute that this kind of attention detracts from the party, David positions the turntables as close to the entrance as possible so that dancers see the floor and not the booth as they enter the room. In a similar move, he also arranges the speakers so they will draw dancers away from the booth and towards the centre of the floor. Yet in London (much more so than in New York) dancers tend to face David, even though the effect is the equivalent of sitting with one's back to the orchestra at a concert. And at the end of these parties dancers applaud as if he's some kind of saviour, when in fact he's a guy who helps put on parties and tries to read the mood of the floor as the 'sonic trail' unfolds.

Reinforced by a cultural environment that encourages crowds to seek out iconic, authoritative, supernatural leaders, the adulation makes David deeply uncomfortable. 'I'm a background person,' he says.

Even if utopias can't be built without a struggle, and can never be complete, the mood at all of these parties is thrilling to behold. The floors outside New York might benefit from believing more in themselves, yet much of their applause is directed towards the music, as well as the surprisingly rare joy of being able to dance among friends in an intimate setting.

That feeling has come about because, after years of dancing together, people now recognise each other to the extent they are entirely comfortable about welcoming in new faces. 'It's unbelievable,' said a female dancer who came to her first London party with her two daughters. 'The people here – they make *eye contact!*' Eye contact might not be very fashionable, but then the Loft isn't about fashion. Rather, it's about putting on a party with friends. And because it doesn't follow trends, it's been able to outlast every other party in the ephemeral (yet eternally hopeful) world of dance.

RUBBISH RAVER

I am, and have been for almost twenty years now, a rubbish raver. I'm a rubbish dancer, rubbish at drugs, rubbish at fashion and especially rubbish at the particular brands of pack-bonding dark sarcasm and untethered gibberish that keep the scene's social mechanisms moving through its endless long and chaotic nights. I've always been destructively picky and over-analytical: as a writer, I sometimes feel voyeuristic, a betrayer of secrets, a spy in the house of love. I'm not a natural joiner, I don't like to toe a party line, and, well, frankly I'm a bit too uptight to get involved with something that by its very nature demands cutting loose, going with the flow, letting it all hang out and all the rest of it. I also – and this is crucial – need a lot of sleep. I am, as today's younger clubbers might put it, a 'wasteman'.

And yet, and yet . . . throughout my adult life, I have loved dance music and all its multifarious splendours; it and the cultures that surround it have fascinated me even as they frustrated and frightened me, and they have inspired to one degree or another almost everything I have done professionally or creatively. I love that same acid sense of humour that I'm so bad at joining in with, I love the hyperactive and compulsive communication and I love the marshalling of utter chaos into something splendid and ridiculous for no reason other than that it's fun. I'm no gorblimey back-in-the-day nostalgia bore, nor starry-eyed hippie twit blinded to the grimnesses and exploitations that go on in the name of night-time pleasure, but, when the lines are drawn there's a part of me that can't help feeling a certain loyalty to club culture. Dammit, I can actually say 'club culture' with a straight face: a statement in itself. In a time when received media and entertainment industry wisdom says that there is no such thing as alternative lifestyles, that everything is assimilable at the spin of an iPod wheel and nothing is new, the idea of something that you belong to, that you must make the active choice and commitment to be a part of, is, I think, as important as it has ever been. So while I may be an old, inconstant, creaky and rubbish raver, I am a raver nonetheless, and proud.

If the potted musical memoir that follows seems self-indulgent to you – well, it is. This is my story, and I revel in it. But in these years of immersion, I've had a lot of time to absorb and observe an awful lot of the foibles and twists of subcultures and subsubcultures as they appear, mutate and either take on a life of their own or are re-absorbed into the larger body of nightlife – and I hope my humble tales of not-quite-fitting, of raves attended and just as importantly of raves missed, can cast some light on the changing ways in which people have tried to find a sense of belonging as they've groped their way through that nightlife these past few years.

....

I was fourteen in 1988, a middle-class country boy at a small-town comprehensive and acid house went over my head a bit. I'd already graduated from glam metal through Billy Idol and the Sisters of Mercy to a vaguely indie eclecticism; I'd had my first Lambert & Butler-flavoured kiss at a school disco where they played 'Pump up the Volume' and 'Jack Your Body', and I'd just begun to dip into John Peel's show where the stranger corners of electronic music started to pique my interest. But the coolest music I owned was probably an LL Cool J cassette album and a vinyl copy of *BBC Science Fiction Sound Effects*; I'd barely even got drunk let alone high, and when friends' older brothers began to talk about acid raves it may as well have been in Lithuanian. The closest my friends and I came to dancing was still putting an Anthrax tape on a ghettoblaster in the park and mock-moshing till we got dizzy. The market town in which I grew up was not big enough to support real subcultures: there were three punks, a couple of 'scooter boys', some moth-eaten teds and one mixed-race – but racist – skinhead, all of whom seemed to drink together. The closest to a sense of human existence outside the day-to-day was the appearance every year or two of the traveller convoy on the nearby Berkshire downs, which would provoke untold excitement – I recall one child at my primary school pelting in one morning wide-eyed, panting, 'The 'ippies are coming! My mum says if you go near 'em they'll inject you with drugs and make you into an 'ippie and all!'

At fifteen, I discovered pot, going to gigs, awkward sex with goths, reading Burroughs and Huxley, playing De La Soul, Spacemen 3 and the Shamen, and with my friend Edwin (whose brother had DJed at parties, done LSD and been to Manchester) I contrived to get to Reading Festival unaccompanied by anybody responsible. There, in between marvelling at New Order, boggling at the Butthole Surfers and nervously sipping pints of pissy lager, I wigged out moderately to someone playing an S'Express acid remix through a guitar amp in the back of a van by a campfire quite late at night and started to think I knew what 'raving' was. That autumn the Berlin Wall came down, and at Christmas I was lying stoned in bed when I heard the Orb for the first time on John Peel, their session version of 'A Huge Ever-Growing Pulsating Brain that Rules from the Centre of the Ultraworld' unwinding expansively over a half hour and leading me to think all the rules of music had dissolved along with the Cold War fears and certainties we'd grown up with. I was so taken away by it, I even forgot to nerdily note that the track's title came from my precious science fiction sound effects record. The world was changing: 'Cubik', 'Killer', 'Good Life' and 'Pump up the Jam' were staples at village-hall dances, and the Happy Mondays were on *Top of the Pops*, singing, 'We'll take a bit of this and that.' It was a time of excitement, newness and wide-open possibilities, but we weren't so hip that the distractions of GCSEs and drinking cider while singing Levellers songs in graveyards couldn't get in the way of more momentous things. A peak experience at this time was less likely to be about losing our shit on the dance floor than about collapsing in giggles at Andy who'd gone AWoL from the navy and lived in a tent lip-syncing 'Freebird' into the mic of his helicopter as we sat around smoking bongs in the older lads' house next to the gasworks.

I discovered how little of a clue I really had about what raving actually was a few months later when, with my friends Danny and Pete, I took my first blotter trip (a Purple Om, if you care about such things), played some Super Mario World on the SNES as we waited for our brains to start fizzing, then went to the

Big Life Records   14'6

Adventures beyond the ultraworld vol. 1

The Orb

Huw Gwilliam

fortnightly Prism club in Oxford. It was the real deal, no question: the UV artwork on every wall a crashing melange of hippie and Illuminati motifs, Keith Haring dancer figures and graffiti characters, lights strobing constantly and gurning faces and twisted limbs lurching around on every side of us, merging into the acid visuals. I knew enough to vaguely understand certain bits of music as American house, some as techno, and some as what was becoming known as hardcore, but I didn't recognise a thing specifically, bar a 'move move move any

mountain' here and a 'Cubik' riff there. Every cliché I'd read about races and classes coming together in the pursuit of hedonism proved true, there was a jaw-jutting grin and thumbs-up from seemingly anyone whose eye one caught, free ice-pops were handed out, and the audio-visual stimulation just kept coming, never giving the adrenalin and disorientation of that first trip the chance to tip over into panic.

Rather than dance, I spent most of the night barrelling about the place in my tie-dye hoody, frayed denim jacket painted with Orb and De

La Soul logos and bloody stupid purple hat, literally bouncing off the walls and almost certainly irritating proper ravers as I tried to take in as much of the experience as possible; at one point I found myself outside a side door through which a few people at a time were being allowed out onto the roof to cool down, and realised that not only did each person who came out have steam rising off them, but a vast column of it was rising from the entire club up into the clear sky. It wasn't until later that the force of this image struck me – at the time, I just fleetingly thought 'Cor, brilliant' and barrelled back in to seek out more noise, heat and movement. I don't really recall the end of the club, just a continuation of this pinballing motion through crowds until we found ourselves in the living room of some polytechnic students' flat, the peak experience wearing off and physical weariness setting in. As Pete and Danny bantered in a corner, I zoomed in and zoned out on the tape that was being played, completely captured by the tempo wind-down of Orbital's 'Belfast' and the stentorian 'music of our 'eart is roots music' sample and echolocation bleeps on the Moody Boys' remix of 'What Time Is Love'. I realised that electronic music wasn't just for the dance floor but could stretch and mutate to fit any circumstance, that sampling and processing meant a good idea was no longer condemned to be repeated forever in one form but could be adapted to any culture's needs, that this is how music was going to be from now on, that computers could express emotion, that sound itself was as dense a conduit for information as we had . . . Oh, I had it all worked out. Then I tried to eat a Marathon bar and almost choked to death. Eventually we stumbled back to Danny's mum's and I fell asleep on a couple of sofa cushions, glowing rows of icons flickering rhythmically across the inside of my eyelids, a bit uncomfortable and wishing the other boys weren't in the room so I could have a wank.

All of this should have been prime epiphany material. I should perhaps by rights have hopped on the rave bus and never looked back – thrown out my Pixies albums, got some massive Spliffy jeans and an MA1 jacket and grown a Balearic ponytail and 'got on it' every weekend, as indeed did many of my friends – but for some reason I didn't feel 'changed'; maybe I lacked the commitment to go the whole hog. My attachment to electronic music certainly grew – I inhaled those early WARP bleep records, Depth Charge, Boys Own, R&S, Rising High, Italian piano bangers, DiY deep house rave tapes, 'Blue Lines', Renegade Soundwave, 'We Are IE' and 'Sweet Sensation' and got so excited by 'Higher Than the Sun' that I sat outside HMV waiting for it to open on the day of release, followed A Guy Called Gerald's awe-inspiring progression from 'Voodoo Ray' into mutant hardcore, became, like so many fanboys, fixated on Andrew Weatherall and Creation Records' Balearic excursions.

I did microdots and watched rainbows explode out of the top of my mates' heads to 'Philly' by Fluke in the garden of Tim's mum's semi in Grove. I sat in the back of Edwin's van grinding my teeth to Ratpack tapes as we sat in a traffic jam – sorry, convoy – looking for a rave on some railway tracks in Eynsham which dissipated as soon as we arrived. I hitch-hiked to Leicester, ate mushrooms and fancied I'd discovered how to dissolve time itself as Weatherall played into the small hours after a Primal Scream show. I tried half a pill at the Brixton Academy with no effect. I became a de facto DJ as fourth- and fifth-generation copies of my lovingly compiled tapes of Sweet Exorcist and ambient rarities became the soundtrack of choice to smoking sessions across my home town. I joined a band and we tried to play 'dance versions' of Hendrix songs at micro-festivals up on the Ridgeway. But while my

Rubbish Raver

friends ventured increasingly further afield to bigger and wilder raves – to Ektos in Swindon, the Eclipse in Coventry, the Astoria in London, to Fantazia, Helter-Skelter, World Dance, yadda yadda yadda – I found myself too much of a sickly waif (suffering badly from glandular fever and self-pity), too averse to gigantic crowds and too fond of sleep to join them, and on the few occasions I did make it to big events or even back to the Prism, they almost never matched up to the pictures I conjured listening to the music at home, or to the experience of getting wasted in an intimate environment with good friends and good music that we were in control of. Despite all my attempts to be cutting-edge and free, I was still a Depeche Mode and Cure fan with propensity for black clothing and misery. I was not, in a word, cool. As the rest of the world got on one and went mental, I sat on a deckchair and watched the boat sail off.

NICK KENT

1973

The hype surrounding cocaine was that it somehow opened up the gateway to thinking brilliant thoughts but the reality was invariably more brutal: sudden jagged mood swings, dry mouth, scary heart palpitations. The first time I tried it – backstage at a Hawkwind concert in October 1972 – I almost fell down a long flight of stairs when the brain rush actually kicked in. The second time I was with the Flamin' Groovies a month later and we all got pulled over by the police outside the dealer's Earls Court house. If someone hadn't tossed the incriminating packet of powder into a nearby garden, we'd have all been facing criminal prosecution.

God was evidently trying to tell me something, but I steadfastly refused to listen up. By early 1973 I was wasting one or two nights of every week snorting the devil's dandruff in the company of other young London-based pleasure-seekers. By the time dawn broke through the gaps in the drawn curtains of their basement lairs, I'd be feeling very brittle and twitchy indeed. The simple fact of the matter was that the drug didn't agree with my central nervous system and made me plain jittery. But I was too much of a schmuck to walk away from its temptation and most of what I consumed was offered to me for free anyway. I duped myself into thinking it would be impolite to refuse and carried on numbing my sinuses whenever the opportunity arose.

At the same time I was getting ready to launch my personal invasion on the land of opportunity. By early February everything was in place: I'd drawn all my funds out of the bank, paid for an open-ended return airline ticket to Michigan and had a special US visa stamped into my passport. In the middle of the month I boarded my flight and some ten hours later was standing on US soil.

At first the customs authorities didn't want to let me in. 'Are you a homosexual?' one of them kept asking me. If I'd said yes, they'd have sent me straight back to limey-land. But I simply told them the truth until they relented and grudgingly allowed me entry into the Motor City. Soon enough I'd hailed a taxi and was sizing up my new surroundings: a big motorway covered with humongous gas-guzzling automobiles bordered by huge billboards and head-spinning changes of scenery. At one point we dipped through downtown Detroit and the streets there seemed as menacing as they were congested. But then another strip of highway would open up and the buildings would look suddenly cleaner and the sidewalks a lot less threatening. Continuing seventeen miles north-west of Detroit, we arrived in a well-appointed residential area on the outskirts of Birmingham, Michigan, where Debbie Boushell and her nouveau riche parents dwelt.

This would be my home away from home for all of one evening. After that I was on my own.

I'd always envisaged the Motor City as a Mecca for tough-sounding quality music but by the time I arrived there, the home-grown musical culture was facing a steep recession. A local heroin epidemic had killed off the MC5 and forced the Stooges to relocate in Hollywood thus depriving the state of its two most promising hard-rock bands. Others like Bob Seger and Ted Nugent would still have to wait several years before they could start creating any kind of impact for themselves outside of Michigan. The one exception was Grand Funk Railroad – a shallow, bombastic power trio from Flint, Michigan who played populist stoner rock specifically aimed at a new and disturbingly prevalent US demographic – teenage barbiturate gobblers. Their godawful records always seemed to be shacked up in the highest echelons of the Billboard and Cashbox top ten best-seller listings or polluting the airwaves in the early '70s. Like herpes, you just couldn't get rid of their feckless racket.

My first night in the Motor City is now something of a foggy memory – and perhaps that's just as well. I recall Debbie and her boyfriend driving me to a bar in the evening where an atrocious live band played the Top 40 hits of the day. I recall a biker offering me some PCP which I politely refused. I then recall a tall blonde girl giving me a quaalude – American Mandrax – and suggesting we both repair to a nearby motel, book a cheaply priced room and partake in sexual congress together. I can even recall entering the motel room with her, surveying its tawdry interior and thinking that Sam Cooke met his end in similar circumstances. Everything after that is a blank. I was knocked suddenly unconscious by the impact of the quaalude on my already jet-lagged metabolism.

When I awoke many hours later, daylight was streaming through the windows. I was alone in the bed and a bird-faced Hispanic cleaning lady was standing over me ranting in an incomprehensible form of pidgin English. Debbie arrived soon after that – and boy, was she pissed off! The girl I'd accompanied to this godforsaken fuck-pit turned out to be one of her sworn enemies. She'd stormed out soon after I'd passed out, mistaking a drug-induced coma for callous rejection. I'd been in Michigan less than twenty-four hours and already had two of its native daughters on the war-path after me. Time to activate plan B.

Birmingham, Michigan – unlike its plug-ugly namesake in the English Midlands – was an attractive middle-class suburb boasting good schools, high-end property, condos, classy boutiques and chintzy antique stores. But sedition still lurked within its carefully manicured borders: the town had lately begun to pay host to *Creem* magazine and its rowdy editorial staff. The ferociously irreverent monthly had recently upped its national sales to 150,000 per issue and celebrated by splashing out on new office space on the second floor of the Birmingham Theatre building. Publisher Barry Kramer also rented a nearby house – 416 Brown Street – for the magazine's key employees to share. That's where I'd be spending my second night in the United States of America and most of my subsequent days and nights in the Midwest.

It had been a dream of mine: to link up with Lester Bangs and learn at the feet of the master of new rock journalism. Now my dream was about to come true. Once again I owe Debbie Boushell a debt of gratitude for helping to make it happen. She was the one who actually phoned *Creem*'s headquarters and told them about my plight regarding immediate accommodation until they relented and offered me a room for the night. She even drove me to the location. Mind you, we arrived well after midnight and I was – oh dear – once again under the foolhardy influence of the dreaded quaalude. I may have even consumed two earlier in the evening in order to calm my nerves. I suppose I was looking to attain chemically induced courageousness. What I arrived at instead was mush-mouthed slobbering stupidity.

I remember staggering into a dimly lit living room and being surrounded by three male figures. One was short and bespectacled and introduced himself as Dave Marsh. A second – taller, California-blond and more muscular – answered to the name of Ben Edmonds. And the third was Lester Bangs. I'd never even seen a photograph of him before this night so it was the first opportunity I ever had to gaze upon the physical reality of the man behind the byline. My first impression: he looked like a rodeo clown without the make-up. Or an auto worker on a beer break. He was a big guy with tousled black hair that was neither long nor short and a full moustache plastered across his manic grinning face. You wouldn't have called him 'handsome' but he wasn't ugly either. Right away his basic sweet nature became apparent to me. There was a soulfulness about the guy that was palpable in its outstretched humanity.

Consider the situation for a moment. A complete stranger turns up at your front door after midnight – dressed like a goddam professional ice-skater and visibly fucked up on tranquillisers and God knows what else – in the hope of finding shelter for the night. Would you let him into your humble abode, make him welcome and even attempt to converse with him at some length? Of course, you wouldn't.

But Lester wasn't like most people. He empathised with fuck-ups because he was often one himself. He gamely sat down and talked with me uncondescendingly for over an hour. He even took me upstairs to his bear-pit of a room and played me his just received white label copy of *Raw Power*. I don't remember if it was during that hour or the morning after that I asked him to be my teacher. I explained my situation

anyway: young university drop-out lucks out at the *NME* but still needs to find his own voice as a writer in order to make the most of his good fortune. I craved guidance I couldn't find back in merry old England. Could Lester show me – by example – how to reach my full writing potential? Would he even be interested? 'Sure – OK, then' was his immediate unblinking reply.

Just thinking about his generosity of spirit still makes my eyes moist. I didn't know it then but other young would-be rock scribes had already personally contacted him for tips and career guidance. One of them, Cameron Crowe, of course, would later go on to write and direct an Oscar-winning film in the 1990s called *Almost Famous* that evocatively transposed his real-life teenaged tutelage at the feet of guru Bangs on to the big screen. But I was the first to have made the trip all the way across the Atlantic in order to seek his indulgence, so maybe that's partly what sealed the deal. That and the fact that we both liked to get wasted. But mostly it was down to him being such a big-hearted guy.

Two days after linking up with Lester and his *Creem* co-conspirators – bingo! – I had my first face-to-face encounter with David Bowie. I'd spent a goodly portion of the previous year trying to finagle a meeting with the man – all to no avail. But in Detroit it actually came to pass. I need to thank B. P. Fallon for making it happen. The imp-like Led Zeppelin publicist happened to be passing through the area with a group he was promoting called Silverhead, a London-based glam-rock quintet whose lead singer, Michael Des Barres, was already a drug-buddy of mine. When we met up in downtown Detroit, I happened to mention that Bowie and his Spiders from Mars were playing at the nearby Cobo Hall that very night. Fallon immediately got it into his head that we should go to Bowie's hotel and make our introductions. This was a mad scheme. Bowie at that stage in his career had purposefully made himself as unapproachable as Greta Garbo. And none of us had ever actually met him before. But 'Beep' had once been Marc Bolan's PR and felt that this prior connection would suffice as a calling card. He was right too. Bowie's huge black bodyguard stationed at the door of his boss's imperial suite was handed a written note by Fallon, took it to the singer inside and came out to inform us that 'David' would be delighted to make our acquaintance later after tonight's performance. He advised us to return just after midnight.

The show itself was another mind-boggler. Not for Bowie's performance per se – he was boldly previewing his *Aladdin Sane* material some two months before the record's actual release. He was great – more self-assured, more self-possessed – but I'd seen him live so often throughout 1972 that I already knew what to expect. No, what left me thunderstruck was the audience.

Back in little old England, Bowie's concerts had been peppered with young people dressing and behaving outrageously but it was mostly self-conscious silliness, a Mickey Mouse pose. They wouldn't have known real decadence if it had come out and bitten them on their bum-cheeks. But over in Detroit Bowie's followers were like something out of Fellini's *Satyricon*: full-tilt pleasure-seekers devoid of anything resembling shame, limits, caution or moral scruples. I distinctly remember a local lesbian bike gang riding their bikes into the foyer of the concert hall and revving them loudly just prior to Bowie's arrival onstage. This had not been pre-arranged between the girls and Bowie's management. These women just turned up unannounced and were so scary no one dared bar their entrance.

Meanwhile the toilets were literally crammed with people either having sex or necking pills. The whole building was like some epic porno film brought to twitching life. Back in London's West End, the best-loved theatrical presentation of the hour was an asinine farce called *No Sex Please, We're British*, a title that pretty much summed up the United Kingdom's awkward embrace of its libidinous potential even during the so-called permissive age. Put that reticence down to a mixture of instilled Catholic guilt, cold showers, single-sex schooling and 'steady on, old boy' stoicism. Our young American cousins however had no such inhibitions to curb their lust. And with no life-threatening diseases then in evidence to cause further pause for thought, they were up for any kind of carnal and pharmaceutical hanky-panky you could throw at them.

This was not lost on David Bowie whose new *Aladdin Sane* songs were clearly part-inspired by their composer coming into direct contact with the Babylonian sexual frenzy of young America in the early '70s. Two hours after he'd left the stage in triumph and had been driven back to his hotel, we gingerly approached his suite in the hope that he was still up for a bit of socialising. His man-mountain bodyguard duly beckoned us into a large room where – seated on an elegant settee – was the man himself. He immediately stood up and daintily shook our hands, welcoming us to his temporary abode. He had pointy carrot-coloured hair, shaved eyebrows, a ton of make-up slapped across his extremely pretty face and a slender androgynous physique – swathed in a red checked blouse and electric-blue Oxford bags – that moved with the studied poise of a movie starlet from some bygone era just prior to the advent of Technicolor.

At first it felt as though he had no fixed sexual identity. His mannerisms were as outrageously camp as those of any self-respecting drag queen but there was a bold streak of jack-the-laddishness immediately apparent in his general demeanour. He'd also chosen to invite several teenage girls who'd been lurking in the hotel corridor into his lair and was eyeing them up and working his charm. By the time we left, he'd already seduced one of them – a black girl. This wouldn't have been especially noteworthy save for the fact that his wife Angie was also present in the room. But she didn't appear to mind: she had her own boyfriend – a Detroit-based singer named Scott Richardson – with her anyway. I hadn't realised it at the time but I'd met her once before at the Stooges' Baron's Court house sometime in the early autumn of 1972. While her husband was busy touring the world as Ziggy Stardust, she'd been occupying her time consorting with Ron Asheton. Clearly she had a serious yen for rough-hewn Midwestern dudes. And even more self-evidently, the Bowies were committed swingers who enjoyed the most open of 'open' marriages.

I can still recall the first words he directed at me. 'So you're Nick Kent. Aren't you pretty! And here I was thinking that all English rock critics looked like Richard Williams.' (Williams – one of *Melody Maker*'s most prominent writers during the '60s – was a straight-arrow Welsh clergyman's son who had been fiercely dismissive of Bowie's glitzy allure.) He stared at me coquettishly but with a wary glint in his two differently coloured eyes. It was as though he had X-ray vision when it came to sizing up strangers. He looked at you and through you at the same instant. On the surface he was all lightness and breezy charm – the host with the most – but that lightning-fast brain of his hiding under the signature dyed-red hair was always in full effect, never giving too much away. He was drinking tentatively from a glass of wine but he and his wife were both very anti-drugs at the time: a girl in the room who started rolling a joint was ejected by a bodyguard at their behest.

Still he seemed to be having a good time chatting away with other music industry Brit expats caught in the culture shock of discovering America. I remember he kept playing 'Virginia Plain' by Roxy Music on a portable record player he had set up at one end of his suite over and over again. He thought the group was absolutely wonderful, the only other glam-rock act to truly merit his respect. That's when I realised how smart he really was. Almost anyone else in his position would have felt threatened by the advent of Roxy Music – they were UK chart rivals after all – but Bowie was intelligent enough to embrace and study what they were doing and in time appropriate some of their elements into his own evolving 'œuvre'. That's why his career has lasted so long. He wasn't closed-minded like so many of his peers. He was a big thinker and a true professional.

Things went so swimmingly that Bowie – after chatting for a couple of hours – invited us back the next night for an impromptu party following his second show at the Cobo Hall. He told us that he didn't normally do this kind of thing – that his manager liked to keep him sealed away from all human contact as often as possible – but that his manager wasn't present on this phase of the tour and he suddenly felt the urge for mingling with the natives. Detroit's wildest young things then caught wind of this invitation and turned up in hordes to the hotel determined to party down with their new rock deity.

The previous night we'd only been seven or eight in his suite – an easily containable collective. But now the same space was throbbing with bodies and most of them were conspicuously on some chemical or other. Bowie looked distinctly ill at ease in the centre of it all. Detroit had a well-deserved reputation as the most hard-partying city in the whole USA and even he was clearly more than a little taken aback by his gate-crashing guests' zeal for self-annihilation.

Meanwhile, outside his quarters and unbeknownst to him, his Mainman-employed touring minions were trying to initiate a series of orgies in their respective rooms with the numerous kids lined up in the hotel corridors waiting to touch their hero. Bowie's American management enablers during his 'Ziggy' era were some of the sleaziest, most repugnant people I've ever had the misfortune to shake hands with. They were all over-sexed gossip-crazed fame-seekers who'd spent time in the lower rungs of Andy Warhol's Manhattan social circle and who carried themselves with a sense of lofty self-entitlement that made the conduct of the royal family seem humble by comparison. They were so caught up in their own lust for personal celebrity that they couldn't help but resent their employer for being such a rising star himself. Still it didn't take long for Bowie to draw much the same conclusion. Twelve months hence, he'd sack them all and initiate legal proceedings to extricate himself from Mainman's parasitical clutches.

The party wound down somewhere in the early hours of the morning. The hotel's hallways as I left the establishment looked like a modern-day rendering of a scene from *Caligula*. Suddenly I was alone and walking the streets of downtown Detroit in a drugged daze just as dawn was breaking. This was pure insanity on my part, as the zone was known to be rife with muggers, rapists, killers and other predatory forms of human debris.

After stumbling down two or three streets, I decided to take refuge in the only bar that was open in the area at this ungodly hour. Now take a picture of this: me decked out like little Lord Fauntleroy entering a run-down juke joint populated exclusively by seriously pissed-off black blue-collar dudes nursing their drinks and thinking criminal-minded thoughts. Nervously I asked the barman if there was a pay phone on the premises, as I was lost and needed to phone a taxi. He jerked his thumb towards the rear end of the establishment, wouldn't even look me in the eyes.

Laughable as it may sound now, being English was the only good-luck charm you needed back then to be instantly accepted in America. Yanks – particularly the women-folk – had fallen head over heels in love with little old Limey-land when the Beatles 'invaded' their shores in 1964 and the infatuation was still going strong almost a decade later. They couldn't get enough of our quaint, wacky accents, bad teeth and bizarre eating habits. You could even talk in the incomprehensible cadences of a Geordie docker and still travel the continent getting laid from coast to coast.

Not surprisingly, my all-American male cronies at *Creem* were often resentful of all this anglophile ardour running riot throughout their proud nation. 'You goddam limey fops!' Lester Bangs would rail at me, 'What's so great about your fucked-up culture anyway? We produce great art like the Velvet Underground, the MC5 and the Stooges and you retaliate with David fucking Bowie and his Spiders from Mars. Whoopee! You're just re-selling us Herman's Hermits for homos.' I'd retaliate by tartly informing him that unlike him I'd been born in the cradle of civilisation and that we Brits were making timeless art when Americans were still learning how to ride a horse, steal cattle and shoot each other in whore-ridden bar-rooms. That would generally shut him up.

The rest of the time we got on famously. Lester drove everywhere in a garbage-strewn jalopy that was one of his few personal possessions and I would be there next to him in the passenger seat taking in the landscape and making sure he didn't suddenly nod off at the wheel. This sometimes occurred late at night after he'd mixed the liquor and pills and was a matter of some consternation amongst his *Creem* cohorts who'd all experienced the phenomenon and were genuinely concerned that he'd drive into a wall one night and spend the rest of his life in traction.

These fears had recently intensified because Lester had started dating a young girl named

Dori who lived in the Canadian frontier town of Windsor, Ontario, over a hundred miles away from Birmingham. He loved the place: the beer they served was extra-potent and you could buy codeine tablets over the counter at the local pharmacists. As a result, he would make almost nightly treks there and back throughout my stay and I would usually accompany him. Those long journeys driving across the muddy Detroit River with him at dead of night were heady experiences for me. Just five years earlier my schoolboy imagination had been seriously inflamed by reading *On the Road* and now I was actually living the full-tilt Kerouac dream, careening through the nation's ripped backsides in the company of America's latest championship-level wild man and literary blow-hard.

The conversations we had ranged as far and wide as the country spread outside our speeding vehicle. Being in motion – and under the influence of amphetamines – always opened Lester up and he'd talk for hours, often littering his diatribes with intimate recollections from his mostly troubled past. He spoke emotively about his drunkard father who perished in a fire when Lester – who'd actually been christened 'Leslie Bangs' – was only nine and about his infuriating still-living Jehovah's Witness mother for whom he harboured deeply conflicting feelings. Her suffocatingly possessive presence throughout his young life had scarred him with regard to developing healthy loving relationships with the opposite sex as an adult. He kept falling madly in love but the female objects of his worshipful desire – after a brief period of courtship – would almost always be put off by his kamikaze drunken mood swings and his intense, emotional neediness. This was heartbreaking to behold because under his rowdy exterior lurked the beating heart of an incurable misty-eyed romantic, who so desperately craved to share his life with a soul-mate that his ongoing loneliness – and the demons it ignited

– ended up growing like a malignant cancer within him.

Lester was equally unlucky in his choice of personal role models. One time I walked into the *Creem* house kitchen and found him in tears. He'd just finished reading a *Rolling Stone* feature in which Neil Cassady's long-suffering widow Caroline had spoken candidly for the first time about her life with her sociopathic spouse – the Dean Moriarty character in *On The Road* – and Jack Kerouac himself. The portrait she painted in words of the latter – Bangs's most revered literary idol – was far from complimentary. She called attention to Kerouac's inability to establish a healthy loving relationship with any woman, his terminal alcoholism and his hopeless mother fixation. She inferred that he was basically born doomed. It was this revelation that caused Lester to weep so openly. He saw far too much of his own predicament in Kerouac's death-driven depiction.

He didn't do himself any favours in his choice of living heroes either. It's no secret that he idolised Lou Reed to the point of obsession and saw the Velvet Underground songsmith as rock music's most visionary iconic entity. A week after the aforementioned Bowie shows, Reed was booked to play a concert in Detroit and Lester managed to set up his first actual interview with the man and invited me to accompany him to the affair to act as his comerman. It turned out to be an ugly spectacle: two drunks railing at each other over the Formica glass-strewn table of a tacky hotel bar. Reed was – relatively – civil to me but stared at Bangs throughout their long over-inebriated conversation as though he was face to face with some mentally challenged country bumpkin who'd just escaped from the local nut-house.

Lester later wrote up the encounter in a piece for *Creem* he entitled 'Death Mute in a Phone Booth' that's since been reproduced in one of his two posthumous collections. It's a vibrant, one-sided account of what happened that day but it neglects to mention at least one pertinent detail. Driving back to the *Creem* house directly after the interview had concluded, Lester was so distraught he veered into a garage by mistake, smashed into a petrol pump and almost totalled his precious car. For three days afterwards he replayed what he could remember of their meeting of minds and fretted about the contemptuous way Reed had beheld him. I told him that trying to locate anything resembling human warmth, empathy or decency in Reed's personality was as futile an exercise as trying to get blood from a stone. Then I bid him and the rest of the *Creem* corps a temporary adieu and boarded a flight direct to Los Angeles. I'd been entranced by visions of the Wild West ever since I'd seen my first Western at the age of six. Now the time had come to kick up some dust of my own within its untamed borders.

SIMON REYNOLDS
Sound Envisioned
Science Fiction and Future Music
(aka Sonic Fiction, Part Two)

You're familiar, I expect, with that old chestnut about the futility of writing about music? But how much more absurd would it be to boogie to buildings that haven't been built yet, fantastical edifices that are just the fever-dream blueprints inside an architect's over-heated brain. Yet that's what the science fiction writer who seeks to imagine tomorrow's music is attempting. It's enough of a challenge to describe already existing music, but to take something so abstract and elusive, project forward from its present forms to the future, then try to evoke the flavour of these phantasmal sounds . . . well, the results are likely to be unconvincing, or embarrassing, or both.

My curiosity about the deficiencies (and rare triumphs) of the science fiction movie sound track was sparked by *Stars Wars* and its famous scene in the lowlife bar where the alien band play really far out music that turns out, on close inspection, to be just Benny Goodman-style swing. When it comes to SF writers and their visions of sound-to-come, the intrigue started with William Gibson and, specifically, *Idoru*, whose whole storyline concerns pop but which strangely lacks a soundtrack, as it were. Gibson's novels brilliantly imagine the near-future but are oddly mute when it comes to music – even as a vague 'rock'n'roll'-ness suffuses most every page. Interviewed about *Idoru* when it came out in 1996, Gibson suggested that 'There's never

been a successful science fiction rock'n'roll book, not in my opinion.' An interesting assertion – and a candid admission, given that the genre he helped to pioneer contains the word 'punk'.

I asked Bruce Sterling, who has collaborated with Gibson and is considered cyberpunk's co-inventor, about SF's difficulties with music. The analogy he came up with was 'the old jazz muso' who, interviewed by a journalist about where he feels music is going next, replies: 'If I knew what the future of jazz was, I'd be playing it already.' Sterling, whose own 1999 rock'n'roll novel *Zeitgeist* was set in the present, argued that while it's 'pretty easy to write about future models of the music *industry* or future *roles* for musicians within future societies', describing 'what music *sounds like* in the future is kinda tough'.

Despite this, according to one encyclopaedia of science fiction I consulted, 'of the arts, music is the one most commonly featured in SF'. And it's certainly true that the genre is littered with passing references to outlandish instruments, from the 'three bass radiolyn' in Samuel Delany's *Out of the Dead City* to the ultra-cembalo in Harlan Ellison and Robert Silverberg's 'The Song the Zombie Sang'. There are also a fair few appearances of alien music that is incomprehensible, traumatising or simply inaudible to the human ear. Isaac Asimov's early story 'The Secret Sense' features Martian music woven out of the flickering patterns of electric

Simon Reynolds

current and therefore beyond human perceptual thresholds. And in Samuel Butler's *Erewhon* (1872) there are Musical Banks (all mercantile transactions are accompanied by music, albeit 'hideous to a European ear') and sinister Stonehenge-like statues sculpted with holes that catch the wind and produce an unearthly keening music, 'a ghostly chanting' such that 'however brave a man might be, he could never stand such a concert'.

Erewhon is not, strictly speaking, about an alien civilization; it is about an undiscovered land on Earth. A similar scenario underpins the much earlier utopian novel, Francis Bacon's *The New Atlantis* from 1627, a time when the voyages undertaken by the great explorers were that era's equivalent to manned missions into outer space. Europeans were only just making their first contacts with the mainland of Australia, and Bensalem, the new Atlantis of the title, is an unknown island in the Pacific west of Peru. Bacon's book contains a remarkable passage about what music might be like in a society that – while not technically of the future – is far more advanced than the European present:

> We have also sound houses, where we practice and demonstrate all sounds and their generation. We have harmonies which you have not, of quarter sounds and lesser slides of sounds. Divers instruments of music likewise to you unknown, some sweeter than any you have; together with bells and rings that are dainty and sweet. We represent small sounds as great and deep; likewise divers trembling and warblings of sounds, which in their original are entire. We represent and imitate all articulate sounds and letters, and the voices of beasts and birds. We have certain helps which set to the ear do further the hearing greatly. We have also divers strange and artificial echoes, reflecting the voice many times, and as if it were tossing it; and some that give back the voice louder than it came, some shriller and some deeper; yea, some rendering the voice, differing in the letters or articulate sound from that they receive. We have also means to convey sounds in tubes and pipes, in strange lines and distances.

In just 174 words there, we have microtonality, the synthesiser, hearing aids, an array of effects and processes equivalent to the modern recording studio and the telephone. *The New Atlantis* passage about Soundhouses was famously tacked to the office wall of the BBC Radiophonic Workshop in 1958 by its co-founder Daphne Oram, to serve as a sort of mission statement defining the ambitions of the unit, which would use then state-of-art tape-editing techniques and sound-synthesis devices to create eerie special effects and incidental themes for radio dramas and (later) TV programmes like *Doctor Who*.

Written in the early days of the Enlightenment, *The New Atlantis* was a straight-forwardly utopian vision of a society organised around rational principles. But by the twentieth century, science and planning were starting to take on a negative colouring, suggestive not of high-minded reason but of high-handed authoritarianism: a technocratic elite who thought they knew best and imposed their rigid ideas on the population. The result was a series of novels that envisioned future societies that look utopian at first glance, or at least considered themselves to be achieved utopias, but are actually dehumanising and totalitarian. In two of the most famous examples of dystopian utopias, Yevgeny Zamyatin's *We* and Aldous Huxley's *Brave New World*, music serves as a potent instrument of social control.

Written in 1920 shortly after the Bolshevik Revolution, *We* was a precocious act of dissidence against the Soviet system: it circulated illegally among Russian writers during the '20s and only saw official publication in the USSR a few years before the fall of Communism. Zamyatin delineates a cold, rationalist society in which every aspect of daily life is regimented and supervised. In the One State, presided over by the Benefactor, privacy has been abolished (people live in glass houses, literally), passion is frowned upon, and sex days are strictly rationed (you need a pink chit to get a shag). Everyone wears identical uniforms and is identified by number not name. The main character, D-503, is an engineer working on building a spaceship, but like Winston Smith in *1984* he's seduced by an erotic dissident, I-330, a woman still in touch with human passion. Music in the One State has been ruthlessly rationalised and enlisted for utilitarian goals. It's made in a factory, the Music Plant, which churns out rousing march rhythms that get worker-citizens moving in lockstep, or generates serene patterns to quell agitations of the nervous system.

In one scene, a lecturer illustrates a talk on mathematics and music by displaying a device called the musicometer, explaining to his listeners that 'simply by turning this handle, any of you can produce up to three sonatas an hour. Yet think how much effort this had cost your forebears! They were able to create only by whipping themselves up to fits of "inspiration" – an unknown form of epilepsy.' An ancient instrument is then wheeled out – the piano – and a Scriabin piece is played to the bemusement and amusement of the audience. D-503 recoils from the 'senseless, hurried clattering', divining in it 'something savage, spasmodic, variegated, like their whole life at that time – not a trace of rational mechanical method'. He contrasts it with:

our present music . . . the crystalline chromatic measures of converging and diverging infinite series and the synthesizing chords of Taylor and McLauren formulas; the full-toned, square, heavy tempos of 'Pythagoras' Trousers'; the sad melodies of attenuating vibrations; vivid beats alternating with Frauenhofer lines of pauses – the spectroscopic analysis of planets . . . What grandeur! What imperishable logic! And how pathetic the capricious music of the ancients, governed by nothing but wild fantasies . . .

Brave New World resembles *We* in its portrayal of a 'negative utopia' (Huxley's term) in which passion and conflict have been eliminated through social engineering and conditioning. Unlike the puritanical world of *We*, though, sex is encouraged along with all forms of entertainment, distraction and sensual pleasure. The removal of tension promotes social stability, so promiscuity is mandatory while romantic obsession is deemed pathological. Drugs are readily available to smooth away every crease of anxiety, doubt and emotional pain. Music likewise is an agent of social tranquilisation. Huxley anticipates muzak with his Synthetic Music Machines: the first one we encounter is 'warbling out a super-cornet solo' in a female dressing room; later, a Super-Vox-Wurlitzeriana fills the air 'with gay synthetic melodies' at a hospice for the terminally ill. As in *We*, music production is centralised, streaming out of a gigantic building in London that contains various Bureaux of Propaganda, floor upon floor of which house the 'laboratories and padded rooms in which Sound-Track Writers and Synthetic Composers did the delicate work'.

In *Brave New World*, there are also concert halls and nightclubs like the Westminster Abbey Cabaret, whose hoarding promises 'ALL THE

Simon Reynolds

LATEST SYNTHETIC MUSIC'. Two of the characters, Lenina and Henry, go there on a date, joining the crowd of couples 'five-stepping around the polished floor' to the complex rhythms of Calvin Stopes and his Sixteen Sexophonists. The band play standards like 'There Ain't No Bottle in All the World like that Dear Little Bottle of Mine': not a paean to booze but Huxley's twist on Al Jolson's maudlin 'Mammy', for in *Brave New World* foetuses are hatched in glass wombs, to spare women the hassle of pregnancy and the agony of birth but also to avoid emotional attachment and all the neuroses created by the Freudian 'family romance'. Hence lyrics like 'Bottle of mine, why was I ever decanted? | Skies are blue inside of you | The weather's always fine'. As the 'tremulous chorus' of sexophonists 'mounted towards a climax' the conductor 'let loose the final shattering note of ether-music and blew the sixteen merely human blowers clean out of existence'. After the band finish, a 'Synthetic Music apparatus' pipes out 'the very latest in slow Malthusian Blues' leaving Henry and Lenina feeling like 'twin embryos gently rocking together on the waves of a bottled ocean of blood-surrogate'.

Elsewhere there's ecclesiastical music (or in *Brave New World* terms, hymns and choral music for a Solidarity Service at the Community Singery), including fanfares from ersatz trumpets and haunting harmonies from 'near-wind and super-string' instruments. Music is also a crucial component of the 'feelies': an omni-sensory update of cinema in which smell and touch are stimulated as well as sight and sound. At one show, the 'scent organ', which Huxley may have borrowed from Huysmans' *Against Nature* (whose decadent aristocrat Des Esseintes composes symphonies with perfumes), plays a

delightfully refreshing Herbal Capriccio – rippling arpeggios of thyme and lavender,

of rosemary, basil, myrtle, tarragon; a series of daring modulations through the spice keys into ambergris; and a slow return through sandalwood, camphor, cedar and new mown hay (with occasional subtle touches of discord – a whiff of kidney pudding, the faintest suspicion of pig's dung) . . .

Meanwhile the music machine unfurls 'a trio for hyper-violin, super-cello and oboe-surrogate' which is joined by a synthesised singer, 'a much more than human voice . . . now throaty, now from the head, now hollow as a flute, now charged with yearning harmonics,' which passes effortlessly 'from Gaspard's Forster's low record on the very frontiers of musical tone to a trilled bat-note high above the highest C' (only once before hit by the opera singer Lucrezia Ajugari back in 1770).

All terrific fun, then, but for the most part the music in *Brave New World* is a technologically boosted, artificially sweetened version of the pop-cult fare of Huxley's day (the book was published in 1932). So Calvin Stopes and his Sixteen Sexophonists are a big jazz band à la Duke Ellington's Cotton Club Orchestra, while songs like 'Hug Me Till You Drug Me, Honey' are modelled on the Tin Pan Alley trifles of the '20s. At the feelies, the Synthetic Music machine operates using a 'sound-track roll' (an idea obviously inspired by the player-piano, aka the Pianola, at its peak of popularity in the '20s but dating back to the 1870s). Even more unimaginative is the Super-Vox-Wurlitzeriana, inspired by the Mighty Wurlitzer pipe organ designed as a one-man orchestra and used in movie theatres to accompany silent films. Considering the talkies were taking over at the time when Huxley was writing his novel, this is frankly feeble as far as extrapolation and speculation goes, especially taking into account the fact *Brave New World* is set *six centuries* in the future. Still, when asked if there is nothing he cares for at all in the modern world, John – the Shakespeare-quoting visitor from the Savage Reservation in New Mexico – concedes 'there are some very nice things. All that music in the air, for instance . . .'

Huxley imagined his benevolently behaviourist New Order of peace, plenty and pleasure to have been constructed in response to the devastation of the Nine Years War and a world economic collapse. But there's not a shred of extenuation for *1984*, George's Orwell's vision of a totalitarian society organised around perpetual war. Just like *Brave New World*'s caste system based around IQ, the Britain of *1984* (which is actually part of a superstate called Oceania) has rigid social divisions. There's the Party (the political class, itself split between low-level bureaucrats and an Inner Party who make all the decisions) and then there's the proles, 85 per cent of the population, powerless drones mired in squalor and pacified by mindless entertainment. This pop-cult pabulum is created mechanically, via 'mills' that churn out novels with stereotypical characters and prefab narratives. The same goes for music, with songs being 'composed without any human intervention whatever on an instrument known as a versificator.'

In one of the most famous scenes in the book, the dissident Winston Smith stares out the window of the love nest in London's proletarian quarter where he and his lover tryst, entranced by the sound of a prole housewife singing one of these assembly-line ditties – 'It Was Only a Hopeless Fancy' – while hanging nappies on a washing line.

> Whenever her mouth was not corked with clothes pegs she was singing in a powerful contralto . . . . She knew the whole drivelling song by heart . . . Her voice floated upward with the sweet summer air, very tuneful, charged with a sort of happy

melancholy . . . The woman sang so tunefully as to turn the dreadful rubbish into an almost pleasant sound.

Winston is confirmed in his belief that if there is hope it lies with the proles – still in touch with basic human emotions, still grounded in the earthiness of the primal and ageless. Like lions after slumber, in unvanquishable number, they'll rise and throw off the Party.

But later in the book, 'It Was Only a Hopeless Fancy' – the big hit tune that season with the proles – starts to be eclipsed in popularity by 'The Hate Song', the theme tune for the upcoming Hate Week, and which, from its description, sounds a bit like Oi! or the more shouty kinds of rap such as crunk.

> A savage, barking rhythm which could not exactly be called music, but resembled the beating of a drum. Roared out by hundreds of voices to the tramp of marching feet, it was terrifying. The proles had taken a fancy to it . . . The Parsons children played it at all hours of the night and day, unbearably, on a comb and a piece of toilet paper.

The rise of this ugly chant, even among the apolitical proles, seems to prefigure the grim conclusion of *1984*: the inevitable triumph of ideologies that feed off hatred and mob rage, the sinister Inner Party apparatchik O'Brien's vision of the future as 'a boot stamping on a human face – forever'.

Ray Bradbury's 1953 novel *Fahrenheit 451* fuses aspects of *Brave New World* (soul-eroding hedonism) with *1984* (the Party's ruthless drive to strip the poetic and emotionally expressive power from language and turn it into the instrument of ideology). The core of *Fahrenheit 451* is the black joke of the firemen of the future being sent out not to extinguish blazes but to use a flamethrower on books, considered socially disruptive because they arouse the imagination but still kept in secret private libraries by dissidents and eccentrics. As in Huxley and Orwell, music is considered to be on the side of sedation not sedition: it dulls the mind in tandem with TV, which in this near-future has evolved into a four-wall mega-telescreen apparatus. Music can be peppy, an emptily effervescent upper so loud it drowns out conversation: 'The walls of the room were flooded with green and yellow and orange fireworks sizzling and bursting to some music composed entirely of trap drums, tom-toms, and cymbals.' But mostly it's bland and emollient, doping the listener just like the legal tranquilisers that Mildred, wife of the fireman Montag, constantly pops.

Mildred also wears 'audio-seashells' – tiny transistor radio earpieces – all day long. One night, Montag returns home late and opens the bedroom door:

> Without turning on the light he imagined how this room would look. His wife stretched on the bed, uncovered and cold, like a body displayed on the lid of the tomb, her eyes fixed in the ceiling by invisible threads of steel, immovable. And in her ears the little Seashells, the thimble radios tamped tight, and an electronic ocean of sound, of music and talk and music and talk coming in, coming in on the shore of her unsleeping mind. The room was indeed empty. Every night the waves came in and bore her off on their great tides of sound, floating her, wide-eyed, toward morning. There had been no night in the last two years that Mildred had not swum that sea, had not gladly gone down in it for the third time.

Like *Fahrenheit 451*, Anthony Burgess's *A Clockwork Orange* reflects the anxiety felt by your typical literati worried sick about people not reading books anymore on account of the rise of 'admass society' (J. B. Priestley's 1954 term for the complex of advertising, mass communications and consumerism). The quirk of *Orange* is not to blame the advent of a pleasure-principled post-literate society on Americanisation, the typical bogey-man in this scenario of popular culture as mass zombiedom, but on its Cold War adversary. Burgess's novel is set in a near-future Britain whose pop culture has been corrupted by 'subliminal penetration' from the Eastern Bloc and where teenage slang is largely composed of pidgin Russian. (Of course, in *reality*, it happened the complete other way round: jeans and rock and Hollywood made Comintern youth eager to Westernise). Anti-hero Alex is the fifteen-year-old leader of a gang of 'droogs', who belong to a larger youth subculture modelled on the teenage tribes of the early '60s. Fusing the yobbery of rockers with the razor-sharp elegance of mods, these dandy hooligans dress 'in the height of fashion' (at the start of the book, that's ultra-tight black tights through which show the bas relief patterns of decorative abdominal protectors, plus lapel-less jackets with padded shoulders) and prowl the nocturnal streets, where they fight with rival gangs and brutalise defenceless citizens. Equally recognisable as early '60s is *Orange*'s urban landscape of high-rise 'flatblocks' and foreboding power stations.

In classic SF style, Burgess took the present – brutalist architecture, youth's new insubordinate arrogance, a rapid-fire turnover of fashion trends, rising crime and drug use, the popularity of milk bars and cafes as places for teenagers to hang out and listen to jukebox rock – and exaggerated it. In *Clockwork Orange*'s near-future, the milk bars sell state-sanctioned psychoactive potions like 'synthemesc' and 'milk with knives in it', the terms Alex and his pals use for a speed-shake that puts them in the mood for ultraviolence. Pop music is naturally central and like the teen argot mostly originates from the Communist Bloc. In the Korova Milkbar, the jukebox plays Berti Laski's golden oldie 'You Blister My Paint'; later, we come across Russky pop stars like Johnny Zhivago, Ed and Id Molotov, and Goggly Gogol.

Unlike his peers, Alex is not interested in all this pop pap. In one of those curious expressions of authorial narcissism that novelists often cannot resist, Burgess inserts, implausibly, his own preference for classical music into his lead character. For Burgess was a prolific composer who only turned to writing as a second choice and who churned out Elgar- and Holst-influenced symphonies, concertos, and fugues throughout his life. Alex owns a top-range stereo and a large album collection, funded by muggings and burglaries. And he finds that the tempestuous romanticism of composers like Beethoven stirs up the Dionysian emotions, stoking his appetite for destruction and sexual cruelty.

In one scene, he hurries down to his local record store Melodia (which happens to be the name of the state record label of the former USSR) to see if a new version of the Ninth Symphony has arrived. A pair of ten-year-old, precociously sexual girls tease him for buying such square and crusty stuff, rather than the hit parade tunes they're into, like 'Honey Nose' by Ike Yard and 'Night After Day After Night' which, sneers Alex, is 'moaned by two horrible yarbleless like eunuchs whose names I forget' (I'm guessing the inspiration for Burgess here was the Everley Brothers or the Four Seasons). Alex invites the girls back to hear their teenpop platters on his mega-system (like putting some horrible fizzy kid's drink in a fine wineglass, he complains). Then he whacks on Beethoven and, suitably stirred, subjects the girls to 'the strange and weird desires of Alexander the Large', leaving them 'bruised and pouty' and punching him with 'teeny fists' as they scurry out the door.

Despite Burgess's evident disdain for pop, *A Clockwork Orange* had a huge influence on pop groups. The Human League titled an early EP *The Dignity of Labour*, after a mural in Alex's high-rise, while the offshoot band formed by Ian Craig Marsh and Martyn Ware took their name from *Orange*'s fictional group the Heaven Seventeen. Clock DVA derived its own name partly from Nadsat, the Russian teen-slang all the young droogs speak. Another group from the same Sheffield post punk scene, Molodoy, had a whole look inspired by the Kubrick movie version of *A Clockwork Orange*, as did punk group the Adicts. Other homages include the band Moloko (nadsat for 'milk'), the record label Korova, and the New York-based, Factory Records-signed outfit Ike Yard.

Often, though, the SF novelists who feel most 'rock' on account of their influence on musicians seem to have given the least attention to music in their work. Philip K. Dick has inspired everyone from Sonic Youth and Royal Trux to the Human League and (via *Blade Runner*) countless techno and drum-and-bass producers. But I can't recall that many appearances of music *in* his books – which is odd, given that he was a music nut with a huge collection, worked in a record store, once entertained ambitions to compose, and even performed in an ensemble led by Harry Partch (albeit only playing the triangle). I only recall a wee thing in *The Three Stigmata of Palmer Eldritch*, where the Earth is afflicted by chronic global warming: one apartment block's air-conditioning fails, causing a resident's record collection to melt into a single blob. In *The Simulacra*, there's a pianist character who has the telekinetic capacity to play piano using his mind and there's also an early short story, 'The Preserving Machine', about an inventor who aims to save the canon of works of classical music for all time via a machine that turns them into animals that can be loosed into the wild, with disastrous consequences.

J. G. Ballard had an even greater impact on rock, influencing all the usual post punk suspects (such as Joy Division, Cabaret Voltaire, Throbbing Gristle and Mute Records founder Daniel Miller who as The Normal wrote the Crash-inspired 'Warm Leatherette') along with Gary Numan, the Buggles ('Video Killed the Radio Star' is loosely based on his short story 'The Sound Sweep', more about which in a moment), Radiohead, The Klaxons, and dub-steppers like Kode 9 and Burial. Yet Ballard often remarked on his lack of feeling for music, claiming to have a 'tin ear' and almost boasting of never having 'bought a single record, cassette, CD or whatever. I don't own a record player of any kind.' He enjoyed the cultural convulsion of punk, but his Desert Island discs were barely middlebrow: 'The Teddy Bear's Picnic', a Bing Crosby and Andrew Sisters version of a Cole Porter tune, Noel Coward, Marlene Dietrich, various light classical pieces, plus 'The Girl from Ipanema'.

'There's no music in my work,' Ballard once declared. 'The most beautiful music in the world is the sound of machine guns.' Certainly there is a kind of hypertrophy of the eye in his fiction that makes all the other senses dim next to his monstrous visual intensity, from touch (*Crash* is about the arrangement of limbs and objects in compelling patterns, about geometry rather than sensuality) to sound. The Ballardian narrative is a machine for generating landscapes and tableaux: where Burgess was a frustrated composer, Ballard had originally wanted to be a painter like the surrealists he so admired.

That said, music and sound did feature here and there in his work, and when it appeared it was handled more imaginatively than many of his more musically sensitised SF peers. Mostly it's early in his career, perhaps before he realised precisely where his gift lay, with the drastically transformed landscapes painted in post-cata-clysm novels like *The Drowned World*. Indeed his very first published story, 'Prima Belladonna' from 1956, concerned music. The protagonist is the owner of a shop selling 'choro-flora,' mutant singing plants that typically have a twenty-four-octave range and can hit notes like K sharp and high L. The story is full of delicious wisecracks (references to 'mixed coloratura herbaceous from the Santiago Garden Choir', the 'Kew Conservatoire', and so forth) but also pre-cociously features the unique Ballardian atmo-sphere of uncanniness and psychological fixation, with its narrative about the strange love/hate relationship that develops between the 'specialty singer' Jane Ciracylides and a 'beauti-ful but evil' orchid. Set in the same indolent-yet-eerie dreamscape of Vermilion Sands, 1962's 'The Singing Statues' features sonic sculptures that respond to the sounds of their immediate environment, including the 'body tones' of their owners. 'Sonic sculpture was now nearing the apogee of its abstract phase; twelve-tone blips and zooms were all that most statues emitted. No purely representational sound . . . a Mozart rondo or (better) a Webern quartet, had been built for ten years.' The plot echoes 'Prima Belladonna' with its wealthy female art collector forming a morbid obsession with one particular sound-sculpture.

In between these two early Ballard shorts came 1960's 'The Sound Sweep', quite possibly science fiction's very best story about music. It's set in the near-future, a few decades after the discovery that sound leaves residues, like the build-up of scale in a kettle, an after-resonance of staleness and agitation that's bad for health and environment alike. Sound-sweeps, em-ployed by the Metropolitan Sonic Disposal Service, use Sonovacs to suck up all the 'em-bedded sounds' in public spaces and private homes. It's not always a simple process: some residues, such as the seven centuries of Gregorian chants that have soaked into a church, are like the picturesque weathering on a building's brickwork, and so a delicate restoration job is required, retaining these 'tonal inlays' but removing the coughs and rustlings left by congregations over the decades. The sound-debris is emptied at a dump way out in the dunes on the edge of the city, a sort of sewage plant for sound where the waste frequencies are corralled in complex arrays of baffles. Cue for a classic Ballardian landscape that's also, for once, a soundscape: 'a place of strange echoes and festering silences, overhung by a gloomy miasma of a million compacted sounds . . . The cacophonic *musique concrete* of civilization.'

This scenario ought to be sufficiently fertile to sustain a forty-page story, but Ballard, in the full flush of his early creativity, adds another layer: in this near-future, music as we know it has been outmoded by the introduction of 'ultrasonic' music, which employs

> a vastly greater range of octaves, chords and chromatic scales than are audible by the human ear, [providing] a direct neural link between the sound stream and the auditory lobes, generating an apparently sourceless sensation of harmony, rhythm, cadence and melody uncontaminated by the noise and vibration of audible music.

An ultra-sonic trumpet, for instance, is strictly speaking silent but its 'fantastic glissandos . . . like frantic eels' charge the air 'with gaiety and sparkle'. Best of all, ultrasonics leaves no stagnant residue behind, the 'leaden and tumid' after-tang you'd get from playing, say, a Mahler symphony. Ballard adds another witty tweak: ultrasonics catch on with the general public and completely replace audible music in part thanks to a further invention, the short-playing record. Spinning at 900 rpm, the SP condenses a forty-five-minute Beethoven symphony into twenty seconds but delivers the same amount of 'neurophonic' pleasure – indeed

it's distilled into a deeper hit of bliss, the classical music equivalent of the crack high perhaps.

The actual plot of 'The Sound Sweep' (and the bit that semi-inspired 'Video Killed the Radio Star') is a *Sunset Boulevard*-like *mise en scene* involving a decrepit, delusional opera singer, Madame Giaconda, and her magnetic hold over the sound-sweep Mangon, who's somewhere between a vassal and a lover, and, for inverse symmetry, is also a mute. With Mangon's help, the prima donna attempts to relaunch her career and bring about a 'sonic revival'. Here's where, for all of Ballard's prodigious inventiveness, we encounter the familiar SF problem of imagining music of the future. The fact that the story's based around an opera diva and that Ballard imagines ultrasonics not leading to some unimaginable form of post-music but the re-scoring of the established classical canon (complete with new-old instruments like the ultra-tuba and triple bass) indicates how hard it is to think beyond the musical limits of one's era.

Things remain equally date-stamped as we reach the psychedelic late '60s. *Stand On Zanzibar*, John Brunner's 1968 classic, is set in an overpopulated early twenty-first century. As with most near-future SF, everything is extrapolated from the trends of the day, from sexual permissiveness to then recent scientific advances like genetics. Using a revolving cast of characters and a large number of plot lines to offer a panoramic view of this world at every social level and in many corners of the globe, Brunner's execution is generally inspired. *Zanzibar* features a number of cute and imaginative ideas about music, albeit mostly just tantalising hints. We follow a night-time walk through a megalopolis, music coming 'from everywhere, mostly hits from the current pop parade in which two or even three disparate rhythms clashed randomly on semitonal discords'. Some of these sounds

Simon Reynolds

issue out of 'radio-dresslets': garments fitted with tiny speakers. There's a passing reference to grooving on 'the random sounds of a Whyte Noyse generator'. At a party, someone talks of visiting Detroit, now a ghost town full of abandoned car factories and whose only living inhabitants are squatters, and going to a squat party with 'a zock group playing full blast under a steel roof five hundred feet long. Didn't need lifting [drugs] – just stand and let the noise wipe you out.' That sounds more than a little like an illegal rave, and in Detroit, the historical birthplace of techno, too. Not bad at all, Mr Brunner. But, um, 'zock group'?!?

The party is a retro theme event thrown by society hostess Guinevere, a queen bitch who's decreed that anyone caught wearing something that dates after the turn of the millennium must pay a humiliating forfeit. The retro idea is itself pretty prescient, since in 1968 it was barely discernible as an undercurrent within pop culture (indeed the word 'retro' is not actually used in that chapter of *Zanzibar*). It's also a cool manoeuvre that allows Brunner to recap some of the pop-cultural fads of the intervening decades. So the soundtrack is '70s, with 'divisible-by-two rhythms' that seem 'banal and boring' after the more complex rhythms like 'five against eleven' that emerged in the '80s and '90s. There's a reference to a currently popular style of 'chants san paroles' in relatively 'bland monotonous rhythms of five against four and seven against eight'. Guinevere catches a guest doing the zock – a 'this minute dance' and worse, the perpetrator's doing it with 'the genuine, free-fall touch' – and the poor sod is forced to do it with a dish of honey between his elbows.

Later, there's a whole chapter about 'zock'. It's split into two columns, Aud and Vid, to convey the musical and visual aspects of this hybrid entertainment form. Here's an extract of the Aud channel:

Trackin hiss
Pick up 7-beat bass below aud threshold
Synch in five-beat
WAH YAH WAH YAH
WAH
Sitar picks up 5
7 beats express takeoff
Octave up bass
Bass up 2nd octave
Bring in at 4-beat intervals tympani,
Lasry-Bachet organ, pre-cut speech tape
MANCH/total recall/SHIFT/man that's
really someth/WHIP/ah whoinole cares
anyway/GARKER/garker/GARKER/gar
ker (ad lib)
Snatch of Hallelujah chorus
Leader talks over gp:
YOU GOT THE OFFYOUR ASS FOR
BOTH OF US MY SPAREWHEEL
AND ME AND SHIGGY MAKES
THREE
Las-Basch FFF waltz-time
Acceleratube passes by
Resume speech tape
I GOING BUST MY
SKULL
Kiss loudens synch with
Resume bass, sitar . . .

The visuals meanwhile are a colour-saturated blur of nudity and simulated sex ('shiggy fondles own breasts', shiggy sucks the longest glass column of "the Las-Bach organ" ') plus random psychotropic imagery.

It's the sitar that gives the game away: this is all just an amped-up version of 1967 and '68 . . . Hendrix, Jefferson Airplane, the White Album . . . coloured-oil projections oozing while Floyd go into 'Interstellar Overdrive' at the All Night Happening. 'Lasry-Bachet' is another period-piece reference, albeit fairly esoteric: it's a reference to the Crystal Organ, fifty-four chromatically tuned glass rods that produce sound when rubbed with wet fingers, which was invented in 1952 by Bernard and François Baschet and played by Jacques and Yvonne Lasry.

Written a few years after *Stand On Zanzibar*, Robert Silverberg's *The World Inside* grapples with some of the same contemporary anxieties as Brunner – overpopulation, mega urbanisation, permissiveness – but is set four centuries into the future. The year is 2381 and most of the world's 75 billion population live their entire lives inside gigantic city-size skyscrapers that tower one thousand stories high; the rest of the planet's surface is devoted to agriculture to feed this ever-expanding population, which continues to grow because there are no restrictions on breeding and total sexual freedom is promoted. *The World Inside* is unique, I think, among SF novels for having a whole chapter devoted to a detailed description of a single sound check-cum-performance by a band. Dillon Chrimes plays 'vibrastar' in a 'cosmos group' that tours up and down the three-kilometre-high building, which is divided into forty-floor-tall 'cities' that bear names like Rome. Other instruments include comet-harp, orbital diver, gravity-drinker, Doppler-inverter and spectrum-rider.

Dillon and his band arrive at the auditorium on the 530th floor of Urbmon 116, which has a stage that hangs like a toadstool in the centre of the space and around which is concentrically strung a web on which the audience will nestle. The vibrastar is so heavy it requires a robot to manoeuvre it on to the stage: it's as if Silverberg couldn't imagine synthesisers ever getting any less unwieldy than the Moogy monstrosities prog rock groups lugged with them on tour. The group's output is visual as well as audio, and in full improvisational flight that night the effect is like a planetarium reprogrammed by acid heads to make the trip as spectacular as possible. 'The spectrum-rider . . . skis off toward the ultraviolet

in a shower of hissing crispness.' Then Dillon takes a solo: he 'coats the ceiling with dripping nebulae', gives the audience 'the stars in one skullblowing rush' and on impulse let's rip with 'an eclipse of the sun – why not? let the corona crackle and fry'. The climactic blast sends the 'flaccid data-stoned audience' apeshit: they give the band the ultimate ovation, slapping their own cheeks. As with Brunner's zock, all this noodlesome out-there-maaaan-ness is just the slightest of projections forward from what cosmic rockers like Tangerine Dream, Hawkwind and the Grateful Dead were doing in the late '60s and early '70s. As if to signpost this more sharply, the floor that Dillon and the group live on is called San Francisco and his wife, Electra, even paints 'psychedelic tapestries' for a living.

A decade or so later, cyberpunk would also reflect its moment. The term was coined in 1983 by Bruce Bethke, who used it as the title of one of his short stories, but it really took off with William Gibson's *Neuromancer* in '84. Although *Village Voice* would hail cyberpunk as a 'hip, musically literate high-tech movement' that was rejuvenating an SF genre that had lost its edge in the pulpy post-*Stars Wars* era, by the early-mid '80s 'punk' as a reference point could hardly be described as cutting-edge. If anything it was played-out, suggestive as much of London tourist postcards depicting spiky-haired punks down the King's Road or Billy Idol's lip-curl sneer on MTV, as of cooler inheritors like Jesus and Mary Chain or Husker Du. (Idol would actually attempt a career comeback in 1993 with the album *Cyberpunk;* at his insistence, journalists were obliged to read *Neuromancer* before interviewing him, although – it turned out – he hadn't actually read it himself.) But then the punk in cyberpunk wasn't really about musical allegiances but 'attitude': tough, speed-wired, effectless. There was also a punk-like minimalism to the hardboiled, clipped-and-stripped prose, while the genre's worldview and mindset, if not quite nihilistic, was certainly dark: the enforced cynicism and paranoid wariness of renegades in a world dominated by sinister corporate entities.

Mirrorshades, the 1986 short story collection edited by Bruce Sterling, brought together all the luminaries of the young genre and featured several stories that directly dealt with music. Pat Cadigan's 'Rock On', a sketch towards her 1991 novel *Synners*, is set in about 2025, a time when rock'n'roll's spirit has faded from the world apart from a handful of battered survivors from the olden golden age – like the protagonist Gina, who remembers being taken as a toddler by her mom to see the Rolling Stones's 1981 tour. By the third decade of the twenty-first century, rock has become an audiovisual entertainment fed directly into the brains of fans via sockets in the skull. But uniquely endowed individuals, people like Gina with a special feel for a-rockin' and a-rollin', are needed to mediate this stimuli before it can be turned into the tapes that fans buy and channel into their nervous systems. These 'sinners' – short for 'synthesizers' – seems to be something like a studio engineer or mixer, except they don't really have agency in the process; they're perhaps closer to a pre-amp, a prism that sharpens the signal. Young upcoming bands and entertainment conglomerates alike compete to get hold of one of this dying breed of rock'n'rollers.

The scenario – a meretriciously flashy audio-visual distraction that needs the substance of true rock to give it any real life – looks suspiciously like the mid-'80s, when American radio followed MTV's lead and filled the airwaves with British pop tarts and flamboyant fake-rock from Motley Crue to . . . well, Billy Idol. There's even a give-away mention of Bow Wow Wow and Oingo Boingo, MTV one-hit wonders that Gina is just old enough to remember (while still preferring her mother's

Hendrix and Who albums). Having the lead character be a relic from an earlier era is a neat ruse too, a way of avoiding imagining the music of the future.

Oddly enough, the *exact same ploy* is utilised in 'Freezone', the other main music-based story in *Mirrorshades*. Author John Shirley is widely credited as having pioneered cyberpunk with 1980's *City Come A Walkin'*, which introduces the squalid yet glittering cityscape later familiar as the Sprawl of *Neuromancer* and other Gibson novels. *City* also has a rock'n'roll thread running through it: its cast of characters include a music club owner and a tough little rocker (called Catz Wailen!). Gibson hailed Shirley's book as 'less an SF novel set in a rock demimonde than a *rock gesture* that happened to be a paperback original'. Shirley didn't really need to write about rock'n'roll because he *was* rock'n'roll: former drug addict, the spiked dog-collar wearing front man of various punk bands (including Sado-nation, whose songs included 'Our Love Is Like A Death Camp' and 'Kill Myself'), a writer of lyrics for Blue Oyster Cult (he named his first novel after their 'Transmaniacon MC'). Gibson's adulation of this dude who walked it like he talked it gets pretty icky: 'I look at Shirley today, the grown man, who survived himself, and know doing that was *no mean feat*. A cat with extra lives.' And pretty yukky: he describes *City* as 'quite literally, a seminal work; most of the elements of the unborn Movement swim here in opalescent swirls of Shirley's literary spunk'.

Gibson pinpoints the proto-cyberpunk hallmark of *City Come A-Walkin'* as its *mise en scene*, 'a "near future" that felt oddly like the present (an effect I've been trying to master ever since)'. Written in 1985, 'Freezone' conjures a near-future (early twenty-first century) that feels oddly like its own recent past. Hero Rick Rickenharp is a 'rock classicist' who sings songs like 'Pain Is Everything', sports sunglasses after dark and wears a battered leather jacket reputedly worn by John Cale when he was in the Velvet Underground. His band Rickenharp are on a downward trajectory: the nostalgia wave that had carried them peaked long ago, their latest holovid isn't getting airplay. So the band are muttering about changing their look (to 'minimono', streamlined and muted-toned) and style (to 'wire', a music form that is 'danced' by performers, with the movements triggering sounds in a manner possibly inspired by the theremin). We witness the wire act NewHope, a sexless, emaciated voidoid whose muscular contractions of limbs and torso are converted, via 'impulse-translation pickups', into 'long, funereal pealing' and 'bagpipe-like riffs'. The minimono-styled audience respond with appropriately complex geometric dance-moves. Rickenharp tries to get into it, to accept it as 'another kind of rock'n'roll' . . . but concludes: 'Real rock is better. *Real rock is coming back* . . .' He finds the music that minimonos dig mechanistic and inhuman: 'The stultifying regularity of their canned music banged from the walls and pulsed from the floor . . . you felt a drill-bit vibration of it in your spine.'

You don't have to be too sharp to twig that NewHope is most likely inspired by Gary Numan or maybe even the writhing dancer that Howard Jones used to have in his videos, while Rickenharp is a stand-in for Shirley, whose Stiv Bators-style punk has been outmoded by the New Romance's synths and drum machines. As a practising rocker, Shirley is good at evoking the magic and chemistry of a gig when it all comes together for the band: Rickenharp, playing what may be their last show as a rock'n'roll group, hit a righteous groove and slay an audience, most of whom have never seen a live drummer before.

But overall Shirley is happier writing about clothes and hair than sound. There's a fashion parade in 'Freezone' of near-future subculს:

neutrals, flares, rebs, chaoticists, preps, minimonos, retros. But even the most extreme of these (the chaoticists with their filed teeth, pierced nipples and skinhead crops with painted sides) are barely further out than the modern primitives of '80s industrial or the freaks of Leigh Bowery's Taboo scene. Similarly, William Gibson's *Count Zero* from 1986 – part of the Sprawl Trilogy that started with *Neuromancer* – features style tribes straight from the early '80s: Gothicks, all lacquered hair and leather and 'graveyard pallor', versus Kasuals, blonde and healthy in cottons and loafers. This mysterious persistence is all the more odd given that *Neuromancer* had featured an oft-quoted passage about the incredible rapidity with which fashion trends and subcultures germinate, blossom and disappear on a monthly basis within the youth population of the Sprawl, a conurban spread that's transformed the East Coast of America into a single gigacity.

But it's *Idoru*, Gibson's first and only book to put pop music centre-stage, that really flinches from the challenge of speculating about music's future. As he admitted in an interview, 'I was a little shy with that . . . I'm not a musician, I'm not musical enough.' In what looks to be a hallmark of the cyberpunk approach to music, a Gina/Rickenharp-like out-of-time rocker is the novel's central figure: Rez, ageing frontman of Lo/Rez, a guitar band who've released twenty-six albums in the decades since their debut for Taiwanese indie label Dog Soup. Lo/Rez are classic retro-rockers, quite possibly modelled on Black Crowes or Lenny Kravitz, as they seem to have been behind the times even when they emerged in the '90s. Asked on TV about the accomplishments of axe hero Lo, 'a venerable British guitarist in wonderful tweeds' declares that 'They hadn't really expected the next Hendrix to emerge from Taiwanese Canto-pop.' Kathy Torrance, an executive at the infotainment company Slitscan, regards Rez as 'a living

Simon Reynolds

fossil, an annoying survival from an earlier, less evolved era'. Another throwback band in *Idoru* is the Dukes of Nuke 'Em, whose Billboard smash 'Gulf War Baby' caused 'diplomatic protests from several Islamic States'. Appealing to the 'meshbacked' audience (i.e. redneck, after the trucker-style caps), they play Republican rock that's 'all about hating anything that wasn't their idea of American'. Gibson's inspiration here, I suspect, was the intolerant opinions expressed by raunch-metal groups like Guns'n'Roses and Skid Row.

Yet nothing musical actually *sounds* through *Idoru*'s pages. The book's real subject is celebrity and fan culture. The plot concerns Rez's decision to marry an *idoru*, a literally manufactured pop idol from Japan called Rei Toei who puts out records and videos and has fans, but he doesn't exist, he is just a software agent, a data-spun figment. The wedding appears to be a mixture of publicity stunt, performance art gesture and philosophical statement about the nature of fame. For Rez the human being has long ago been subsumed within a fantasy-figure superself, woven out of crisscrossing threads of publicity and fan(tasy) projections. Gibson has sharp perceptions here: he notes how Lo/Rez's 'fan-base had refreshed itself over the years with a constant stream of pubescent recruits, girls who fell in love with Rez in the endless present of the net, where he could still be the twenty-year-old of his earliest hits'. But what seems like the most speculative and futuristic element in the book – Rei Toei , the artificially engineered pop idol – was overtaken by reality in the gap between his handing in the manuscript and the book being published: there actually was a virtual *idoru* known as Kyoko Date, with a website and animated videos. Then again, you could say the Archies got there first in 1969 with 'Sugar Sugar'.

Gibson legendarily wrote his books while watching MTV and his fiction is littered with rock references (a spaceship called Sweet Jane, an *Idoru* chapter titled 'Fables of the Reconstruction', phrases like 'meat puppets', etc). But as he admits, music rarely appears in the narrative, instead figuring as 'a kind of offstage influence'. Cybertheory academics go gaga for the passages in *Neuromancer* concerning the Rasta space station Zion, where dub basslines echo through sensimilla-scented corridors:

> When they'd strung the cables . . . they hung them with battered sheets of yellow plastic. As they worked, Case gradually became aware of the music that pulsed constantly through the cluster. It was called dub, a sensuous mosaic cooked from vast libraries of digitalized pop; it was worship, Molly said, and a sense of community . . . Zion smelled of cooked vegetables, humanity, and ganja.

When I first read this I did wonder how come people were *still* listening to dub in the twenty-first century, a good fifty years at least after King Tubby invented the genre . . . Still, credit where credit's due: what Gibson describes *is* slightly ahead-of-the-game; 'a sensuous mosaic cooked from vast libraries of digitalized pop' doesn't sound like reggae in 1984 but like the *idea* of dub that emerged in the '90s, promoted by figures like DJ Spooky and Kevin 'The Bug' Martin via his *Macro Dub Infection* compilations: dub as process not genre, closer to remixology or sampladelia than a band-played form of music like reggae.

Fifteen years after *Neuromancer* came *Needle in the Groove*, science fiction that's not only all about a band and music-making but is deeply informed by the de-Jamaicanised notion of dub that emerged in the '90s. Author Jeff Noon's earlier novels like *Vurt* and *Pollen* offered a British post-rave counterpart to cyberpunk: urban grime, subcultural colour, drugs, musical references. A former musician himself, Noon had been involved in a late '70s moment that pre-echoed all those '90s ideals of musical boundary-crossing and mixing-it-up. He played guitar in the Manchester post punk outfit Manicured Noise, whose singer Owen Gavin (now the journalist Frank Owen) told me about the group's formidable experimentalism: they'd lay down 'military beats, over which we'd recite poetry by Mayakovsky' and combine that with elements inspired by film soundtracks and primitive funk learned by copying Chic singles slowed down to 33 rpm. Talking about the post punk era, Noon argued that the discovery by white youth of dub reggae's bass pressure and disorientating spatiality was the most significant musical development in the last few decades: 'from that moment comes everything we now listen to', by which he meant electronic music, drum and bass, post-rock, trip hop, Timbaland-style R&B, and so on. 'Everything' is stretching it a bit, but those were the sorts of claims being made for dub in the mid-'90s, among a certain *Wire*-reading and *Wire*-writing sector of the population. In the '00s, we'd hear a lot less of this kind of talk, but if he were making that comment today Noon could certainly add dubstep to the 'everything' list.

Needle in the Groove's acknowledgements section doffs its cap to outfits like Autechre, Microstoria and others operating on the post-rave/post-rock fringes of '90s music. And Noon has often talked about how he has 'such an intimate relationship with music. My writing is all tied up with it. I listen to it all the time, writing to the rhythms.' So how well does he do, then, with *Needle in the Groove*? Noon didn't set himself a massive challenge since the novel is set in the very near future: *Needle* came out in 1999 and because of the main character's age (twenty-four) and his time of birth (summer 1978), you can tell the story is set around 2002/2003. The location is familiar Noon territory, a Manchester where the streets are named after bands or records (State 808 Street, Ian Curtis Boulevard and so forth). The protagonist/narrator Elliott is an ex-junkie bassist who joins a band called Glam Damage: like Manicured Noise, a mixed-gender, experimental-but-danceable outfit, but here updated for the rave era. There's the brilliant enigmatic drummer 2spot, the sultry black girl singer Donna, and the female deejay/sampler-whizz Jody, who throws scratches and samples into the mix in real time, and is also a drug fiend.

So far, so '90s, then. The futuristic and speculative factor added by Noon is that Glam Damage, through their patrons Zuum (a club/label), have gained access to a new recording format that captures music in a liquid: a technology identified at various points as 'wave recording', 'wave-sonic technology', 'aquamatics' and 'hydrophonics'. Instead of a reel of tape or a DAT, there's a golf-ball-sized vessel full of sky-blue gel veined with darker strands (these hold the music). Like a child's snowscape, this globe can be shaken, causing the music to remix itself in a potentially infinite number of ways as the strands settle into new patterns. And the harder you shake it, 'the deeper the mix', explains DJ Jody. Elliott gives Glam Damage's 'Scorched out for Love' a good jiggle. What results is 'Elliott's Bad and Busted Remix'. And a wodge of prose poetry (the first of several) that's something like a William Burroughs cut-up using only issues of *Melody Maker* from the early '90s:

> the creeping two-shot spots of a flow-
> down drumfall and the rim of skin-beat,
> in a snare-dancer's downtime rhythm-loop
> explode lament/where all the rain cymbals
> sing/the contours of the voice, waiting for
> the bass to steal, the sliced and crazy
> feel/shots of the lost/the hidden sound
> chant knowledge caught and twisted, now

stretching guitar burst/a drag from the fingers/holding, releasing/noise caressing the blade-song/I wonder what colours you'll burn, when the bass returns/bruise of crackle-pattern, vinyl screech-pop of string . . . incisions of chorus, made of mad magic/amplifies the heart crying out, injection dance/cuts of motherloading bass honey, off-kilter dripping deep, and then word by funky word, passion splinters the tragic splice tactics/on the caught samples singing it all away/all the tripwire scratching kaleidoglide of a strange groove/deep jesus bass of music, catching the shimmer/the final crackle of silence/holding, releasing, dissolving

There's loads of tricks you can do with this new plasmatic recording technology. At the Zuum club one night, where ravers trance out to 'cheapcore', 'fleshcore' and 'techzak' (terms indicative of Noon's professed disdain for the more functional forms of dance music), Jody puts vinyl versions of 'Scorched out for Love' on both turntables and cuts back and forth, then uses an eye-dropper to siphon some of the liquid version of the same track out of the little blue orb, squirts it on to the twelve inches and scratches the needle over these wet spots. This makes 'the music slip away and slither | become a river', until the ravers are pounding on the glass wall of the DJ booth and screaming to know what the hell this freakadelic tune is. Cue more prose poetry from Jeff, aka the 'Club Zuum Remix':

Loop-dancer dripping a deep lament
Of mad magic scatter honey
Found
Exploding bootleg skin splinters
Nerve poison scraped from the shimmer
Working a pop drag screech from the
    heart lost

And taking a hit from blade strings
Injection's dance fires up the groove glide
Along the decks of tripwire
Found
In the snare-time rain of cymbals
    drumfalling
Through scratches of rhythm stolen and
    kissed
Kaleidofunk dissolving
Lost in the tangle and crackle

Wave-sonic music gets made illegal before the book's end, but not before the band work out you can inject the liquid intravenously. The samples in the track become portals through time taking them back to when/where they were recorded (in this case, the punkfest at the Electric Circus in Manchester, October 1977, as recorded for the live album *Short Circuit*). But is it just a mindblowing hallucination or actual time travel?

In interviews Noon talked about 'the way we live now, I call it Liquid Culture, and I think to find the prose equivalent of that is great'. The concept/conceit of *Needle* is that the method of its composition is in tune with the digital era's cutting-edge music. Or at least, the prose-poetical 'mix' chapters are, since it's those bits that have been sluiced through the 'Cobralingus Filtering System'. Noon characterised this writing technique in terms of the array of effects and processes offered by a studio mixing desk or digital audio workstation. He talked of channelling his prose through 'filter gates' (overload, 'ghost edit', 'add virus', randomise, decay) and 'drug'-like treatments such as 'metaphorazine' and 'repititorphan'. But it turns out that Cobralingus was closer to a set of instructions and options à la Brian Eno's *Oblique Strategies*, except that Noon didn't bother to make them up as a pack of tarot-style cards: this technology of the imagination was a purely imaginary technology, existing only as 'the strangely twisted pathways inside [my] head'.

Noon had dabbled with literary counterparts to dub's versioning in his earlier *Nymphomation* and *Pixel Juice*. And after *Needle*, he'd go further still, writing a whole book of 'remix fiction' actually titled *Cobralingus*. Here he sampled text from sources like Emily Dickinson, Thomas De Quincey, and Ecclesiastes, then shoved the literary signal through 'a series of gates'. In one story, Shakespeare gets melded with Zane Grey. It all sounds a bit like Kathy Acker's iconoclastic remakes of canonical novels like *Don Quixote*, updated from the era of No Wave and Cindy Sherman to the age of Warp-style electronica and all those 'remix albums' that cluttered up the latter years of the '90s and whose versions increasingly bore no resemblance to the original (and in some cases no *relation* either, since they featured not a single sonic shred of the remixed track).

A prototype version of *Needle* featured a female character called Toop (short for Tupelo). Bizarrely Noon hooked up with David Toop to create an album based around his novel: *Needle in the Groove: If Music Were a Drug, Where Would It Take You*, released via Scanner's Sulphur label in 2000. Or not so bizarrely, really, given that Toop was the perfect choice, as one of the principal theorists for 'liquid culture' with his 1996 book *Ocean of Sound: Aether Talk, Ambient Sound and Imaginary Worlds*, which contained passages like this:

> Disco began to work on the principle of decomposing songs into modular and interchangeable fragments, sliced and repatched into an order which departed from the rules of Tin Pan Alley . . . Songs became liquid. They became vehicles for improvisation, or source material . . . that could be reconfigured or remixed to suit the future. In a humiliating way, musicians became technicians, alongside recording engineers, tape ops, editors and all the other technocratic laboratory assistants cleaning their glasses in the back room. At the front end of the medium was the DJ, ruling the disco, playing music and people as one fluid substance.

In terms of its SF premise and the storyline, but also at the level of the text itself, *Needle* attempts to implement this very ('90s, technotopian) notion of dub/remixology as deliquescent and deterritorialising. For the resulting fictional music to be then realised as sound by Toop, one of the great theorists of 'sonic fiction' (Kodwo Eshun's term), made for a perfect circularity: what flows around comes around. It's also, as far as I know, the only time an attempt has been made to create the future-music imagined in a SF novel, and with the involvement of the author to boot.

So what does *Needle in the Groove: If Music Were a Drug, Where Would It Take You* sound like? Kudos to Noon for the cojones . . . but frankly, a little underwhelming, after the 'remix' passages of the book, and after Noon's burbling in interviews about the 'mind-boggling' thrill of going into Toop's studio and being confronted by 'all this digital stuff they've got [nowadays] . . . they can do absolutely anything. They can manipulate the musical input, the signal, any way they like.' The track 'dubbedoutforlove (Dubgeist Remix)', for instance, doesn't sound ahead of its time but if anything, slightly behind it: ambient chill-out infused with a fragrant tang of 'modern exotica', it's all a bit mid-'90s, in the vicinity of Mouse On Mars's *Iaora Tahiti*. The track sways on a gentle bass-pulse, draped with ripples of hand percussion and twangy curlicues of steel guitar redolent of Eno's *Apollo* soundtrack, an album Noon listened to while writing *Needle;* bobbing like a corked bottle in the waves is a sing-songy Mancunian voice, Shaun Ryder's dotty uncle – Noon reciting lines like 'boomsonic boomsonic/kaleidofunkphonic'.

This mellow, atmospheric approach was taken, Toop explained, because it's 'impossible to read in a flexible, expressive way over hard-edged dance music' but also because he 'heard something other than dance music in the book . . . a weird soup of skiffle, blues, hip-hop beats, Manchester rock and psychological noise'. Toop did take a stab at achieving something close to the liquid remixing in *Needle*: he took 'a huge collection of fragments and jammed them all together in the computer'.

But the very idea of remixology/dub-as-process, signposted so heavy-handedly with the 'Dubgeist Remix' subtitle, was already past its freshness date by the turn of the millennium. (Indeed the passage from *Ocean of Sound* quoted above was itself cut and pasted from an article on remixing Toop had written back in 1992 for *The Wire*). Dance culture in the '00s would abruptly veer away from the totally unrecognisable remix version like a Music and Video Exchange bargain basement employee swerving to avoid toppling a stack of un-resellable 'remix albums'. Instead there were vogues for 're-edits' (remixes that largely consist of the original song, but structurally resequenced – a reversion to how things were done in the '80s, in other words) and for mash-ups (chimaera-like composites stitched together out of amputated parts from two or more highly recognisable tunes).

Needle in the Groove the album, like the novel, proves once again the difficulty of thinking ahead or outside of present conceptions of music. To imagine the music of the future and then convey that in prose you'd need to be a mixture of accomplished critic, musicologist and practising musician (and if you were the latter, as Bruce Sterling suggested, you'd be making the music already). Futurologists are no better at this game than SF writers. Take Ray Kurzweil, the inventor who pioneered optical character recognition, text-to-speech synthesis and a number of keyboard synthesizers. In his 1999 book *The Age of Spiritual Machines: When Computers Exceed Human Intelligence* he drew up a timeline of breakthroughs that the twenty-first century was set to unfurl. He postulated that around 2009 a computer would have become sufficiently intuitive to be able to 'jam' with a human musician: a 'marvel' that dates him to the era of Carlos Santana and Jerry Garcia.

Futurologists and SF writers both tend to do much better speculating about technology, geopolitics and social mores than arts and culture. Especially with science and machines, the cause-and-probable-effect trajectories are far easier to track; you can see the gaps in contemporary knowledge or technical capacity that could be filled, the breakthroughs that are required for the currently impossible to become possible. There are magazines and specialist journals that are all about speculating about developments, proposing goals and solutions. But art and fashion don't have a 'way forward' that you can map out in this fashion; there is no teleology, no immanent logic set to unfold in ways we could predict. The history of pop music, especially, is full of swerves, double-backs, bolts-from-the-blue. Twenty-five years ago, at the height of synthpop, or even fifteen years ago, at the peak of techno-rave, few would have predicted the massive revival of interest in folk forms and acoustic instrumentation that took place in the '00s. Similarly, people who heard 'Tomorrow Never Knows' and 'Are You Experienced' when they first came out might have thought that rock music was just going to get weirder, more studio-phantasmagoric and drug-frazzled (John Brunner and Robert Silverberg certainly did). One or two strands of rock did pursue those trajectories, but most of it went into completely unexpected and unforeheard directions (the singer-songwriter boom, glam's warped echoes of '50s rock'n'roll), and some of it deliberately went the opposite way (The Band, Creedence, country rock, et al.). Music can offer a potent *sensation* of the future-now, but it is rarely an actual glimpse of the shape of sounds to come. And it is only looking backwards that you can see what were the harbingers of, or flash-forwards to, our sonic present: at the time itself, the germs and heralds of tomorrow's music were more often than not ignored, undervalued, unnoticed.

Perhaps the very idea of 'tomorrow's music today' is one of those Wittgensteinian wrinkles in language, a nonsense produced by the peculiarities of tenses and grammar. If it's made today, or even *conceivable* today, then by definition it's no longer *of* the future, it's already here. In music journalism, one of the standard-issue ways of praising something (usually old music, a reissue or something that deserves to be reissued) is to say it was 'ahead of its time', that a certain record 'looks ahead to' or 'anticipates' something much later, that with a particular song Band X 'invents' the much later Band Z. No actually existant music can really be ahead of its time but it is possible for popular taste – the general public, or a particular, wilfully backward-looking sector of it, like indie-rock – to be *behind its own time*.

What about the idea that music itself is the vanguard of culture, the furthest-extending promontory into the oncoming ocean of the future? This notion is aired in *Idoru* – 'popular culture is the test-bed of futurity', observes Mr Kuwayama, the boss of the company that created Rei Toei (which makes ye olde rockisme of Lo/Rez all the more lame). As outlined in his classic book *Noise*, Jacques Attali's theory of music's evolution hinges on the notion that music is already in advance of the rest of culture, that its current forms are somehow prophetic of future modes of social organisation. The theory is too complicated to examine here, but the part that is most relevant and suggestive concerns the present era, what Attali terms the age of 'composition': after a long period of music being a specialist profession and consumers 'stockpiling' recorded sound and listening to it passively and mostly in private, the punters get to make their own music. Attali (whose latest book *A Brief History of the Future* doesn't mention music) wrote *Noise* in the mid-'70s and there have been varied interpretations of what 'composition' would look like: some have pointed to punk and to the do-it-yourself/release-it-yourself culture of post punk, others to the more recent micro-undergrounds of noise, improv, drone et al. (where music is home-recorded and circulates in tiny editions of cassettes and CD-Rs among fans who are most likely practitioners themselves). But perhaps the most convincing candidate for 'composition' is DJ culture and related genres based around sampling (from hip hop to various post-rave styles to mash-ups). This is literally com-position, the putting together of shards of pre-existing music either in the DJ's mix or as a sample-collage, resulting in the reanimation of 'dead' energy trapped in stockpiles aka record collections. But all these candidates for 'composition' fit Attali's theory in so far as you could see them prefiguring new social forms based around transactions within networks of autonomous individuals.

....

I really like this idea of music being the forward sector of culture: as someone who's dedicated their life to writing about music, it appeals to my professional patriotism. If music had the capacity to herald change (if not actually effect change by itself), that would certainly ratify the excessive importance that some of us have invested in music. The latent futurity of music would also go some way toward explaining why so many SF writers are influenced by music, why so many pop groups have been inspired by SF, and indeed why so many rock critics started out

Simon Reynolds

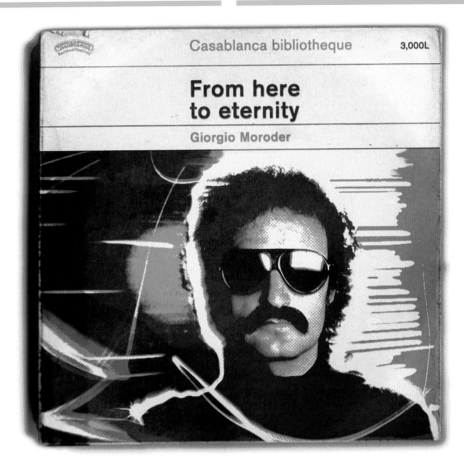

From here to eternity

Giorgio Moroder

as SF fans (Greg Shaw, founder of the pioneering rock mag *Who Put the Bomp* had a long history doing science fiction fanzines beforehand, as did Paul Williams, whose *Crawdaddy* is generally regarded as the very first magazine devoted to rock criticism). Part of the allure of being a music hipster is the idea of being *in on the future*. I don't know why I've never before connected my own interest in music's cutting-edges with the fact that science fiction was the thing I was into immediately before I discovered punk and the UK rock press; before I wanted to be a music writer, I wanted to be a SF novelist. The big post punk festival of the era, headlined by groups like Public Image Ltd and Siouxsie & the Banshees, was Futurama in Leeds, and it was originally billed as the World's First Science Fiction Music Festival.

This Attali-derived notion of utopianism as the latent content of music, or *some* music, actually fits the feelings that music, or *some* music, stirs up: the vertigo of limitlessness, inordinate hope, unstoppable energy. It's the same scary-euphoric rush that the best SF gives. But if music *is* the future-now, it only figures that dreaming up in prose the future form of that future-now is going to be a tall order.

KEV KHARAS

Private, Post-generic Truths and the
Bedroom Club Belief Eke

For too long too many have toiled for the promise that music is somehow imminently poised to change the world. 'The' world! There's barely a 'the' world left for music to change, and even if there were – supposing there will always be some thin strand of empathy knotted round our necks – why would it choose to surrender now to the morass of men with stubble and guitars and morals? Why is it always stubbled, guitared, moralled men who so sorely ache to change 'the' world? Maybe it was possible for them once, I don't know. 1965? You can't help but think that if it's time for a change of anything, it's a change of tack, boys. Regardless, I for one (and not for all) very rarely feel like part of 'the' world for anything longer than a few hours. Part of my world? Yes. Near-constantly. That much should be obvious. But my world's 'a' world and there are an infinite trillion of those for music to alter – and if it wants to it can, with relative ease. It can change tens of thousands of 'a' worlds at once if potent enough, irking reality for a moment to sink upon brain or room or field like a dubious vow – one that alleges, 'Yes, we are together.'

What?

'Look, how this groaning bass swell rattles our teeth and wobbles eyeballs in their sockets. Can you feel that synth cutting up under your ribs? It is the sound of a jet's chrome heart slapping blissfully against the horizon, great, big bird on window, slithering down slow leaking silver unity ooze. I flung the jet heart. You are the horizon. I know you know exactly what I mean.' If it's convincing enough you go with it for a while, permitting – maybe even reveling within – the bounds of its tampered reality, and why not? When 'the' world grows tedious – tedious labour, tedious water, tedious air, zzzzzz – it's only natural to seek its transformation. Clubland is designed with this in mind – it will provide you booze, drugs, steam, stairwells, darkness, lasers, confusion and sweat-wet skin, all of it to help obliterate the distance between you and everyone else. With any luck, a skewed, liquid empathy ensues, one in which dancing, speaking too loud and financial and chemical oblivion are weapons to tote in the glad pursuit of oozy union. Eventually, though, that logic will desert you, in the glare of house lights or the morning or just before 3 p.m. the next day, parched and contorted on somebody else's mattress like it was a beach you washed up on, and suddenly everything music had you convinced of in the dark seems completely fucking absurd.

It's in these collisions, though, that music finds perfection, a type of invincibility. When it gets the chance to impose its very own 'a' world, the necessary collision with yours should be swift, rare, hidden, confusing, absurd and oozy. It should offer an escape hatch from the mundane, not giving you what you want, but bewildering you with possibilities you never even recognised. Music is at its worst when it overreaches itself and arrogantly demands to be real forever – our bearded, guitared, moralled men, again – and when, in attempting to do so, it looks to provoke a kind of mob empathy. Unsurprisingly, it seems to have pinpointed Saturday evening television as a chink in reality's armour. X Factor's an easy target for me, too, but there are reasons for that – watch helpless as it brags and blares its way into your living room, fingering your mother's empathy buttons like an outrageously manipulative stepfather. He'll make her cry then hug her better, all the while firing smirks at you over her shoulder and making wanker signs into his mouth. He's horrible. If he is 'the' world, I want no part of it. I will retreat from it – and where better to retreat to than the bedroom?

Bedrooms are miraculous places, for sticky, age-old reasons, but for newer ones, too. It'd be hard to underestimate the importance of teenage bedrooms (and, in particular, suburban teenage bedrooms) to England's pop history. Michael Bracewell's *England Is Mine* certainly doesn't – an exhilarated, exhilarating inspection of Albion's pop DNA, it follows conspicuous, flown 'suburban dandies' back from city-staged *Bildungsroman* to provincial boredom. Is there anywhere more private than a suburban teenager's bedroom? In such solitude, the mind is permitted to drift . . . ideas and identity are given the time they need to blossom and, when ready, are invariably watered in the dreary hail of small-town heckles. Suburbia, with its relentless repetition and constant, tense promise of the city, is a vast and unwitting incubator of escapist 'a' worlds. Only now the flown 'suburban dandies' of Bracewell's book are few – his and England's would-be pop heroes no longer have to flee to cities in order to conquer them. They don't even have to leave their bedrooms.

....

Joy Orbison is the recording and DJ alias of twenty-two-year-old Peter O'Grady. Peter grew up and still lives somewhere he describes as 'suburban and repetitive but close enough to London that you always feel there's a way out'. His music displays all the benefits of provincial distance and tension – a lean confluence of feminine house warmth, skipping UK garage, junglist delirium and dubstep lumber, it's no surprise to learn that O'Grady's ears have been wed to London's pirate radio transmissions for the best part of a decade. In July, he told *Pitchfork's* Martin Clark about the hours spent 'in my room moving the aerial around trying to catch Flex and Kool FM' and you could see the eternal suburban fourteen-year-old almost immediately, arm in air, waving foil-wrapped antenna, stretching out like a demented sunflower towards urban clamour.

'London was always the obvious place to aim for,' he explains, 'even when I was a kid visiting my uncle's studio I recognised that it all revolved around London, there's no other place that I've really made an effort to play in.'

After years of home-honing with Joy Orbison O'Grady emerged from his bedroom with arguably the most realised and live example yet of a sound that's at the forefront of today's (tonight's?) London club scene – a sound fellow DJ Alex Bok Bok locates 'occupying the uncharted territory between Dubstep, Garage and House' and that's 'deep, epic yet banging, morose'. Tracks like 'Smother', 'Wet Look' and the ecstatic, valiant 'Hyph Mngo' – all terse yearners, stamped with synth overtures and diva stutter – undoubtedly represent a continuation of something pre-existent, evolving from the decades-muddled blood of UK bassland. With allegiance pledged to pirate radio and 'the second-hand culture' of 'raving, record shops and . . . Drum and Bass tape packs', it would seem O'Grady's ripe for adoption into Simon Reynolds's 'hardcore continuum' – the lineage in

British dance that, according to Reynolds, still thrives today twenty years after it was conceived in eve-of-the-'90s rave.

But Reynolds isn't convinced, particularly by 'Hyph Mngo': 'To say it is to sound like you're spluttering in laughter,' according to a recent post on his Blissblog. Damned with the faintest of praise, Joy Orbison's coup de grace is reduced to nothing more than a 'perfectly pleasant little tune' that 'gestures at musicality without actually delivering it', a 'dull' example of 'moist 'n' milky minimalism . . . the minimal of undeveloped, not fully realised, didn't finish the job . . .' Instead Reynolds plumps for the 'maximalist direction in post-Wobble' that leads to tunes like Coki's 'Spongebob', a workout in thugstep cliché that womps along tediously doling out nuggies and farting the word 'generic' into air stale with dead sweat reek and 'roid fumes. 'Spongebob' is hideously developed, pumped and solid to the extent that it leaves no room for any response other than a moody grimace and a flailing fist. Its empathy is aggressive and imposed upon you – the smirking offspring of 'the' world's horrible stepfather.

If that kind of generic thugstep has any value, it's that it's such a potent deterrent. The most vital new UK dance – that 'occupying the uncharted territory between Dubstep, Garage and House' – moves and mutates so fast that no one's had a chance to pin it down and stamp a name on it yet, creating a paradox, whereby the faster it accelerates away from the Dubstep scene it sprang from the longer it seems destined to operate under the Dubstep banner. Go to a party and tell five people, when the inevitable question comes, that you listen to 'Dubstep' – you'll be greeted with at least three screwed-up noses that have taken the word to mean the style in its most notorious form: that generic thugstep meted out by the likes of Coki, Rusko and Caspa that only seems to make sense to moshing males with a heavy sadness in their loins. But in erecting their barrier of semi-erect men, those knucklehead rhythms – as well as the 'Dubstep' label itself – seem for now to be unwitting bouncers for the moving, mutant, most vital strain they share a name with; keeping (post-)Dubstep collisions with producers like Joy swift, rare, hidden and confusing, 'a' world to escape into rather than 'the' tedious world you're escaping from.

There's a need to keep things moving, essentially.

One of the key tenets of Reynolds's hardcore continuum is that it's UK. It's a mutant torn away and separate in rave's break from the Europhilic US dance styles of house and techno that had dominated previously, establishing a club community here, on British turf, that birthed and still houses the 'second-hand culture' passed on to O'Grady and countless others (in Peter's case by older brothers and sisters). Pirate radio, record shops, plants that'll cut and press dubplates, labels that'll put them out, promoters that'll put you on and the clubs they'll put you on in comprise a kind of cottage industry that sustains and is in turn sustained by those dancers, DJs, MCs and producers devoted to UK dance music. It seems a tacitly 'by us, for us' arrangement, made insular by the lack or inconvenience of outside options. While that intimate relationship endures, it'd be hard to argue that UK dance culture still suffers for a lack of outside options – the internet has, for example, made it possible to stream 'pirate' radio and to listen to and buy records from anywhere in the world, all without leaving one's bedroom. 'Hyph Mngo' is drenched heavy in US house and will be pressed in Berlin.

There's been much hype about what the internet's done for music, but little has been written on what the internet's done to it. Pair it up with cheaper home production and recording equipment – as well as a planet's record collection on tap – and the internet isn't just keeping suburban dandies from the cities they once seemed destined for, it's luring those that live already amid the sprawl back to the immersive solitude of the bedroom, a place for minds to drift, dream and plot, bubbles of teenage suburbia quietly annexing metropolitan soil. And within those bubbles, away from the rush and fad and social pressure of the city, burgeon new 'a' worlds.

Holed up with only their own minds and web-bound gabble for company, musicians, producers, DJs are liable to come untethered from communities and scenes they'd otherwise find themselves answering to. Codes and conceptions of 'the done thing' become more lax – you can hear that in the 'nuum transgressions of Joy Orbison's music and in the off-the-map sorties of others into that much-disputed zone between Dubstep, house and garage. Producers like Sully, whose yet-to-be-released 'In Some Pattern' is slippery and skew-whiff UKG that occasionally sighs ecstatic house, or Floating Points, whose 'J&W Beat' finds garage out later than late night, with red eyes and hands clutching after-party vinyl – Theo Parrish, Flying Lotus, Sun Ra. Same goes for the staccato, strobe-lit SND-isms of Untold, the black cab despair that haunts Pangaea, Pearson Sound's dilapidated Funky House and the tracklists of Ben UFO's DJ sets – you can see the jump-off points from what came before, but the thing this latest crop share is that they're all out there on their own, having taken a leap beyond the reach of scene, community or genre. It's a scene of *auteurs*, almost – no one's trying to rip anyone else off or do what someone else has done, only better, louder and faster. There are no variations on a theme or sacrifices made to UK clubland, 'the' world you'd expect this music to eventually inhabit.

Instead you have, if not absolute radio silence, then a dissolution into something more personal and private, music that exists to enchant the imagination, curiosity and initiative latent in its makers' skulls rather than to seek the loyalty of any community. If people ever decide to talk about what the internet has done to music, rather than fret incessantly over digital marketing opps and unshifted units and all that other shit that makes me want to crush my vomited heart in my hand, they'll come to arrive at the same irony I have: that all those telephone wires and router cables are working to bless music with the means to exist isolated in 'a' world of its own, rather than toil and loiter bored in 'the' one of hoary social mores and obnoxious mob empathy. It's not just post dubstep – the sweep of bedroom dissolution is as evident in Joy Orbison's remote welding of Chicago house to London bass as it is in the agoraphobic lo-fi of Blank Dogs; Zomby's feverish re-animation of himself as eerily undead as the lonely croon of Jens Lekman, swung rat without pack. At the moment music feels like it doesn't need genre, particularly – instead it'll give you still-twitching blocks of its own raw brain or heart or rib as intimate, undiluted sound, full of colour, either pre- or post-*mores*, but definitely without them, definitely post-generic. We've had *auteurs* before, that much is a given – but so many, so dominant of new music, all at the same time? It feels like the start of a severing of ties. It doesn't give you what you want, but it often gives you things you never even knew you wanted, things like chrome jet hearts (Zomby again). And its empathy with the work of post-generic like minds is found in a mutual desire to endure, first and foremost, within the reclaimed sanctity of 'a' bedroom, skull and, by extension, universe of its own.

....

You enter SALEM's bedroom at your own risk. Heather says she 'used to fuck this guy who was a high member of the Church of Satan'. From

Kev Kharas

their skull comes a track called 'Skullcrush'. Their universe – one oppressed by codeined lethargy, permanent kohl cover and synths in reverse – is a heavy one.

'I think it's the same feeling we're all trying to bring out, but we do it in different ways,' explains Jack Donoghue, when asked what it is that he, John Holland and Heather Marlot are trying to communicate.

Can you put words to that 'same feeling', Jack?

'Nah . . . I think there's a certain bleakness and, uh . . . like disappointment and acceptance and sad . . .'

He trails off. An acceptance of sadness?

'Like . . . accepting that we're still alive so we're gonna make music instead of just saying "peace out" . . .'

Peace out? Is that the only alternative?

'I don't know . . . I guess there's a lot of alternatives but not making music and not doing things would be the alternative. To not get up.'

You realise what a bind that'd be when Jack says he only sleeps for an average of between two and two and a half hours every night. For the duration of the interview he seems only half-there – caught between waking and dreaming, as if permanently ensnared by sleep paralysis. SALEM's music is just as physically affecting – it's some of the most physically affecting music I've ever heard, I think; beats Chopped and Screwed into an alien, upsetting moonshine of futility, remorse, wonder, torpor and just unbearable fucking sadness.

'I don't feel obligated to be alive,' Donoghue drawls. 'So I really just hate when I don't feel anything. That's a horrible feeling. So I don't want to feel just "inspired" or "sad" or "happy", I really wanna be feeling like I'm experiencing and actually doing something and not just fucking numb.'

The other thing you ought to know about SALEM's music is that when Heather sings it's every bit as as pretty as it is sad . . . unbearably so. Of course it is. The self-imposed sleep-deprivation, the codeine, the dubious statements goading religious sects, the kohl-eyed hip-hop tremor . . . it's a collusive chaos the three of them conjure to elude 'the' world and its lame, prefab emotional sets. SALEM want to slip through the gaps. They don't wanna feel 'just "inspired" or "sad" or "happy".' It's never as neat as that, those words ultimately just inadequate labels for vague glowing feelings in the gut or a millennia-long ache behind the eyes, arcane signals that come groaning from the snatches of primordial gloop still latent and despotic at human core. The gloop isn't solid nor is it reliable. It flounders dumbly in an ambiguous dark somewhere between balls and brain but SALEM are intent on fumbling after it, olms glimmering and glowering in the dim murk where it's hardest to tell if they're fucking or fighting.

'If someone tells you they love you,' Jack continues, 'whatever that means to them doesn't necessarily mean the same thing to you. Or me saying "I'm sad" . . . doesn't have to mean the same thing [to you]. Some people have said they're really sad to me and I see them laughing and having way more fun than I could if I was sad. I dunno . . .'

SALEM's crusade to exist in a penetrated world beyond the shield of easy labels is a trait common to post-generic music. It's that desire to strip everything back – received opinion, unquestioned practice – and communicate itself in elementals that moves it beyond genre. In the case of Bristolian producers Joker, Guido and Gemmy that elemental is colour and their favourite colour is purple. Hence Bristol's 'purple sound'.

'It's not a genre, but purple is the colour we all get along with,' Joker told the *Guardian* in June, before dismissing the idea that he 'suffers' from synaesthesia, the disassociative brain condition that pours colour into the ears of its hosts and plays melodies upon their tongues.

'I can hear a sound and write a colour down,' he continued. 'My friend was playing me a tune the other day, and I'm like, "Your bass line sounds kind of orange."'

Listen to the totemic 'Purple City', a track slung down into the earth by Joker and fellow Bristolian Ginz earlier this year, or to Gemmy's slathering 'Purple Moon' and you'll start seeing what they see: G-Funk's dub fantasies come dripping from the dark with warm daubs of colour, hung-tongued bass lines that slobber purple all over the side of your face.

Teengirl Fantasy's music is just as colour-drenched and seems to emerge from a similar dark, but the shades and the inspirations aren't as blatant as purple, G-Funk-sloppy dubstep. Instead, Ohio-based pair Logan Takahashi and Nick Weiss sap colour from house, early US garage and Kosmische then sever ties; scenes, codes, guidelines, genre and community pressure all dissolving in an Impressionistic wash of gauzy synths and ecstatic afterglow.

'I've often associated colour schemes with our songs,' explains Weiss. 'We both agree "Portofino" is obviously blue with black edges and "Now That's What I Call Volume 2" emanates a softer pink or orange.'

The colour world Teengirl Fantasy immerse themselves in is one that seems to melt forever from one escape route into the next, fluidly and constantly moving between vaguely remembered dreams, gut ache and flashback giddiness. It's 'a' world that seems destined never to escape from itself – club music you wouldn't play in a club, dance music you can't really dance to. Weiss seals his own post-generic fate with talk of early internet web host Angelfire as 'a great place; free, unpretentious . . . almost as open and welcoming as somewhere like [cherished New York nightclub] the Paradise Garage was'. Tracks like 'Hollywood Hills', with its blurred retreat into internal headspace and the rhetorical, telltale refrain 'have you ever been | alone in a room?' seem to betray the fact that Weiss and Takahashi's experiences with Angelfire and the Paradise Garage hail from the same time – around the turn of the last century, to be exact, at least a decade after the Paradise Garage closed its doors to 'the' world. Teengirl Fantasy's image of the nightclub seems that of a pair of trespassers, cobbled together from personal reflections on the records that span there, as well as the archives of Wikipedia and YouTube documentaries – truly 'second-hand', stolen, even.

But it's a shared stolen nostalgia, one that's articulate of itself and that others obviously connect with – see that for yourself in the temporarily flushed, flickering film Baltimore video artist Mark Brown made for Teengirl's stellar Telepathe remix (tinyurl.com/teengirlfantasy). A similar demonstrative and engaged empathy could be found until recently at SALEM's MySpace page. It's lighter now, but used to routinely crash my laptop with its absurd weight; the music it offered up apparently so potent in its evocation of SALEM's 'a' world that it compelled all within earshot to return with grotesque offerings of their own. Cue a comments wall plastered with absurd, disturbing images of masturbated cocks with eyes, children bearing arms, wolves somehow dead and stranded on overhead phone lines.

Post-generic empathy – a new way to dance? On walls? To architecture? At least it's not imposed. The understanding's coming from both directions, interactive, non-spectacular; a head-on collision rather than a crash. And if answering art with art or sound with sound is the new way to relate, then Andrew 'FaltyDL' Lustman can take UK garage from London just as Peter O'Grady has taken Chicago house from America.

Wait, this is confusing . . . FaltyDL?

'It's a strange name, I know, but it's been mine since I was 12, before before,' explains the New Yorker, who grew up on Jungle and has a surname I'm not sure I'd be so keen to shed. 'I feel like I can hide behind it a little . . . regardless of whether or not you know my real name or face or home address I can create this sound that I've been hearing in my head forever.

'I'm working on this harmony that has been in my head literally since I was fifteen,' he says. 'Falty will eventually bring it out.'

He says all his producing goes on 'late at night, in isolation' but both debut album *Love Is a Liability* and the new *Bravery* EP seem conjured from thin, dark, fresh, urban air. Tracks like the astonishing 'To New York' breathe in a way that seems buzzed and unconfined: the repartee between burbling synths, garage skip and wordless, sampled vocals like a city talking to itself when human noise stops, a banter of ricocheting echoes and mysterious, mechanical throbs emerging from midnight stairwells and subways.

I've no idea what that harmony in Lustman's head may sound like, but I'd guess it was originally found wandering the streets late at night. What's just as important is his belief in the bedroom as a place to eke that harmony out – his belief in the bedroom as a place to believe in, if you will. By introducing one hidden zone to the other, he confirms the reality of both and multiplies the possibilities of each, establishing between street and bedroom a skewed, liquid empathy. That's where FaltyDL's music exists – hanging over the city like a spell at the exact moment of swift and rare collision.

What are you looking to collide with, Falty?

'Just the groove, the rhythm in your step. You, yours! I watch you people all day long out my window.'

Through that window comes hip hop, soul, psychedelia and, most importantly, fresh air for Lustman to breathe in; blood sending it up to brain where it can be warped into something private and profound, and that's the overriding desire, I suppose – to create something 'a' and 'own'. But we can't just stay lonely in bedrooms forever. That would just be unbearably sad.

'I'd say all of us are pretty disinterested in things as they are,' muses SALEM's Jack Donoghue. 'Things just being totally straightforward. It's like, creating interest in things for ourselves, do you know what I mean? Even if we're aware of it, we'll have to make things even more beautiful than they are to even want to participate at all.

'All of our bedrooms are really aesthetic and beautiful,' he says, before laughing nervously. 'You know what I mean?'

ROB CHAPMAN
In Conversation with John Walters

In 1987 I interviewed John Peel's producer John Walters for a book I was writing about pirate radio and the early days of Radio One. The man could talk for England and filled two C90s for me while barely drawing breath. His career took in spells as an art student and art teacher, trombone player with the Alan Price Set and twenty years, as he himself put it, as 'John Peel's representative on Earth'. His death in July 2000 was as unexpected and as untimely as that of Peel four years later. To those of us who got nine-tenths of our musical education from them, their absence is still keenly felt. Listen to the output of most generic radio today and it's as if Peel and Walters never existed. There is already a generation of kids in their late teens to whom they are just dim and distant memories handed down from older brothers and sisters. Pretty soon their names will be as remote as those of legendary radio figures like Uncle Mac and Archie Brough. (Ask yer Grandad!)

Peel once famously said that Walters was 'sustained in his retirement by his determination to deliver the eulogy at my funeral. This eulogy will be unbelievably long and more about Walters than about me!' That statement has an unbearable poignancy about it now. What follows is barely a tenth of what Walters bellowed at me that day in his cramped shit-pit of an office in Egton House, former home of 'Wonderful' Radio One.

I Thought I'd Get a Pamphlet

I was playing with Alan Price at the time. Doing a session in Maida Vale for one of these programmes called 'Swing into Summer' or something like that, those old Light Programme shows which had a lot of live guests. It was all very simple stuff. All the brass round one mike. And the balance was like, 'Move the tenor sax in six inches. Stop there. Now play the same thing again.' There was no mixing, or anything like that. Everybody was packing up to go round the pub, and I was standing watching and they were all messing around behind the glass and having a bit of a laugh and a coffee and, frankly, I remember looking at it and I thought, 'Actually those people behind the glass seem to be doing approximately nothing, y'know.' And I thought, 'There must be jobs in here, ways of earning a living.'

In the band we never met other people. We never met, say, the Who. They were always working somewhere else. So if you were in Manchester you didn't see the groups who were in Leeds and so on. Everybody thought you did, but you didn't. But I thought if you could work at the BBC, then you're in show business all the time. And so I simply wrote to the BBC. The strange thing was, I thought I'd get a pamphlet. I mean I wrote, really, for a pamphlet and got a job.

They said, 'Come in and see us.' I'd got the 'gift of the gab'. I'm reasonably articulate, decidedly verbose. They said, 'Hello, come in. So you're with one of these bands. . .' We were in the charts at the time so they were pretty impressed. I think they'd seen the Beatles' films and thought it was like that, which really it wasn't at all. It wasn't even like that for the Beatles. And so I babbled away and told a few jokes and they were clearly wildly impressed. 'Look, we'll be in touch,' they said. 'We've got something coming up.'

Radio One. It Was All the Same: Groovy

I didn't know what Radio One was. Nobody knew what it was at the time. But obviously it was being worked out. From having an occasional pop music radio programme, they'd suddenly got 'em all day and they needed something like twelve or fourteen new producers as far as I remember. We did a show called *Scene and Heard* with Johnny Moran. A pacey magazine programme. Rather embarrassing when you hear it now. Instead of letting it breathe and be fairly natural, it was one of these 'Hey, there! Hi! Ho!' sorta things. It didn't matter whether it was Paul McCartney or Engelbert Humperdinck. It was all the same: groovy!

Jimmy Savile – It Was the Nearest I Got to National Service

I think he'd done Radio Luxembourg and BBC Television, but never BBC radio. I think they picked me because I was young and inexperienced. I was naive and new to the business. They didn't want to pitch Jim as a strong figure against one of their more experienced guys with these preconceptions about the role of the disc jockey and producer, and how things worked and who made the decisions. 'Cos they knew Jim was gonna be his own man and not easy to cope with. They said, 'Well, this is what we're gonna do. Jimmy going round the country. We'll give him a Uher [tape recorder] and he'll meet people and talk and we'll call it *The Savile Scene.*' And I said, 'Oh, come on. It must be better than *The Savile Scene*. What a boring name.' So I said, 'Well why not, obviously like *Gulliver's Travels*, make it *Savile's Travels.*' It was just a little pun and, God, they went mad. It was one of those wonderful moments – Jimmy immediately went, 'Oh!', as if he'd discovered me. And he just got a cigar out and went 'Oh – there we are – have I got the right man here? I have picked the right boy – doctor, doctor, I told you – I said "I can pick 'em".' And I thought, 'I don't even know you.'

I got the impression that I was then his protégé, the brains behind certain things. He'd get on the road and I'd be in the lab working. I thoroughly enjoyed it, but it was hard work. I used to wake up from a dream that a train was pulling out with Savile waving on it and I was running down the platform, y'know what I mean? I couldn't keep up with the bastard at all and couldn't make him do things. Instead of bringing me what I wanted, which was about twenty-five to thirty minutes of speech to edit down to eighteen, he'd bring me about twelve to eighteen to edit up! You had to pad it out. And on occasion we had to fake it. I had to get, like, a fucking record of a beach, put it on with seagull effects and Jimmy was 'clearly with somebody', let's put it like that. 'Oh, isn't it great, you and me lying here on the beach? Can you see that gull up there?' and I'd think 'God, this is terrible!' But the sheer cynicism of it is why it's so wonderful. Savile's always been like that, I've always had great respect for him because he is sort of 'the enemy' to anybody who's had any ideals about what can be done. And yet he does it so well. He's like somebody who plays against your team, but you've got to admire it. It's like watching Maradona or something. It was the nearest I got to National Service, 'cos you went in a boy, came out a man. I'd like to have worked more with him over the years. He was as streetwise as they come.

Peel – I Didn't Need All That Hippie Shit

At the time I regarded Peel as a rather jokey figure, a rather irritating figure – all the hippie shit, y'know – all the shoulder-length hair and love and peace and 'Hey man, let's do it for free!' And all that bollocks. I didn't want to do it 'cos I hated that hippie shit, and Peel knew this. I remember that classic interview, when Donovan was being launched as 'The British Dylan', the first interview in *Melody Maker*, where he said, 'Oh, sometimes I just go down to Brighton and just look at the sea. And I think what's it all about?' [Laughs] What kind of answer is that? I mean once you've done four years' art school and been a teacher, and played with jazz musicians, I didn't need all that 'hippie shit', y'know what I mean? And I didn't like it, and the 'Hey man, we don't pay the roadies, we trade in smiles', kinda thing.

The very first thing we found we had in common was W. C. Fields. He knew I was not like him at all – I was a groovy kind of ex-soul man and a man down the pub. He was none of these things. But I took him out to lunch, to try and get to know him, and we had a laugh and I thought, 'Well we're getting on better than I thought.' 'Cos I remember going round to my secretary at the time, and I said, 'You'll never guess what's happened.' I'd just had this call. I said, 'I'm coming off the programme we're doing and d'you know what I'm gonna do?' 'No, what?' I said, 'John Peel, *Top Gear*.' He said, 'Oh, no!' And I remember it was one of the first times I ordered spirits. A vodka and tonic, 'cos I thought, I really did, 'God, all that moaning and hippie nonsense, and long records and hairy people.' But again, I had to make the best of it. We were getting on a bit better by the end of lunch. We'd had a giggle, and I just said to Peel, 'Actually I'm going up towards Regent's Park, 'cos I want to see the W. C. Fields Festival.' 'Oh,' he said, 'I didn't know. I love W. C. Fields.' So I said, 'Well, why don't you come in with me – it's only a couple of hours. Just two or three old shorts.' And we went in there and we pissed ourselves watching this thing. We came out thinking, 'That was really good.' And suddenly we realised that in our own different ways, we had certain things in common, a certain outsidery and slightly cynically humorous view of reality.

I found that things like Marc Bolan, whom I'd seen as a joke – once I got in the studio with him was an amiable little chap. But also the work was a lot better than I'd thought. And although it's not the kind of noise I wanted to hear, I could see that there was some ability with him. He was a more creative bloke than I'd thought. And I suppose we both united on the bluesier, jazzier end of things, y'know the Cream, Fleetwood Mac. He was on a more fey 'Tinkle, tinkle little star' trip, bloody strato-spherics, Floyd and so on, which I thought, 'Oh, no.' And all this well-meaning smiles and stoned nonsense was no good to me. But the harder end we both liked. It wasn't until later that we got into more or less liking a lot of the same stuff.

Sounds of the Seventies. Rag-Eye Music

It was quite a 'culty' thing, that post Woodstock era. They [the BBC] didn't realise that it was actually more than was being played on the Peel show. There was a lot of it about – the record companies were all looking round for tame hippies, bringing out their own labels. Peel had his 'Dandelion' label, and there were all these things like RCA's 'Neon' and CBS had its own, with all these bands like 'It's a Beautiful Day' – those sorts of bands. The hippie sort of 'West Coasty' kind of thing, and they packaged them all together and issued them under a special logo. And EMI had Harvest. Decca had an awful label. So they all had something along those lines, which apparently are very collectable now. Wish I'd kept them, 'cos they were practically all awful and totally unmemorable, as far as I can remember. Except, of course, I can't remember them now. Anyway, all this was going off and I think the Beeb suddenly thought, 'Hang on, there's a lot more happening than just on this one *Top Gear* show,' which was Saturday afternoons. And so they suddenly decided to start *Sounds of The Seventies*. I remember Douglas Muggeridge, who was then controller of Radio One, announcing it at the time. 'We're going to have all these different aspects of the progressive rock scene. We'll be having a folk rock evening, and one for progressive rock, folk and jazz.' And another one – I'll always remember how he pronounced it – he said, 'and one for 'em . . .' groping a bit, y'know, 'progressive rag-eye.' Which gave the whole game away, because there wasn't really any progressive reggae: obviously reggae did progress in a sense, into the dub thing, which was a big step. But on the other hand, by the nature of the beast and the nature of the people who did it, it wasn't a modernist movement. But it's the fact that he pronounced it 'rag-eye', having only read the word and been to public school, like sort of 'reg-eye, reg-ore and reg-est, magester, magestorum' – y'know, it sounded like a school motto.

In the Ghetto – It's an Instinct They've Got
It was decided to open up the very late area, ten o'clock onwards. And they put Peel in there, ten till midnight. And it did segregate him – it was a sort of ghetto situation – because real Radio 1 stopped at 7.30 in those days. And then Radio 1 and 2 combined, then Peel came up with the weirdo stuff. And we rather felt they've given us that to make it quite clear that there is a normal Radio 1 and we have to [laughing] accommodate these other people as well. So we went five nights a week doing that.

At the time we used to think, 'Why aren't they playing some of these during the day?' You didn't want the Soft Machine on *Housewive's Choice* as I always used to say, 'cos it wasn't suitable. But Fairport Convention and people like that were quite pleasant to listen to. But that segregation still happens today, I mean I've walked through an office and somebody's been playing the Cocteau Twins – which I find to be rather erring on the side of 'beautiful music', in the sense that it's a perfectly pleasant, romantic kind of sound, swirling and whirling away there – and had secretaries stop typing and say, 'Can you turn this down?' And you think, 'But you're listening to other things that are really hard to listen to, that are in the charts'. But they have a funny switch-off point. I remember walking through an office upstairs when Billy Bragg was in the charts with 'Between the Wars'. And one of the daytime shows put it on and one of the girls, who's very much the kind of 'Oh, Stevie Wright, he's a laugh' [sort was] typing away there. And Billy's record came on. Just his little guitar and wistful voice. And she stopped typing and said, 'Can we turn this rubbish off?! What IS this row?' And I thought, 'This is really odd, 'cos my mind doesn't work like that.' I don't particularly want to hear Billy singing 'Between the War' or Mel and Kim but I can't see that one's allowed and one's not. But you realise that you're up against something a bit bigger. It's an instinct they've got. It's like walking into the disco with the wrong collar, y'know? They know straight away.

At this Point Peel Walks into the Office.
Peel: Walters obviously will be telling you that he hasn't got any time, he can't talk just now, and hasn't stopped speaking for half an hour.
Walters (studiously failing to rise to the bait): He was asking the age-old thing – 'Wouldn't it have been better not to have had like the Peel area and all those Rock areas and Reggae areas as separate ghettos, but have it mixed in during the day.'

Rob Chapman

Peel (impassioned to the point of angry incoherence): Given things like a Smiths' record, it's in the charts and is programmed and then they'll just drop it. I went and checked the paperwork. In the week that the Smiths' new record went into the charts at number thirteen, that week it was played three times on daytime programmes, whereas a Five Star record that went in at eighteen was played thirty-something times.

Punk – Short, Sharp Sets which Sweep You Away on a Tide of a Racket

I'd experienced it more than he had. 'Cos he was five nights a week by that time and couldn't go out to gigs. I'd seen Siouxsie, he hadn't – and I'd seen The Fall, he hadn't – and so on. So I'd come back and report to him and I was as enthusiastic about what was happening as he was for the first time ever.

I liked going and listening to the punk bands, mainly because they went on about the right amount of time, which was about a minute or two minutes or something like that. There are very few things in life that are worth going on for more than about two minutes. Ask my wife! I mean, I went down to see the mods at the time, not because I wanted to listen to mod music. I went to see all those bands and kids climbing on the stage, shouting 'We are the mods' and tramping off through Leicester Square, waving things over their head. I loved the idea of it. And I liked the idea that it was still going, so I went to see the punks. I went to see Test Department, not to tap my feet, y'know what I mean? I like to see what's happening. All the Stupids and people I've been to lately, when they find a haven and places start to put on those sort of bands regularly, I'm in there. They do short, sharp sets which sweep you away on a tide of a racket, banging and shouting. And I enjoy it – I don't wanna listen to it at home. I don't want to have people say, 'Let me pour you a dry, white wine and put on *Jesus Meets The Stupids*.' 'Cos at forty-eight, same as Peel, I don't think he puts anything on for pleasure when people come round to the house. And neither do I much – except probably old jazzy things, once you've had a couple of drinks, or old rock things, or early '60s. Girl groups, Shangri-Las, Little Richard – that sort of thing.

The Two Johns – Jack Spratt and his Wife

He sees somebody do something quite barmy, with a great air of confidence, like Wild Man Fisher or Viv Stanshall, and there's a great admiration on his part, of 'Gosh, I wish I could've done that.' He'd love to be able to be an unhinged voice and a Wild Man Fisher himself in many ways. And when he's had a couple of drinks he will get a lot wilder. But basically he would like to do that and appreciates it. He's got a feel for the offbeat and the quirky, the wildly unhinged.

My background was different to Peel's when I got into the music business. I was more into musicianship, something I don't have much time for these days. My background was as a player and a critic and lecturer in jazz and so on. Therefore, you were brought up with the kind of musicianship then, which I don't respect today. Every time I go to Ronnie Scott's now I think, 'This is incredibly boring.' There's always a support. Often it's quite good – it may be Ronnie's band. I mean they play well – the musicianship's there. But as soon as they've done the chorus, there's a piano solo – then immediately there's a trumpet solo – two choruses – then there's two choruses on the tenor. And then there's usually a chase between let's say, the tenor and the trumpet, the drummer, and then they all go out on the chorus. And it's the same for every, damn number. These days I've got past musicianship.

Peel never had any education of a serious nature, but he has this gift, which is a most strange gift, of being a kinda grown-up child who is excited – genuinely – by music. The other day our secretary phoned me. Peel was coming in; she got all his pile of records which you can see around you – that the record companies leave in envelopes and cardboard and stuff. And to help him she opened them all, and just stacked them here to save him the trouble. He just flicked through them and he said, 'Aw – don't tell her,' – 'cos he didn't want to offend her – but he said, 'Try and stop her opening them all. I like opening them.' You see what I mean? It's that aspect. I do open them, but I don't like opening them much. I'd just rather flick through 'em and say, 'Well, that's all right, that's not.' But he's got the real delight in it. I am more detached. So it's 'Jack Spratt and his wife' a bit.

I remember talking to a senior chap here some time ago. They were talking about looking for a disc jockey, not to replace Peel but they've always had difficulties in the pre-Peel spot. The senior man said, 'We had a really good tape from somebody in local regional radio. A guy who's very well thought of in his catchment area. And we thought, "This is the man. Come down and talk to us and let's see how you get on." He came down.' And he said, 'He had a grubby T-shirt, sneakers and jeans, and – totally unsuitable to fulfil the role of a Radio One disc jockey. Didn't he understand? We couldn't possibly consider him.' I said, 'You mean the tape was all right, but his image was not?' 'No,'

he said. 'I mean imagine – he couldn't have done *Top of the Pops* or a quiz show.' They suddenly thought, 'This man is not gonna look good standing beside the goodie wagon and saying, "OK, I want somebody to bring me up a pair of knickers!" on the Radio One Roadshow.' And I thought, that is the yardstick. D'you see what I mean? And it goes right back to old, showbiz traditions – the bingo master. And they sort of like it like that. Let's put it like this, if Peel came today, there is absolutely no chance of him being taken on.

But I can't see in the foreseeable future Peel not having a place on Radio One. Even though there are people here who don't like the music he does. That's still the same. You still get it. I heard it the other day. One of the daytime jocks said, 'OK, we're coming up to the news time, just twenty seconds to fill, before the Shakattack record. But don't forget, you can hear Stevie [Wright]. He'll be up with those wacky characters, then it's Bruno. Oh, and Janice Long's special guests are the Alarm and Sisters of Mercy. And then John Peel.' And they never say, 'And he'll be here with . . .' Or occasionally it will be, 'John Peel with . . . his kind of music.' Y'know, kind of, 'We all know what THAT is.' As I said, there is an instinct. They know the enemy. And it's very odd, 'cos we're not really the enemy. Peel never saw it as 'this should replace them'. He just wanted it to be 'there is more to life than the Chart Show'.

PAUL MORLEY
An Awfully Big Adventure
Michael Jackson in the Afterlife

Michael Jackson died in June 2009 from high levels of drugs in his body, including the powerful anaesthetic Propofol, more commonly used on hospital patients before surgery.

Two

I first thought, when I heard the news, how did anyone ever get to be so lonely? And yet, at the same time, the centre of so much attention, as he moved among us, sometimes so fluently, so far inside and outside his own body, using his feet to communicate with us, about the miracle of light, and time, it seemed like he'd flown in from another universe, and landed in such a way that his feet were yet to hit the ground. He visited earth, and never quite connected. This lack of connection was endlessly fascinating, whether represented persuasively through the moves and demands of a sensational entertainer born to amaze, with a voice that soared God-how-high, as clean as if cut with a diamond, or through how his trapped, unstable mortal energy was ruthlessly processed and packaged as pure pleasuring product, or made grotesquely explicit through the alarming ways that his skin turned to paper, his flesh started to leak and his eyelids turned to dust.

Sometimes he moved so nervously, so awkwardly, so damned tentatively, it seemed like he was not human, or at least had once been human, and then became something else, or he was slowly, painfully becoming human, transforming from something alien and removed. Sometimes, as he moved among us, on the way from one sort of peculiar ceremony to another, with a frantically rigid look on his face, it could make you feel sad and confused, he seemed so brave and tragic, it appeared he didn't actually know what to do with his feet, or his hands, or the thoughts, agitated shreds of sensation, that must have been ganging up on him inside his head. His eyes were black holes swallowing, rather than reflecting, light.

By the end of his life he looked like this exotic being from another universe who had once soared among us, possessing a dancing body that could change shape in sudden mid-flight, and then a famous scarred body that changed shape for vain, sick reasons, a pitiful, trapped creature that had finally landed, and met the earth, not with an elegant, cushioned softness, but with a horrible, catastrophic wallop. He crash-landed on to earth, and his body, mind, sanity, vision and memory splintered, and he moved among us like an extravagantly deformed casualty that was both banal and mystifying. We couldn't bear to look at him, this 'it' containing so much devastated promise and so much visible oddness and sadness, and we couldn't take our eyes off him.

Then I thought, I suppose, now I came to

think about it, that I had always heard loneliness in his voice. He was always on his own, and even at the height of his fame, the time when he seemed most alive, and in control of his self and his surroundings, he seemed distant and preoccupied. He moved among us, super present in his songs, extra vivid in his videos, desperate to ensure that the second after we'd heard him, or saw him, we would not forget him. If we forgot him, it would be like he had never existed. If we forgot him, what was the point of living? Who would ever know he'd been alive?

He desperately needed to be desperately needed, and he choreographed an existence dedicated to ensuring he would never be forgotten. He laboured so hard to establish an indelible identity, even if this meant stretching his skin and mind and sanity to such an extent eventually everything would snap. He was so keen on making sure that everyone knew who he was – so that he would feel wanted, and he sang confessional, often furious songs that exposed so much about his paranoia, insecurity, prejudices, distress and anxieties, he revealed so much about his miserable childhood, his sexual bewilderments, his emotional burdens, his eccentric desires, his diseased self-control, his macabre obsessions, his poignant dreams of happiness, his restless sentimental craving for some kind of calming religious certainty, his humiliations, his raging boasts – but he never let anyone get to know him.

Three

'The prosecution paints a disturbing picture, in which moms jockey for status at Neverland by offering up their little boys. Meanwhile, Michael is fickle with his attentions, moving on to a new special friend every year or so. There was Wade, Brett Barnes, the '93 kid. As a local writer suggests to me, 'Michael's like the Matthew McConaughey character in Dazed and Confused *– he gets older, they stay the same age.'*

Four

To be honest, my very first thoughts upon seeing and hearing that Michael Jackson had for certain died, in circumstances that were undeniably and inevitably suspicious to the point of seeming scripted, were professional. I thought about myself.

I thought, what the hell am I going to say, when someone asks, as they surely will, very soon, what my opinion is about Michael Jackson? I didn't think about the sad, broken man who had died in agony inside an anonymous rented Los Angeles mansion apparently located in the centre of a local celebrity-spotting route. Died in monstrously shabby circumstances facing excruciating pressure both from those that loved him and those that hated him.

I didn't instantly consider the real person dealing with the collapse of an empire and the disintegration of a reputation, the ever-accelerating deterioration of his youthful zeal, the wrecked, fastidious individual who must have still existed inside the mauled and massacred body it had become so easy to mock and marvel at. The body that had turned him into a pitiful modern freak show – more manufactured mechanical puzzle than living, breathing, feeling person – that surely made it increasingly difficult to take seriously or at least fully comprehend his once-upon-a-time-actions as motivated showman, guileful, passionate musician, cryptic creative catalyst, surreal businessman and slick, knowing audience manipulator.

I didn't immediately think what the news of his death might have been covering up – the fact that he had been dead for days and now was the time, organised by business, family, television, shady conglomerate, whoever was now in control of the estate, the idea, of Jackson, to reveal the truth. Or the fact he had been dead for years and it had been decided, days before Jackson was due to play a stupid amount of live shows, that it would be more

Paul Morley

commercially shrewd to exploit a dead body, and a sparkling new show-business legend, than risk the possibility that it might be spotted that Jackson had been replaced by a slightly too eager look-a-like or a not quite paper-thin-enough hologram. And then, of course, he might not be really dead at all, and this was some ludicrous trick of the light, some monstrous publicity that would lead to the news a few days later, on the eve of the fifty shows he had been signed up to play in London, that he was still alive. It was, in some way, yet another mask, another cover-up, another way of fooling us into believing what Michael Jackson, whether a person, an insurance scam, a company, a conspiracy, a small island off the coast of Mexico, a slice or two of corruption, a stubborn drain on our emotions, a mere pop singer with ideas above his entertainment station, wanted us to believe.

I thought all this eventually, as you can see, but not in those first moments after I had seen and heard the news.

Five

What is Michael Jackson according to Google #1

Michael Jackson was whipped into shape by his father
Michael Jackson is a freak
Michael Jackson is soooooo sexy
Michael Jackson is #1
Michael Jackson is back
Michael Jackson is a weird motherfucker
Michael Jackson is a father again
Michael Jackson is black????????
Michael Jackson is in 3D
Michael's father performed with The Falcons
Michael Jackson is a dance
Michael Jackson is Joan Crawford's daughter
Michael Jackson is leaving Sony
Michael Jackson is the worlds leading consumer

Michael Jackson is a way of life
Michael's mother is a God fearing Jehovah's witness
Michael Jackson is still a werewolf
Michael Jackson is dedicated to bringing Michael Jackson fans worldwide all the latest and official news surrounding the king of entertainment
Michael Jackson is saying when you're strong and you're good, you're bad
Michael Jackson is beautiful
Michael Jackson turned down a part in *Men In Black*
Michael Jackson's birthday is August 29th
Michael Jackson is the whole business of money and sex mixed up with something primitive and deep
Michael Jackson is confessing to Oprah Winfrey
Michael Jackson is a eunuch
Michael Jackson is jealous of Eminem for being able to play the MTV game the way he'd always wanted to and in tears when he sees Eminem make fun of him
Michael Jackson is innocent why did he pay off the witnesses he makes fantastic music but he should not be above the law
Michael Jackson is pictured at the University of Oxford Union
Michael Jackson is the king of hearts and the king of music
Michael Jackson is alright
Michael Jackson's Smooth Criminal is the seventh single from Michael Jackson's *Bad* album
Michael Jackson is one of a kind
Michael Jackson is only at home on stage
Michael Jackson is a southerner
Michael Jackson is actually a cyborg sent from the 24th century to halt the current trend in music
Michael Jackson owns the bones of the Elephant Man

Michael Jackson is mentally unstable? yes/no

Michael Jackson is more than just an extraordinarily popular singer and wonderfully gifted dancer

Michael Jackson is a hoax

Michael Jackson does not clean his own house

Michael is taking his milk of magnesia

Michael Jackson is saying that he respects the obligation of confidentiality imposed on all of the parties to the 1993 proceedings

Michael Jackson vividly speaks their thoughts and dreams

Michael Jackson needed plastic surgery to restore his appearance after suffering horrible burns filming a Pepsi commercial

Michael Jackson is debatable

Michael Jackson is realising how the debris of the past and present can be salvaged to make up a different identity

Michael Jackson is clinging gingerly to the bobbing raft

Michael Jackson has reached the lying in state stage where it remains to be seen if his remains will be seen

Michael Jackson is saying 'I was a veteran before I was a teenager'

Michael Jackson is poured like ketchup over everything

Michael Jackson was fourteen minutes long with a beginning, middle and end

Michael Jackson and all that shit is ass backwards

Michael Jackson was born in 1958 in Gary, Indiana

Michael Jackson is bewildered at the lengths people will go to portray him so negatively

Michael Jackson is being teased and ridiculed by his father

Six

First of all I couldn't help but wonder – as a journalist and broadcaster, knowing that I would soon receive calls from various parts of the media asking me to comment on radio shows, and TV programmes, and in print – what my position was in terms of his music, his image and reputation, his existence and now the non-existence. The non-existence that would now mean an endless, horribly sincere parade of those randomly appointed broadcasting judges and insiders with a point of view on just how heroic, or perverse, or exceptional, or irrational, or *compos mentis*, or just plain medicated he really was.

Did I have a point of view? I wasn't sure. I just knew that I was about to be asked, and really, whoever would be doing the asking didn't really want any kind of answer other than one that just filled some time and added to the atmosphere an amount of whatever was required to ensure that the atmosphere surrounding this news struck viewers as being given the circumstances more or less correct.

Seven

The defence calls Lisbeth Barnes, the mother of Brett Barnes. She says she let little Brett go on tour with MJ all over the world. She let Brett sleep in Michael's bed the entire time. She's asked why she let Michael sleep with her son. 'Why not? You just feel when you trust someone and when you don't, and I had total trust in him.'

She says she discussed with her husband whether it was appropriate for Brett to sleep with Michael – but their only concern was whether Brett would be imposing on Michael's privacy.

Eight

Within minutes of the announcement that Michael Jackson was dead the news flamed across the web, the news channels, the intimately connected social network, in a blast of gossip, supposition, sympathy and composed shock, the result of perhaps his most ostentatious move as commercial artist since the 1982 NBC TV *Motown Special* moonwalk. (The

Paul Morley

moment when he most perfectly expressed his celebration of America – and the American dream filtered through black history, minds and bodies – in motion.)

It was also apparent that the future of Michael Jackson as item, icon, aura, memory and pure self-referring information was going to be fought over by a toxic combination of those acquisitive hustlers swiftly racing across the headlines and tweeting and mourning and lamenting to claim with best stricken expression put first that they knew him best. The history, reality and commercial future of Michael Jackson were being claimed by those who found themselves in the best and nearest position to take possession.

Obviously, this meant his family, or at least the still-functioning, visibly show business part of it that relied on Michael to give the Jackson name any enduring credentials, because even though to some extent Michael was a has-been, past his best, deeply creepy, all but totally done in by an excess of attention and indifference, the family itself without him was useful for very little apart from appearances on reality TV shows. This once mighty show business family without Michael and everything he brought with him was a little lifeless, verging on the completely empty. Not even Janet, the Jackson sister that had seemed to maintain a certain physical and emotional balance despite being a Jackson, and at times a radiant singing and dancing star, could help maintain the Jackson brand to the extent the family were used to.

It was Michael who helped sustain whatever interest there still was in the Jacksons as a financially viable show business family, however far he exiled himself from the family, however distant he was from that particular faded circus. Michael drew attention to the family, as the member of the Jackson 5 that most confirmed that glorious early promise and maintained possible future interest in any kind of adult version of the group, and as the most visible and obvious sign of what can happen to an immature, innocent young kid inducted, willingly and yet against his will, into show business.

He was the one male member of the original Jackson 5 singers, Michael, Jackie, Tito, Jermaine and Marlon, who ever had a sophisticated appreciation of the pop business. Younger brother Randy arrived later, once the Jacksons had left Motown, signing in 1975 with CBS's Philadelphia International Records. He replaced Jermaine, who was married to Motown chief Berry Gordy's daughter. Randy had more of the multitalented Michael aptitude for wanting to write and play, although Jackie would also write, and occasionally even sing a lead vocal. Michael, though, was the dominant lead voice, and the lead imagination. Michael had an intuitive understanding that to succeed and then succeed even more in a business that was all about the latest craze and distributed craziness, and then to keep on succeeding, even if everyone else thinks you are failing, involved much more than just a mere musical talent.

It involved an economic, psychological, cultural, technological and political reading of just how the myths of fashion and music work, and an ability to invent yourself, and reinvent yourself, in ways that kept pace with changes in expectations and trends. Whatever else Jackson was, he was definitely an analyst, once spectacularly accurate, and gradually a little off the beat, and then finally fairly out of focus, of his own position in the public imagination and how to adjust it so that he always featured prominently in that imagination.

Michael was the most inquisitive and purposeful, he had the sharpest aspirational visions, perhaps because he had been weaned on his father's almost vicious need to improve his family's lowly status and rank, and he had been educated inside the streamlined Motown school, where self-styled black capitalist Berry

Gordy Junior had pulled off the modern miracle of selling joyous, free-thinking black pop music that didn't completely betray its roots in gospel and rhythm and blues. Michael, so the story goes, forced the divorce from the controlling, cautious Gordy, and encouraged the Jacksons' move to another ingenious soul-based commercial corporation, run by the studio designers of the deeply beguiling tough and tender Philly soul sound, Kenny Gamble and Leon Huff. (Gordy and Motown kept the plain but undeniably alluring name Jackson 5. The boys were now, even plainer, and never as fabulously, the Jacksons.)

Michael became fascinated watching Gamble and Huff write and record, closely witnessing how they dealt with musicians and operated the mixing desk. They happily shared with him their experiences and techniques in the recording studio, the way you could experiment inside it as though it were a laboratory, work on different ways to stack and manipulate vocals, and their uplifting soft-hearted themes and messages for songs, the love, unity, harmony, togetherness, would have a strong influence on Michael's more plangent, heart-warming songs.

Working, hard, with Gamble and Huff was a significant part of the education of Michael Jackson, making him appreciate the part the recording studio would play in realising those ambitions he had, inspired by the more adventurous Motown acts, to succeed not just as a performer and interpreter but as a writer and studio technician. This opening up of possibilities and an acquired technical expertise prepared him for his partnership with his greatest showbiz sidekick, Quincy Jones. Meanwhile, the rest of the Jacksons never followed their brother into the pulsating wired-up depths of the recording studio, where true magic could be found, and reproduced, and rewound. That was for others. That Michael wanted to be one of those 'others' who could play with sound, and learn how mental energy could make it on to tape, and use sonic possibilities to enhance and finesse a song, to supply it with an amount of distinctiveness that could emphasise its commercial appeal, was one of the things that separated him from his slacker, weaker brothers.

Disciplined in the arts of self improvement against unruly American odds, never doing enough to please his disciplinarian father, and then never doing enough to please himself, to live up to his own standards of excellence, Michael developed the most ruthless iconoclastic ambitions. He had, even if initially reluctantly, done the kind of homework that the rest of the Jackson boys had evaded. As one of a family group, he was inspired from the very beginning to find ways to stand out, to not just be A Jackson but to be The Jackson, to sustain the factors, even if just that he was the youngest and cutest, the fastest and snazziest, that made people single him out. He could not lose, once he grew up, whatever amazed audiences because he had such stunning natural skill as the kid once he grew up: he had to find ways to recreate that initial sense of shock and delight people felt when they saw him as this supersonic ultra-cute boy.

He studied what it takes not only to transform your compulsions and manias into sound, but also how to match that sorted sound with a combination of dance and appearance and a physical hint of mystery that helped brand you, and make you noticeable. The rest of the Jacksons took for granted that there were those who could do this for you, but Michael approached the formatting and framing of his own personality and charisma with forensic attention to detail. Working out what kind of character you were selling yourself as was as much a part of music as the song and the dance, and inventing this character so that it appealed to the right kind of audience requiring a certain sort of pleasing was both an art and a science. Michael got it. He was very good at it. He was so good at it that it would run away with him – addicted to the giddying process of changing his image, trapped by his own appetite for constantly proving he was ahead of the rest, always the pop pioneer. Constantly establishing his difference, because being different, for better or worse, and therefore free, was everything that he was about.

He worked out that success in the music business involved constructing plausible facades, and that impersonating, or replicating a form of sincerity was actually more useful and durable than simply being sincere. You shouldn't be too nice, but you should seem to be very nice. You should charm the public without it seeming that you were using nefarious means to charm the public, and thrill them without it seeming that you had desperately rehearsed to the point of blankness the exact gestures you would utilise in order to thrill them. There was a fakeness about the whole thing, a fakeness he had a special relationship with, because he was a kid faking being an adult, and he seemed to understand how to achieve and maintain this fakeness and disguise it with fluid levels of sincerity and controlled spontaneity.

He had the ability to motivate colleagues and fans to believe in his talents, ultimately a slippery, agitating skill as a kind of illusionist convincing those around him, and eventually that number ran into the millions, that he was exactly what he pretended to be – the king of pop. Without Jackson's professional and meta-physical agility as he mutated from enchanting teen idol to challenged adult superstar, it was unlikely that the other Jackson boys could have lifted themselves out of the '70s as anything other than a shrivelled nostalgia act acting out their gay, fancy hits with frayed cabaret glibness. As Michael fulfilled his plans, his schemes and dreams, and succeeded in moving out of the disco-daft '70s and into the different, tricky, image-mad '80s as though he himself was in control of the whole new decade, he dragged the rest of the Jacksons with him, even if he didn't particularly want to. He extended their lifespan a few times over, even as he fell from the sky.

As Michael plotted his wild rise, and suffered his wilder fall, as the plot twisted way beyond his control – or was it all part of his plan, if we decide the plan was sort of cosmically conspiratorial and way beyond the realms of reason, the graphic wished for outcome of all this convoluted manipulation of his and his fans' desires? – the Jacksons were always a possible gateway to Michael, and therefore still had a use for a media chasing sensational, squalid or stupid news about Michael and his strange ways. As soon as Michael died, the Jackson show business family received a jolt of much needed energy, and quickly adapted to their new position as grieving keepers of the sacred flame and proud protectors of the imperial image as if in the end this had been their purpose all along – to be the dignified collective widow, the conscientious organisers of the tributes, memorials, souvenirs, films, the controllers of the posthumous career. He'd fought so hard to fight his way out of the family's claustrophobic, blackmailing control and assert his independence that in many ways it had killed him. Now safely dead he returned to the bosom of the Jackson clan, as much a member as he had been in the days when he was the darling showy tiny one in the Jackson 5.

Nine

The defence calls Karlee Barns, who is Brett's older sister. She's the smiliest, bounciest witness yet – a cute young lady with darling dimples and a twinkle in her eye. When asked to describe Neverland (she, too, has been staying at the ranch while she's here in town), she sighs as she says, 'Every time I go back it feels like I'm going home.' This elicits a group 'awwww' from the fans at the back of the courtroom.

Ten

Then there were those that were in place very quickly representing themselves as close friends of Michael, the special few that knew the 'real Michael', who had the virtual key to his heart which they naturally kept close to their heart. The key to revealing that you knew the real Michael involved confidently confiding that the soft, fluttering voice Michael used in promotional public, as part of a much greater distraction, a more serious sleight of hand, was nothing like the way he usually talked. The voice he used when he was playing himself – so there was such a thing! these self-styled close friends said so! – when he was issuing instructions, passing on orders, throwing tantrums, can you imagine even shouting at those that disobeyed him, was a deeper, manlier thing. This was presumably another way the contradictions inherent in Jackson's complex psychological make-up manifested themselves – there were the two, or even three, skin colours, the two, or three, sexual placings, or even no sexual shape at all, a sort of sexual less than zero, a gap in the market so to speak, and there was the way his voice could be gentle and yielding when that suited the occasion, and tough and purposeful when that was required. Both voices were used for protection – the weak, heartbroken, boyish one for those moments in mostly televised public when he felt accused and misunderstood, the strong, self-assured grown man one for when he was sorting out business, closing in on a deal, instructing lawyers, or dealing with some friendly rough and tumble. Maybe he used it when he was ordering room service.

These alternative voices conveniently reflected the two extremes of his music – the flimsy, vulnerable, pity me ballads, and the hard-on macho don't-underestimate-me frantic dance pop anthems. Or perhaps neither voice was the real thing. Both voices used in certain circumstances hid a real voice, another sound altogether, something known perhaps to so few people no-one could honestly describe what it was like, perhaps a voice used when he was in conference with Quincy and his studio team, the normal voice of a normal man of his age and race, one that got used less and less, until Jackson himself lost sight of it, and he was reduced to using the pretend publicity put upon whimper, or the put on and purposefully surprising baritone. Perhaps toward the end the only time anyone would ever hear this voice was when he used it, without even knowing he could still use it, to plead with whatever aide or servant or hanger on or medic happened to be nearby to 'help me.'

Eleven

The Robsons in particular from the defence point of view are extremely strong witnesses. They come off as honest, reasonable people. (If totally blind to the notion that a normal middle-aged man would not sleep with small boys.) Of the three kids who've said they were molested, two won millions of dollars stemming from the accusations. The third is from a family that's notorious for grifting off celebrities.

Twelve

The self-described close friends that crawled into position as soon as the switch was pushed that projected Michael into a golden coffin were a morbid collection of eccentric, excitable self-promoters and professional boasters, all of them ultimately superfans to the extent of being stalkers, all of them echoing the narcissistic stress lines, freaky nervous tics, speech impediments and physical peculiarities of their lord and master. They saw many of their own vulnerabilities exhibited in an exaggerated somehow comforting form in the way Jackson dealt with the outside world.

The fired-up freak friends leapt into action as though they had long been preparing for this moment, the moment when they could become apostles of the faith, spread the word, and gratefully draw in some of the glow and power of their mentor, never letting anyone forget that they understood him, supported him, believed in him, loved him. Their job was to protect the memory of Jackson from the damaging, heretic assaults of the suspicious, cynical and ignorant. They faithfully built the halo, and set it into position, so that they could feel secure and holy under its dazzling light.

Perhaps they had been specially selected by Michael all along, as the right kind of insistent, thick-skinned, voluble and undoubting persuader/defenders whose shrill, convinced praise could cut through messy callous media noise and sustain the crackpot, faith-healing edge of Jackson – a long way from the Jackson and Jones team that produced entrancing and relatively radical middle-of-the-road psycho-pop drama – that ultimately had proved the major perpetuating element in the Jackson brand.

The self-important illusionist Uri Geller, the quasi-crazy preacher and activist Al Sharpton, the cynically self-mocking celebrity loon David Gest, all of them with skin, hair and tone clearly derived from the face and fakery of their idol, breathlessly delivered their scripts and well-rehearsed anecdotes. It wasn't clear whether they had last met their master in the past few months, years, decades, how often they were actually in Jackson's company, what they ever talked about: such details were necessarily kept secret in case they gave the game away. You got the feeling that even if they had only ever met Jackson once or twice for a few minutes this promoted them to the standing of friend and confidante – they had got close enough to have made it as an insider, one whose anecdotes

about Jackson could marvellously feature the luminous man himself, who, naturally, revealed who he really was only to them.

These supporters could be seen as extreme examples of the kind of loyal, credulous fan that Jackson attracted in what we could describe as his declining years, the controversial years, the rotten years, the pathetic years. Now, officially, and more than just a story, The Final Years. The fans of Jackson who stayed loyal in those sorry final years recognised in their troubled but triumphantly famous hero someone who knew more than anyone what it was to be so emotionally and intellectually at sea, who understood the confusion chaste loners and outsiders felt in a world that tended to doubt the feelings of those craving security and solace and attempting to stave off despair in oddball, untraditional ways.

These fans, and the I-alone-knew-the-real-Michael-friend-fans, possess such purity of belief, such devotion, which seems to the cold and judgemental outsider to verge on the hysterical, that at times you wonder if, in honour of the object of their worship, they had feigned a kind of madness, or had actually gone mad – after all, there is a world where Jackson feigned madness because he decided this is what people expected of him, and his whole career for better or worse was based on him giving people what they wanted, what they found intriguing about him, even if it wasn't the music, or the performance. By the end of his life, perhaps the last twenty years, he had decided, as someone who had traditionally always been in control of the choices that were made about how he appear to the public, that he was not expected to act normal. So he would not act normal. He would play up the debauched quirkiness, the withdrawn weirdness, the enfeebled mutant, act out the idea that he was still the poor, unhappy and misunderstood little boy living behind sequined bars at Neverland who needed a normalising mother even after the grown-up president of Jackson Inc. had fought to buy the rights to the Beatles songs and vigorously deflected the savage accusations of those that considered him monstrous. This appeared to work – even when there was no music, no songs, or the music didn't quite live up to the lightning flashes of the Quincy Jones-era hits, or the mercurial Motown fun, he forced his way into our imagination, and stubbornly stayed there. He held over his fans, and the self-justifying media that supplied the fans with all of their information and motivation, the tyranny of a plan, of withheld secrets and staged revelations. He replaced the hit single as a way of impressing upon people his presence and, as far as he was concerned, importance, with a series of regular updates, related to his apparent corruption, or seediness, or innocence, or unorthodoxy, or, quite simply, the fame that had wrapped his fame in more and more fame. His attitude was, if they want me to be mad, I'll show them madness.

His feigned madness then seemed to implode into an authentic madness, or at least an inability to understand that his behaviour was not now seen as the charming, entertaining, dangerously indiscreet but image-strengthening way-out antics of a fantasy pop star living out sweet, juvenile fantasies, an astute subversion of the hurtful wacko image that others had created for him, but an alarming, lurid sign that he had lost sight of reality and of what was appropriate for a middle age man to get up to.

For the loyal, unwaveringly devoted fans, and the primitive disciples that Geller, Sharpton and Gest instantly became as though it was their destiny, Jackson represented – and to the judgemental outsider this seemed so unlikely that it achieved the quality of a peculiar kind of miracle, or at the very least a dynamically achieved illusion – absolute goodness. The more he was accused of unspeakably seedy acts of abuse, the more he actually started to facially adopt the painted, cruel look of an uncanny comic-book villain, the more disturbed and disturbing he became, the more the true believers truly believed. To them, he was being maliciously misunderstood by unforgiving forces aggressively keen on removing Michael's special powers. Michael was being lobotomised by this menacing opposition, and therefore the worst, the most frail and helpless he seemed, the more intense the support and companionship; the more he actually needed them, which then seemed to multiply how much they needed him.

To the fanatic, overwhelmed by the idea of Jackson as erotic sorcerer, singing mystic and shape-shifting angel of mercy, he, as in He, happened to live in a crude, nasty and suspicious era when such goodness and humility was persecuted. It was up to them to explain to the ignorant mob that in fact Jackson was being punished, and actually being ripped apart, not for the alleged acts of molestation, for the loss of originality and magic in his music, for the obsessive, disfiguring cosmetic surgery, for his weakness for the sensational, for the gothic, ritualised ways he organised becoming a father, for the ways his idiosyncratic lifestyle seemed to mock the very standards of decency and fair play he professed to support, for the self-pity, for the stunted development, for the succession of fake marriages and the surrogate mothers, for the ways he seemed convinced his life was only worth living if he could live it as a child, but because, through it all, despite his psychic frailties and the constant abuse, he was a pristine world-changing symbol of hope and love. He was, according to the gospel spread by those who for their own particular reasons saw only resonant purity, threatening not because of his neuroses but because he was so powerfully a proponent of a kind of fragrant, intoxicating positivity. And those that did not love him, or like him, who in fact actively hated him, were simply jealous.

Paul Morley

Thirteen

What is Michael Jackson according to Google #2

Michael Jackson is known everywhere on the planet

Michael Jackson is the sexiest man alive

Michael Jackson is a ten year old boy trapped in a 49 year old man's body

Michael Jackson is suing British television company Granada

Michael Jackson is the best singer I know of

Michael Jackson proves that many times in life the people that have the least to say end up saying the most through their actions

Michael Jackson is pictured at Exeter City Football Club in Devon on June 14

Michael Jackson is protesting that Sony failed to promote his recent album

Michael Jackson is staging a comeback

Michael Jackson is talking only to himself in an empty universe

Michael Jackson is hitting out at the record industry again

Michael Jackson is universally known as Coca-Cola

Michael Jackson is Peter Pan

Michael Jackson was the fifth member of Abba

Michael Jackson is where God emptied himself into man

Michael Jackson has yet to reach the climax of his psychodrama

Michael Jackson is in legal combat mode again

Michael Jackson is a freak who abuses children

Michael Jackson is seen outside the high court

Michael Jackson is losing it

Michael Jackson was very pleasant

Michael Jackson is ready to emerge from his debasement

Michael Jackson told Martin Bashir that he allowed kids to sleep in his bed thinking people would think of him as an innocent child but he was very much misunderstood

Michael Jackson's songs were all about how we lose the people we love, we lose our vigour, and we lose our lives

Michael Jackson is my hero contrary to the press about him lately

Michael Jackson is such a gentle man

Michael Jackson has buried his identity

Michael Jackson hangs on the cross forever

Michael Jackson once met Victoria Principal

Michael Jackson 'sang for the famine-stricken of the world as they endured the impotent extremities of starvation' and if that sentence was say the shape of his nose when he was fourteen years old then this sentence 'he had come to realise that there was no deep sense in things, that nothing and no one had real dignity and real deserving, that 'the world' was just a jumble and a rubble and a dream' was the shape of his nose when he was forty four except in fact the nose was now only the size of the word 'rubble.'

Michael Jackson was scheduled to perform 50 sell out concerts to over one million people at London's O2 arena

Michael Jackson is one sick bastard

Michael Jackson is a friend of Shirley Temple

Michael Jackson is a ticking time bomb waiting to explode

Michael Jackson is my best friend

Micheal Jackson wore white socks to draw attention to his feet as he danced, feet that fought with all their life against the volatile faithlessness of the human mind

Michael Jackson is hermaphrodite

Michael Jackson doesn't recognise himself

Micheal Jackson lives in a dream world but then we all live in dream worlds

Michael Jackson felt the post modern culture revving along inside him

Michael Jackson is oblivious to the protest of Jarvis Cocker

Michael Jackson is knowing what is catchy to a ten year old

Michael Jackson makes sure he is ahead of his time so that his records are played years later

Michael Jackson gazed down on me from above and he had a strangely elongated head and a strange pallor, the pallor of something that had long been deprived of light, a shadowed leaf, a deep sea fish, a grub inside a fruit

Michael Jackson's third child is born in 2002 using his sperm cells with a surrogate mother and an artificial semination

Michael Jackson is a tourist attraction

Michael Jackson is nobody's memory

Michael Jackson says that men who don't masturbate become kind of unstable

Michael Jackson is destroying his face because he doesn't want to look like his father Joe

Michael Jackson loves you

Michael Jackson is going to duet with Madonna on In The Closet but he doesn't like what she wants to do he think she's too rude

Michael Jackson is taken advantage of because of his money

Michael Jackson is pronounced dead at 2.26 pm local time

Michael Jackson proved that just by being your black self you could make the world yours

Michael Jackson is nicknamed Smelly by Quincy because when Michael liked a groove he'd call it Smelly Jelly and he doesn't curse smelly is his way of saying a bad word

Michael Jackson is singing 'you start to freeze as horror looks you right between the eyes/you're paralyzed'

Michael Jackson is what you could call a health nut

Michael Jackson is in racial and cultural exile

Michael Jackson is like all the rich being victimised as much by his own lawyers and hangers on as he is by those on the outside

Michael Jackson is very much a man and he is very loving and very caring and we never had sex

Michael Jackson is set to a melody as lost and forlorn as an orphaned boy

Michael Jackson is almost running out of money

Michael Jackson is beautiful

Michael Jackson is speaking in a whisper and wearing a scarf around his throat to protect his golden voice

Michael Jackson's May 1994 marriage to Lisa Marie Presley was short lived and ended in divorce after 2 years

Michael Jackson is a condition that no amount of money can cure

Michael Jackson is writing songs for himself

Michael Jackson would have found his calling with or without his dad he had a God given talent not because he was beaten down by dear old dad

Michael Jackson's face is on the side of a Manhattan bus advertising Invincible just weeks after 9/11

Michael Jackson's defence attorney is pitch perfect

Michael Jackson is overcome by dread

Michael Jackson is the youngest member of the Jackson 5 the first black group on the cover of the teen magazine 16

Michael Jackson obtained fertilised eggs from Poland and then had them implanted in Debbie to carry them for him

Michael Jackson is grabbing a water gun and joining in

Michael Jackson is used to coarsened and corrupt public sensibilities

Michael Jackson is making plans to escape

Michael Jackson referred to his young Neverland visitors as 'rubbers' as in something to rub against

Michael Jackson is molesting Gavin only weeks after the Martin Bashir film aired

Michael Jackson is thrusting his pelvis

Michael Jackson is a dolphin

Michael Jackson is spending time talking to dead people

Michael Jackson is having a party

Michael Jackson is the only father they knew and I'm sure he loved them

Michael Jackson is tied down, Gulliver like, by miniature dogs dressed in business suits

Michael Jackson is predicting his own death in 1997 song called Morphine from Blood on the Dance Floor singing 'trust in me/just in me/put all your trust in me/you're doing morphine'

Michael Jackson is dead according to TMZ but his Wikipedia page has not been updated

Michael Jackson is the most hideous thing I have ever seen

Michael Jackson's second bride would be identified as Michael's dermatology nurse Debbie Rowe

Michael is dead from an overdose of propofol which causes a euphoria quite like any other sedative

Michael Jackson is singing 'ain't the pictures enough/why do you go through so much/to get the story you need/so that you can bury me'

Michael Jackson is scared by the look in his father's eyes

Fourteen

When I think about Michael Jackson, I don't think about the music. I don't think about the singing, the dancing, the hits, the videos, the perfectionist craving for some ultimate performance achievement that would embed him into history more comprehensively and unassailably than Chaplin, Astaire, Monroe, Elvis, Hendrix, Brando, the Beatles, Prince.

I wouldn't think about the music immediately, not as something that can totally represent who he was, and what he symbolised and inspired. I cannot just think purely of a brilliant but flawed character easily called by many the greatest entertainer who ever lived – because if he was any such thing, or certainly a resolute contender, then that was because he was so crammed with doubts, paranoia, qualms, phobias and funks, all manner of contradictory energies that spilled over into his entertainment. Ultimately it is the dark, afflicted side of him that actually seemed to eat into his face and mind, the florid self-consciousness increasingly made worse by fame and wealth and all that affectionate and poisonous attention, that fascinates me more than the music.

He thought and felt about himself so unlike anyone else, with such voluptuous narcissism, such obsessive self-destructive commitment to his obsessions, that ultimately it is his mind, his motivation for becoming what he became, his capacity for remaking himself, his convoluted and defensive actions as edgy, diffident and allergic mortal victimised for being so different, that is more interesting than his music. If his pop music had anything special about it, the way it reflected his nerve, fear, impatience, oddness, loneliness, brutalised ordinariness, the scorched, lithe craving of an insecure outsider for love and attention, his desire for the sublime and a way of escaping the mess of existence through the needy, often pleading combination of rhythm and consciousness, then it is hard for me to jettison all of that and just hear his songs as songs, as things of value in themselves.

I think of a kind of epic, demonic fantasy as organised by a mischievous, tortured fantasist who was both totally in control of arranging and decorating the fantasy, and completely out of control, beaten into submission by the consequences of the hyperbole, fame and suspicion. A naive, sophisticated fantasist with a monstrous appetite for self-invention who represented through the gloss and allure of expensively constructed and extravagantly distracting commercial entertainment the rapid, disorientating changes in the Americanised world between the late '50s and the early part of the twenty-first century. A surrealist song-and-dance man, who used pop music based on his torrid imagination as a way to invade, and toy with, and trick, our imaginations.

Fifteen

Once Michael had ceased to be more musician than mere celebrity, it was the smirking, deadpan media doing the punishing and scapegoating, greedily feeding on his decline, wallowing in his misery, interpreting his eccentricities as a clear sign of criminal behaviour. When he died, they stepped in, naturally, to take charge of how Jackson's image would be decided upon and distributed.

The media, even above friends and family, who could only do so much sustaining their loving memory of Jackson without being able to generate publicity and access, were in the best possible place to take control of how Jackson would be honoured, dishonoured, remembered and buried. The media, representing themselves, because they could, could manipulate it however they wanted, as the force that most understood Jackson, and, they could maintain, because it was all up to them, that they had the best interests of everyone, fans, family, friends, at heart, and they really took their responsibility seriously in how they presented Jackson to the world.

As a member of the watching, judging media, made up of jostling points of view but somehow always ending up pointing in one direction, did I have any specific position, was there an area of his life where I could be considered an expert? Could I cope with talking about, say, the beautiful boy brilliant Michael Jackson of the Jackson 5 in the post-hippy '70s, this surely incandescent distillation of youthful hope, without considering the disfigured, hunted and arrogant Michael Jackson of the early twenty-first century? Could I smile at the excellently snazzy sight of the innocent but already somehow fictional pre-teenage Michael

obediently popularising for teenybop audiences the bewitching urgency of James Brown, the soulful groove of Marvin Gaye, the defiant alertness of Stevie Wonder, without grimacing at the thought of the disenfranchised and traumatised fifty-year-old Michael, ruined and wiped out because he'd once been this fresh, flashy coquettish pre-teen prodigy, then he was the vivacious, dolled-up, respected emperor of MTV, and then, all of a sudden, he wasn't?

And was the older Michael, the exiled wreck, the gruesome light-skinned apparition, the embodiment of agony, some kind of meta-cultural comment on the existence of the younger, exploited Michael – an explicit warning of some sort, to whoever might be paying attention, that fame is a disease, and that the more intensely it claims you, or you claim it, the more damaging it becomes, the more it breaks up reality and mutilates your soul? That, in fact, to have Jackson's ambition, to want so much to break free of his background, his status and race, to mock ordinariness and limitations, to achieve isolated glory, and therefore to possess his locked-in level of perfectionist fury, can only lead, once reality, and the mundane, actually get in the way, to, if not an early death, then a succession of deaths, a gradual erosion of life, a replacement of one vigorous, visionary being with a wretched, spindly echo.

I tried to think of a situation where I could consider the prematurely soulful, noticeably sorrowful, poignantly trusting lead vocals of the eleven-year-old Michael, the impeccably assembled pop structure of 'I Want You Back', without dealing with the eventual consequences of this early display of commercial ingenuity and enslaved glee – without also appreciating how the young performer would become so spoilt and tormented because he was the nervous, oppressed son of a demanding, dictatorial, bad-tempered father and a fanatically religious, severely controlling mother, working for a series of kind-hearted and/or menacing bosses constantly and possibly aggressively demanding greater levels of precision, charm and sweetness, educating the young performer at such an early age about the ways and means of manipulating a targeted, gullible audience to fall for you, to buy into a fantasy and thus buy the product. To make believe, say, that you are part of a happy, loving, close-knit family when in fact you live in fear of your father and sundry moguls and find the whole process of performing as though you are having the time of your young life a draining, joyless experience. Fans gasp as you jump for sheer joy surrounded by illumination and loving harmonising brothers but do not understand how you had to get up an hour early this morning to clean the yard and if you failed to do it properly you were beaten with a clothes hanger.

He was allowed to experience before he was fourteen the intoxicating, consoling but dubious advantages of being so visibly appreciated and adored for the way you can sing and move and just in a way be. On the one hand he was cleanly robbed of what might be considered any kind of normal childhood, and punished for being so fabulously reminiscent of Sammy Davis Junior and Little Stevie Wonder by being forced as a chirpy, well-mannered little star to fulfil certain paradoxically soul-destroying duties. On the other he was handed various clues how he might achieve through his Motown-framed talents and his well-marshalled exuberance a kind of freedom that went way beyond the potential for independence of the so called normal teenager.

He had, so the story goes, his childhood snatched away, replaced with hours of regimented practice, he was bullied and forced into professional routine more or less as soon as he could walk and talk . . .

Sixteen

Thousands of fans gathered at a public memorial held at Harlem's Apollo Theater, where a nine-year-old Michael Jackson won an amateur night competition in 1967.

Seventeen

. . . and at the same time was offered tantalising glimpses how he might hang on to his childhood forever – a peculiar personal dream of what childhood actually was, seeing as how he was never allowed any kind of real childhood – because the possible reward for the kind of stardom that was clearly in his grasp is the chance to perpetually postpone the conventional responsibilities of adulthood. By having his childhood erased by the unnatural conditions of being a child star, and therefore achieving a radical sort of freelance bohemian flexibility, in fact offered the opportunity of a permanent childishness, or at least a chance to recreate throughout his life a version of being young constructed by someone for whom the natural states of being young, the internal fantasies, the chance to play and wish, were mercilessly distorted by those around him using up his youthfulness for their own nefarious reasons.

The combination of being controlled by specialist disciplinarians driven by how much business your natural energies could generate, and yet being shown a world where you could actually take control of your own destiny because of a certain kind of mysteriously self-possessed uniqueness, eventually contributed to the way that the bright, bushy-tailed and costumed Michael of 'ABC' became, via the imperial, all-conquering, glamorously freakish Michael of 'Billie Jean', the brittle, bitter, defeated and impaired Michael that lingered on and on through the '90s and '00s tragically convinced that he could still move, and move us, as though he was a combination of the spinning teen Michael and the thrilling body-blurring and flamboyantly liberated 'Thriller' Michael.

Could I possibly talk about 'Rockin' Robin' and its positive relationship to a very particular history of black showbiz expression and African-American showmanship, the all-male singing group with a long noble tradition in both religious and secular fields, without infecting the memory by dwelling on the habitual crotch-grabbing and the baby dangling, the accusations of child molestation, of pain clothed in stylistic clichés and the grandiose self-defensive self-pity that swallowed him up whenever he detected that there was a loss of interest in him, at least as an artist, an entertainer, and not as the ultimate, sinister victim of the frightful insanity of fame?

Can we marvel at the ultimate African-American musician channelling decades of black musical progress – ragtime, jazz, blues, swing, rhythm and blues, rock 'n'roll, soul – into the popular white mainstream by adding his own striving sense of extravagance, mystery and competitiveness without acknowledging that his killer instinct ultimately led to such behavioural strangeness it undermined his achievements? It meant that he can never be taken as seriously as he wanted to be, as an experimental populist rewriting the laws of pop music, continually proving that the popular song could be transcendent and endlessly surprising, because, however stunning his music and performance was, it is always overshadowed by the resultant overwhelming tabloid weighted weirdness. He was so driven to demonstrate his originality and his ability to stay ahead of the pop crowd, to confound expectations that he ended up pushing his originality too far. His originality shrivelled up into abnormality.

Could I possibly talk about 'Don't Stop 'til You Get Enough' as a shining early example of the supreme collaboration between Jackson and record producer Quincy Jones, who brought to Jackson his sophisticated commercial under-standing of how to arrange a piece of music so that a magically balanced coherence could be achieved through the sensitive blending of strings, horns, rhythms, electronics and voice – and the space within all that – without mentioning that once Jackson and Jones stopped working together Jackson was left forever trying to recreate the perfect partnership, and never quite making it? Would that be fair – to deny him a greater part in the history of popular music simply because the artistic and commercial success he attained as he fought free of the child star trap ultimately meant he was perpetually stressed trying to equal that impact, and the pressure became a part of what caused him to crash so horrifically?

Shouldn't it be enough that, with Jones, whom he fought to hire despite the doubts of his record label, who felt Jones was 'too jazz' to add anything to Jackson's already solid record sales, Jackson fulfilled his absurd-seeming ambition to equal the (white, rock) Beatles in making (black, soul) music that was the most technologically advanced, the most culturally charged, and commercially the biggest-selling of all time? If the stupendous effort directly caused the slow, painful descent from grace, shouldn't we excuse, or accept, the catastrophic breakdown as an inevitable consequence of the kind of impact Jackson made, and concentrate simply on the musical and cultural break-throughs? Remember Jackson as a strutting, stirring, effervescent African-American super-hero demonstrating how to succeed in a white American world and a major artistic talent who brought the creative best out of Quincy Jones, not as a tortured freak behind an eerie mask with seamy private interests, known for once being incredibly well known, who began to believe in himself as some kind of angel of love gifted to the planet in order to save souls and guide humanity forward.

In fact, perhaps we should actively sym-

Paul Morley

pathise with the pitiful, hounded Jackson, who gave so much to realise his fantasy of success and domination that it destroyed him, as if he sacrificed himself simply so that in an increasingly complicated, demanding and cynical world he could still produce the kind of internationally recognised superstardom that officially ranked with Elvis and the Beatles. He became unbelievably pathetic, embarrassing and even obnoxious, but wasn't that simply the ultimate fate of someone who climbed so high, while so in the spotlight, and was so exceptionally rewarded? That much fame cannot be easily processed, especially by someone who never really had any fully formed memory of what it was like not to be famous.

Of course, even to concentrate on the irresistible fast-moving finger-snapping pop delights of 'I'll Be There' is to ignore the mushy, maudlin side of the young Jackson, or at least that pre-teen girl-pleasing schmaltzy side of Jackson as coordinated by his prudent manufacturing masters and arrangers combined with his own arrested instincts for pleasing hormonally agitated young people who identified with his touching expressions of hurt, confusion and lovesickness.

He was singing 'Got to be There' and 'Ben', and as much as he would pursue the wild dream of blending ethereal black soul passion with macho white rock attack on his best-loved hits, concerned we might consider him too wimpy if there was no such zeal, he never shook off this commitment to the affected, simpering ballad. There was the crotch grabbing, the shrewd attention to dance rhythm detail, the buying in of hard rock guitar heroes for regular doses of mock mayhem, and the constant need to capture in compromised form newly generated urban energies. Always, though, a need for softness, for wrapping himself and all of the world in a blanket of love and affection, where there is no danger, and no angry, possibly violent parental intrusion – where, presumably, there could be some gentle crotch stroking and a mound of mooching.

For Jackson, the airy, tender, pious ballads were another way of tapping into the otherworldly areas where he ended up feeling most at home, and he never freed himself of this early part of the formula – in fact, the gushing sentimentality and epic gentleness metastasised just as much as any other part of the Jackson make-up that was established in those early years, when he was living out a childhood enjoying and consuming pop culture not simply as a fan but actually himself as a pop culture ingredient. (This led to the middle-aged Jackson that was hysterically, and in a way courageously, clinging on to his responsibility as pop culture icon while at the same time basing all his experiences of reality on an imaginative world consisting almost completely of pop culture references. He was never able to escape the idea that the world was a kind of cartoon because in a way from his earliest time as a performer and kid he was already a kind of cartoon himself, literally so in the Jackson 5 cartoon series that placed him squarely in a world of Bugs Bunny and Peter Pan. He felt that he was able to do things to himself and the world around him that you could only do in a cartoon.

In a cartoon, nothing he did to himself, nothing he did to his body, nothing he believed about his own powers, his ability to change the world, to change his race, to change people's minds, to create fantasies around him, to defy gravity, the most unreasonable demands, the most extraordinary moves he made as his body snapped, melted or mutated from one shape to another, whether because of intuitive rhythm or intrusive surgery, none of this would have been beyond the realms of possibility. He lived his life, perhaps, following principles established in cartoons, where reality could be bent to your will, and there were no limits to your appearance, and your powers, and the emotional or physical violence you might cause yourself or others, without ever really causing permanent harm. In a cartoon, you were free, to experiment with your shape, colour and size, to manipulate the details of any contact you may have with others, to touch the sky and freeze time, to dress up as dramatically as you wanted, to talk to the animals, to avoid questions of sex – what is more sexless than a cartoon, where reproduction never requires messy, mysterious intercourse? – and to continually re-imagine your environment. In a cartoon, you can be whoever you want to be, you can glide across the surface of the moon, you can segue from zombie movie to a space station, you can star with Marlon Brando and Eddie Murphy. You can save the entire human race, earn and spend fabulous fortunes, and you never grow old, and all adventures, however scary and intimidating, can be made to lead to a happy ending, and then it starts again, as if you are born again, and ready for anything. You could be who ever you wanted to be and who was going to stop you?)

To just talk about the animated, elated Jackson 5 Michael, the cute whirlwind topped off with an adorable mini-afro deliciously hinting at the far less tamed and far more threatening forces of black power, is to be selective, to ignore the soft-centred, gooey songs he sung that more blatantly exposed the idea that the group were cynically set up to be a mainstream pop phenomenon. This is the thing with Michael Jackson. You can choose what you wish to celebrate, or praise, the cultural radical who smashed through early '80s racial barriers on the white, rockist MTV, the astonishing dancer who catapulted Astaire, Kelly and Nureyev into the shrieking pop future, the post-modern bandleader who coordinated the creation and imagery of a series of lavish set pieces that helped transform him into a video

age living legend and a major internet era topic of conversation – but can you ignore the oddness, accusations and martyred bitterness, the compulsion to entertain by so explosively displaying his psychic wounds? You can dwell on the curious and the perverse, the man whose megalomania was a mask for a great deal of misery, the whitewashed dynamo that burnt himself out by the age of thirty with ankles that resembled his wrists, the putrefying hyperstar leaking the odour of decomposition into the late twentieth century, but can you reject the restless American genius and his sincere assertion that 'human capacities have no limits'?

I waited for the calls to come, and wondered what my take would be. Should be. Could be. What did I believe? Which Michael Jackson did I believe in? Was it possible to believe in only one Michael Jackson? How many Michael Jacksons were there, how many macabre permutations, how many commercial envoys?

Actually, did I believe at all in a Michael Jackson that was in control of a Michael Jackson, or was the thing I believed in not Jackson himself, the fascinating music, the shattered image, the reclusive spookiness, the convoluted history, but the response to Jackson, the coverage and interpretation of the different periods of his life, the speculation about his defects, and drive, and addictions, and self-abuse, that ended up, or could not possibly end up, with a single all encompassing idea of who he actually was and what he really represented?

Did I believe only in the creation of Michael Jackson by an entertainment media – therefore by the end of Jackson's life, just about all of the media, and the emergence of new forms of media created by the internet that favoured the rejection of considered, contextualised analysis of events, trends and circumstances – and the voyeuristic consumers of the media? Was the Michael Jackson I found myself thinking about an invention of the media – and therefore in

Two friends.
Bonded by hardship,
driven by hope.

'LEAN ON PETE CONFIRMS VLAUTIN AS SIMPLY
ONE OF THE FINEST AMERICAN WRITERS
OF HIS GENERATION, BOTH LAVISHLY GIFTED
AND WONDERFULLY HUMANE.'
JOHN CONNOLLY

From the acclaimed author
of THE MOTEL LIFE
and NORTHLINE

LEAN
ON PETE
Willy Vlautin

OUT
NOW

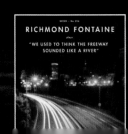
ff

fact the media itself, the media in human form?

The media had itself during Jackson's lifetime become so fascinated with sexual crimes and pornographic details of those crimes, and with sex, and money, and image, and fame, and wide-eyed, attractive young singers of gut-wrenching ballads and gutted electro-rock, and the myth of eternal youth, the obsession with physical appearance, and celebrity humiliation, and celebrity surgical transformation, with celebrities being increasingly positioned as role models, that the '80s Jackson seemed ultimately like an avant-garde experimental anticipation of this new world. Jackson set up a world where the stories that most people were exposed to, and learnt to love, and feed off, were the petty details of some life or another of someone famous for a while or famous for the famous fifteen minutes, a life pulverised by newspaper and gossip magazine headlines. Jackson invented in his detached, histrionic image the mock-world of late twenty-first-century celebrity gossip.

A world where face lifts, nose jobs, liposuction, breast enlargements, cheek implants, tattooed eyebrows, hair straightening and botox were now normal, everyday, actually desirable things, and the idea of the flaws, fights, failures and trivial fuck-ups of styled, sponsored, willingly exploited celebrity freaks being monitored daily by a wacko media and its wacko clients and customers using skilfully engineered music and recycled fashion as forms of reality controlling stimulation and sedation was no longer some dystopian science fiction fantasy.

Was this Jackson I did believe in actually the spirit of the age – perhaps the cause, through no fault of his own, or maybe it was entirely his fault, because he couldn't cope with being the son of a tyrant, and he was so famous it actually really did hurt, and so seduced by a fantasy of wealth – of this neurotic, nervy, selfish,

scandalous world made up of commercially organised, manipulated and titillating image and its constant seductive soundtrack? Michael Jackson's legacy did not lie in a vibrant transference of the militant, soulful, persecuted, spirited energies of his mentors with their active inner lives and their rampaging sensuality, but inside the tatty, lurid details of the Katie Price/Peter Andre divorce, inside Simon Cowell's love for triumphalist kitsch and excess.

This was his influence – as the king of wannabes. As the king of the self-invented minor celebrity. As the king of surgically enhanced frivolity. As the king of the emotional emptiness of modern, Godless humanity who were either trapped by shopping or refused the freedom to shop.

The king of this superficial distillation of pop's cosmopolitan stimulations because of how he looked stitched together out of copied bits of his favourite stars and singers; his identification with the untouchable glamour of stars as framed, filtered and made permanent through film, TV, video; how he behaved, as though it was all about him; the twisted, sentimentalised guilt about the abstractly felt sufferings of others; the excuses he could dredge up to explain his errant behaviour; the way he accumulated great wealth and then indiscriminately spent it; the way he craved a perpetual adolescence where he could play games, party, and have what he wanted; his belief that dancing to brilliantly manufactured electronic pop music could lead to a blissful escape from life's mundane pressures; the sense you got that he never read a book – and if he did, he hid it, because such a thought would alienate regimented post-modern consumers dismissive of any literary ways of expressing, savouring and defining the imagination; the way he represented his fascination with horror and the dark side through hypnotic special-effect spectacle as though this way he could control chaos; the endless ways he transformed himself inside his entertainment zones from cute boy to ghoul, mystic to hooligan, human to animal, pursuing a mutable identity; the strong recommendation he handed on to successive generations that you could break out of a grim working-class background and associated horrors through the power of song and dance, that all problems could be solved by passing an audition, and impressing a select few judges, and powering to glory.

There were also, of course, the ways he regularly altered his appearance as if by doing so he could first of all achieve the dream of everlasting youth and secondly outwit death, and even when he did die, in the middle of an induced sleep that was perhaps even deeper than death, he had by then ensured he would never be forgotten . . . He had, what with one thing and another, succeeded at never being forgotten. Because he was different, and everything he had done to himself was because he had to maintain that difference as everyone started to catch up with just how different he started out being.

No one could now ever forget him, not, perhaps, because of his singing and dancing, but because of the spectacle he made of himself, sustaining his 'difference' through a grandiose collection of gimmicks, publicity tricks, uniforms, silly rumours, gallivanting and delusional pomposity.

His exploits as hero and villain had directly inspired this hollow, self-indulgent pop struck world, one that had slowly taken over even the mainstream news, whether the majority of people wanted it, most surely not as caught up in the machinations of pop culture as the entertainment industry and those invested in its success. He did this by first being commercially fascinating and relishing the hard-edged suspense he could create through song and dance, and then by simply recreating his level of fame by replacing music and imaginative effort with stunts, so that the product that promoted him was not his music and records, produced with the same kind of commitment and self-awareness that led to *Off the Wall* and *Thriller*, but the scandals, the court cases, mysterious illnesses, the paternity suits, the pet chimps, the television documentaries and interviews, the big-budget greatest hit campaigns, the masks, the whitening of the skin, the rumours of various absurd alliances.

This was also Jackson's legacy – not so much passing forward the lessons, vocals and style he had inherited from Wonder, Gaye, Robinson, Ross, Astaire and Cagney but creating a world where pop stars would essentially merely be selling themselves and their bland, branded mega-image, with the music a kind of tightly controlled, highly formularised, technically neat side-product. In his later years, after all, he was more influenced by the death of Diana as a major historical landmark and the relentlessly photographed flaunting of an expensively empty but ever present Paris Hilton as a demonstration of cultural importance than by anything musical. (In this sense you could see how he was the missing link between the elegant, troubled Marvin Gaye and the boorish, aggrieved Kanye West, and a major signpost on an entertainment road to ruin that replaced a certain sort of sonically represented social consciousness and emotional sensitivity with a plain and simple sonic representation of boasting and coasting. He played a vital role in directing a long, courageous history of dissident black music toward it being smothered in capitalist drag.)

By the end of Michael Jackson's life, he was us, reflecting back at us the insatiable, submissive way we now consume pop culture, showing us what the ultimate end can be of a life obsessed with putting on a public face, with permanent play, arrested development and a complete indifference towards a world that isn't dedicated to pleasure and dressing up. If somehow, as a well-regulated apparently discriminating collective of consumers and customers and media addicts, we looked in a mirror to check the recent adjustments to our appearance we would see the ravaged, savaged bashed-in ashen faceless face of Michael Jackson staring back at us. The mirror would then point out, this being a Jackson-based fantasy, that we were still the fairest of them all. And we would believe it.

And when he died, because he had helped create the environment, a flash, tabloid-shaped, app-saturated, ring-toned, Google-searched, twitter-reduced, sensation-seeking, gossip-boggled world of Paris Hilton and Amy Winehouse, Kanye West and Taylor Swift, Justin and Britney, Mary-Kate and Ashley Olsen, Jessica and Ashlee, Beyoncé and Jay-Z, Rihanna and Chris, X Factor and American Idol, E! and TMZ, Cowell and Seacrest, GaGa and Pattison, a world where commercial success was increasingly made the only official sign of creative quality, a certified classic song only one that went platinum, he was not slipped into an aside as simply a famous pop singer from the MTV age dying, shame, weird guy though, and moving on: the requirement was to celebrate him, as something awesome and influential, with any flaws and defects attributed to his unassailable genius.

He had helped build a youth-conscious media world that was now guaranteed to hail the sad passing of an extravagantly eccentric entertainment guru as though it was in fact an event that contained genuine spiritual qualities that marked a significant cultural moment. He had ensured by accident and design that the media followed his methods of faking reality for their own commercial ends, and therefore, when he died, they effortlessly faked a situation where Michael Jackson was more important than being just an impressive crowd-pleaser who sold a lot of records and won awards and worked out

how to play MTV at their own game and made a bit of a hash of dealing with the impact on his tense nervous system of some personal difficulties and an amount of fame that got out of hand. He was in fact, even though it was all a fiction massaged into shape over a few decades, genuinely a special, important royal king with unique compassion who had died before his time.

No comment on how he had been pushed to replace himself with someone, something, else, persuaded to try and become what he was clearly never meant to be – white, sexually conventional, heterosexual, a father – in order to satisfy the no-nonsense conventional demands of American public opinion. The barely there ex-pure electroghost that trailed slime, debt and defeated loopiness around the edges of the entertainment world long after it had reached what was probably the natural end of its life had become so distorted and wretched not least because it had been encouraged to think that if it was white and part of a family, it would be accepted. These edges of the entertainment world that would once have been very rarely checked out could now because of the internet, the entertainment shows that had built up to fulfil the demand for fluffy information about celebrities with something to promote and the twenty-four-hour news channels, be propelled right into the centre of everything. This suited Jackson, the major star of the well-remembered '80s who had never quite reclaimed his position as fully functioning superstar making the hottest, smartest high street records of the day, but was also operating in a grubby twilight zone of intrigue that positioned him at the level of a minor celebrity, somewhere between Pamela Anderson and David Hasselhoff, one who might get a reality show on a camp channel following his every distinctively erratic move and sniggering at his hilarious, hopeless relationship with his children.

Paul Morley

Epic recordings   32¢

Off the Wall

Michael Jackson

When the two sides, the historical pop icon and the trashy reality star, collided, as they sometimes did, there could still be a close reminder of just how potent a presence he was, if not much of a reminder of what it was like to hear the 'Thriller' bass materialise for the first few times, as though it was giving us some radiant clue to how Michael Jackson actually perceived the world – as if he had said a few words to Quincy, about his hopes, fears and aching need for something he couldn't quite work out how to resolve, dropped in a few fugitive images, explained yet again about the other dimension he could reach when he sang, about how it helped him emerge out of the dark and into the light, and Quincy had conspired to come up with this giant-sized warning sound, which captured in its swanky, insouciant attack and intricate machine-maintained minimalism, its delirious sureness, Jackson's fierce anxiety, disordered confidence and perversely nerveless determination.

If you really wanted to get to some kind of truth about Michael Jackson, then somehow you would need to interview the sound of that bass, which would be able to answer with some stunning revelations about Michael's early memories, the enigmatic traumas he suffered, his need to order the world around him through the kind of fantasy songs he was now singing, the way he responded to the right sound as though it was a magic potion that could lift him out of his past, and his present, how he ended up so self-demanding, and it was his way of counterpunching, fighting back against the dark, against his shyness, and the doubters, and sometimes the biggest doubter of all was him, never sure he could be as good as he needed to be, to have such a spunky sound, underpinning such a song, built in the image of his trembling, surging imagination and calculated to reflect right into the eyes of those looking toward him his superabundant nervous energy.

Eighteen
Posted by jon at June 30, 2009-09-20:

'I think Michael was more talented at ten years old than most everyone else (who was not a Beatle) at age fifty. It appears he was abused, and the Jehovah's Witness teaching will hammer any child. Also it appears that he had the emotional level of a child. Not withstanding his hyper sexual/danced music and lyrics. He couldn't kiss his wife in public, its sad. Jesus knows us better than we know ourselves. I am inclined to believe Michael loves Jesus. But I am only someone who never met him. I am sad that he was not able to show what he was capable of in his comeback concert series. No one knows if he will be breathing tomorrow. Michael is now in the hands of our saviour. May God rest his soul.'

Nineteen
No reflection in the immediate post-death news coverage on the particular timing of his major success, during the early Reagan years, where his poised and polished, and extremely expensive, sound, was sexed-up funk and ethereal soul diligently diluted and expertly modified in order to reach the fussy, prejudiced white audience – a black performer introducing white elements into black music as the opposite of Presley more or less kicking this whole dream/nightmare off as a white performer introducing black elements into white music.

Could I say this kind of thing in a radio interview, or on a television show, in the hours after his death, restrict myself to examining how he failed to make the move from immaturity to maturity, plunge into his inner self and examine how it didn't exist, not in ways we can ever fully understand, and remark on the ways the media created the monster, and then dwelt on it, spurned it, fed it, starved it, tortured it, operated on it, killed it? Could I make the point, at a time when we are all more focused than usual on what Michael Jackson really meant, that he was a burnt-out symbol of ourselves and our indulgences, when perhaps all that was wanted was a brief, genial, if slightly guarded comment that Michael was gentle and kind but a notorious perfectionist and intensely dedicated to his craft?

And was it too much to talk about his excessive precocity as a gifted eleven-year-old forced to perform on demand, how he leapt free of his own teenage history, the ominous intensity and biographical melodrama of the beautifully produced 'Billie Jean', how the original title of the Rodney Temperton song 'Rock with You' was 'Eat You Up', his ability to make music that mixed the kitsch and the transcendent, the flow and tension of his dancing, how the title track of *Off the Wall* when his life and career could still follow improvised paths revealed some kind of manifesto relating to his haywire life and polluted innocence – 'the world is on your shoulder | life ain't so bad at all | if you live it off the wall' – and how if you're looking for the truth about why he ended up the way he ended up, the perfect figure to play Edgar Allen Poe in a movie, then listen to his song 'Childhood'–

Paul Morley

'before you judge me | try hard to love me | the painful youth I've had'.

Twenty

Someone asks me if I like Michael Jackson. Now there's a question. And if I like Michael Jackson, what is it, exactly, that I am liking? It seems like a very simple question, and I imagine there are some people who can answer the question very quickly, and emphatically, and with a fair amount of satisfying completeness, without thinking about it too much. They do not find the question particularly troubling. They know what it is to like, or not like, Michael Jackson, and instantly imagine a Michael Jackson, a moment, a memory, a thing, a hook, one thing, one person, singing one song, 'Rock with You', say, that snare drum at the start, snapping you to attention, one person, on the cover of one record, part of a cartoon series, singing about a rat, a favourite period, *Off the Wall*, say, more gritty, less theatrical than *Thriller*, one person, having hits at eleven years old, it's just about 1970, so much enthusiasm and radiance trapped in song, one person, part of the Jackson 5, beyond a boy band but all that a boy band could ever be, one person, when he was sexy, or something mysteriously close, when he was writing songs that sonically explored the idea of sex, in a way perhaps he never physically did, so that the songs he wrote or sang when he was just about twenty and then for a few years were pop as sex, fame as lust, sound as foreplay, rhythm as release, one person, introducing his moonwalk at the twenty-fifth anniversary of Motown, before he was strange, really strange, or was he always stranger, because he was a stranger to himself, moving in public as if such motion solved everything, one person, when he was young and good-looking, really good-looking, one person, singing that the kid is not my son, and the guitar catching up with his thinking, one person, singing another song,

'Beat It', say, the carefree way he presents himself as some kind of warrior with the intention of somehow letting his younger, enslaved self know that everything was going to turn out all right, he was giving himself back, body and soul, to the poor unhappy and misunderstood boy who needed him, giving that young boy the strength, in fact, to ensure that he ends up with the kind of life-loving self-confidence that means he can end up writing and performing and starring in a song as sure, aroused and ecstatic as this, so that 'Beat It' is somehow a gift to his younger self, a rescue plan, a light at the end of the tunnel.

So some people can be asked the question, do you like Michael Jackson, and the answer is obvious, they know where they stand, it was all about the music, he is only the music, and the good times, and the bravado, and the brilliance, and nothing can take away the solvent shrewd-ness and liberating joy, and calls for the metaphorical lynching are unfair, if not actually evil. The music is all we can know; everything else is just pure conjecture, unreliable biography, prejudiced speculation that has got nothing to do with the pure evidence of the singing and the dancing.

Do I like Michael Jackson? That makes me think. Was I ever a fan? Did I ever actually buy a Michael Jackson record? Did I ever really get it out of my head that Michael Jackson was more than the black Donny Osmond – this is something the American dean of rock critics Robert Christgau got out of his system in 1973, noting that for all the 'sweetness and cleanness' here was a 'real interpreter'.

For me, there was always the Donny thing, even as Michael grew up, and began to swerve and swivel through the changes that would never actually stop, until he at last had to stop, because he died, as he went about shaking off the innocence, the lightweight childishness, if not the sweetness, of those early years, as he worked on the greatest relationship of his life, with Quincy Jones, and most vividly expressed all the struggles and contradictions that flooded his sensibility. In fact, even during the Quincy era, when the patience and experience, the general musical wisdom and structural insight of Jones coincided so perfectly with Jackson's private and public yearnings and a series of major cultural and technological shifts in emphasis, the resulting blockbuster music still seemed to be more about sales figures and the accumulation of wealth. Youthful playfulness had merely been replaced with professionally calibrated storytelling that isolated and emphasised brilliantly spotted trends in dance pop music and followed very closely recommendations on how to proceed with the soundtrack to the life of Michael Jackson taken from the results of some market research.

To me, it was still a Donny thing, the creation and marketing of mundanely enterprising light entertainment, however conscientiously motivated, however sensitive it was to the musical movements and efforts of more original talents – and if Michael Jackson was the Michael Jackson to the Donny Osmond of Donny Osmond, then even at his most renowned and record-breaking, even as the 'Thriller' video lifted him on to the top of a world packed with fans whose hearts he'd made race faster, even as he crossed over into a whole new state of MTV being, Michael Jackson seemed the Donny Osmond to the Prince of Prince. The whole thing seemed somehow a mathematical certainty, the inevitable end result of a series of boardroom calculations, investigations, hunches and decisions.

To some extent, as musical as the whole organisation of Quincy Jones was, as in the team he built and the way he approached the architecture of the music, his marvellous assembly of musicians, engineers, tone, style, technology to help fully realise a fantasy of what Michael Jackson's music should sound like, it didn't touch me as a mainly musical thing. It struck me as being the meticulously designed soundtrack to the far-fetched life of Michael Jackson, a life that was being played out like a movie, and in that sense *Off the Wall*, but especially *Thriller*, and then the final Jones album *Bad*, these increasingly industrial constructions, followed increasingly strict notions of what kind of mock dissident, pseudo-spiritual, neo-wanton, tautly plausible music the biggest pop music superstar in the world should sing.

Twenty-one

What is Michael Jackson according to Google # 3

Michael Jackson is intoxicated by his own talent and ability

Michael Jackson enjoys extravagant shopping sprees

Michael Jackson is very cool

Michael Jackson is a licensing agreement

Michael Jackson is saying I am just like everyone else I cut and bleed and I'm easily embarrassed

Michael Jackson turned up for his courthouse appearance more than an hour late in pyjama bottoms, slippers and a suit jacket

Michael Jackson no longer has to experience mundane life

Michael Jackson drinks wine hidden in a soda can

Michael Jackson is the next Elvis

Michael Jackson fell in the toilet and couldn't get out

Michael Jackson's performance was enough for the world but it was never enough for him

Michael Jackson is showing the writer Danny Fields who went on to manage the Ramones a studded vest he had stitched himself and he wondered whether Danny liked it or thought it 'too busy'

Michael Jackson is willingly making his soul available for commodification

Michael Jackson is singing and crying at the end of She's Out of My Life written by Tom Bahler an ex boy friend of Karen Carpenter who left him after she found out he had another life as a married man and father

Michael Jackson is outside the constraints of normal human behaviour

Michael Jackson is destined to be ripped apart by an angry crowd

Michael Jackson is diverting public attention from genuinely pressing issues

Michael Jackson can bring with him into a room such moroseness and then manufacture such crazy revelry on stage

Michael Jackson and Farrah Fawcett Majors versus Elvis Presley and Groucho Marx

Michael Jackson self crowned like Napoleon is surrounded by cheering, hysterical crowds

Michael Jackson was relentless in his quest to help others

Michael Jackson is singing 'there's no need to dismay/close your eyes and drift away'

Michael Jackson is moving effortlessly from quiet to loud

Michael Jackson tried to push Judy Garland off the yellow brick road

Michael Jackson is not changing his behaviour after being charged with sexual molestation of a 13 year old cancer survivor

Michael Jackson hiccoughs in the middle of songs

Michael Jackson is sent to sleep using propofol which can induce priapism in some people

Michael Jackson's edition of Robinson Crusoe was an edition published in 1887 by Estes and Lauriat of Boston

Michael Jackson was Mike to Akon who tried to tell him he didn't always have to be ahead of the pack he should just stick to what made him great in the first place with an added bit of whatever the newest technology was

Michael Jackson is wandering admiringly through a shrine to Elizabeth Taylor

Michael Jackson was going to sing Bad with Prince but Prince said it 'would be a hit without me' so he didn't do it

Michael Jackson gets the blood going

Michael Jackson is walking into a room totally naked with a hard on and the brothers were totally grossed out

Michael Jackson is increasing circulation

Michael Jackson's face is on a $20 bill

Michael Jackson didn't find it easy to smile

Michael Jackson doesn't know if he was his father's golden child

Michael Jackson is confronting rumours about his skin colour

Michael Jackson is still grabbing his crotch

Michael Jackson is forgiven because he is show business

Michael Jackson cannot be rescued by his personal physician

Michael Jackson is moving to Bahrain so is a muslim

Michael Jackson is doubting everything in the world

Michael Jackson craves information about freaks of nature

Michael Jackson is a modern day crucifixion

Michael Jackson did bleach his skin they found the skin bleaching ointments in his home

Michael Jackson is playing 50 shows at the O2 Arena because Prince played a month long season there and he wants to out do him

Michael Jackson obviously needs psychological help

Michael Jackson's death is causing web-traffic havoc

Michael Jackson is using the Beatles songs to stave off debt

Michael Jackson is singing 'it doesn't matter who's right or wrong'

Michael Jackson is talking about his belief in God with Geraldo Rivera

Michael Jackson would have to be invented if he didn't exist

Michael Jackson is being scammed

Michael Jackson's top half looks like the male of the praying mantis whose upper part has been half devoured by the female but who perseveres in his copulation

Michael Jackson appeared on the Larry King show as Dave the day of his burial

Michael Jackson smiles like a lizard

Michael Jackson is reflecting the contemporary cultural struggle to be both hyper-sexual and innocent, to be true to ones roots while trying to make it and assimilate

Michael Jackson will die before the abuse trial ends fears his former spiritual advisor Rabbi Shmuley Boteach

Michael Jackson is the son of a crane operator at a steel mill

Michael Jackson is a puppet made of wood come to life

Michael Jackson is eaten by Free Willy

Michael Jackson had two children with Debbie Rowie, Prince Michael and Paris Katherine Michael

Michael Jackson CD prices are going up in second hand shops

Michael Jackson is cooing in the middle of his songs

Michael Jackson is trapped in an endless web of make believe

Michael Jackson is a sad sight emerging from his Neverland Valley

Michael Jackson is a space alien drag queen

Michael Jackson as a Jehovah witness child is forbidden from celebrating Christmas and now has Christmas decorations hanging up in June

Michael Jackson is ending the song with an angel coming down to hug and embrace him

Michael Jackson's self-destruction is one of our modern entertainment luxuries

Michael Jackson ached with the need to convince himself that he did exist in the real world

Michael Jackson is a believer in the hopeful impulse that makes beginnings and seeks outcomes and imagines adventures in the middle

Michael Jackson is maintaining that sharing his bed with children is an entirely innocent expression of affection

Michael Jackson is addicted to tranquilisers, painkillers and alcohol

Michael Jackson was not breathing

Michael Jackson's father said his father treated him the same way and he thought it was ok because he was raised like that

Then for Michael Jackson time stopped.

Twenty-two

A first call came, within an hour of the glaring death bulletin, for some sort of comment, on some late-night radio show, with – under the circumstances I found myself in, not sure I really had anything precise enough to say about Michael Jackson – the worst possible brief. The one where you are innocently asked to 'sum up his career', no doubt in three minutes, by some poor assistant producer following hastily issued orders from above rifling through numbers of pop journalists hoping for some kind of response from anybody they can get hold of.

I'd been watching the television news channels catch up with the idea of a dead and done Michael Jackson. The timing of his death coincided with many pop journalists and entertainment correspondents camping out at the Glastonbury pop festival. To those that put together news shows, this must have seemed a very lucky break, that the right kind of interviewers and experts were located together where there were handy outside broadcast units all ready to beam back early responses. Surely it was all pop music, and Glastonbury was pop music, and the two things, the festival and the death, were therefore a perfect fit, as if one would become a natural stage for the Lennon-like, Diana-deep grief that was surely going to rage through the pop world.

It wasn't really the same thing at all. In fact it would have been more useful to have had an audience at Wimbledon, a Milton Keynes nightclub or a matinee of *Dirty Dancing* comment on the death, because in fact the idea of Glastonbury represented much about the music business that had frustrated Jackson in his quest to be accepted as a major artistic talent – filled with the kind of alternative music, rooted in punk, and grunge, and a more artsy, and very white, risk-free rock attitude, give or take a sanctioned token flash of rap and soul, that to him remotely represented something very unexciting and cynical. This was a world that could somehow mock the kind of commercial success Jackson was the ultimate, horrendous example of while simultaneously hoping for it as well, and if they got it, enjoying it in their own way as much as Jackson.

Glastonbury appeared to gently represent diversity, positive communal spirit and easy-going open-mindedness, but it was as much a reflection of the vast, controlling entertainment industry of music, the devious pursuit of a shrewdly targeted youth and post-youth audience following specific trends, as anything that Jackson had been involved with. In a way, with its roots in a very white late '60s hippy world, and with a sensibility updated into a predominantly white and anti-theatrical post punk alternative universe, it was a reminder of the dogmatic rock attitudes of the early MTV, of the kind of early '80s commercially and culturally convenient if ultimately impractical racial barrier that Jackson and Jones were so determined to break down.

It was a reminder of the early '90s, when Jackson was under the stress of his fame and a new mammoth deal with Sony, not to seem passé. He was searching for a harder, meaner, post-superstar, post-Quincy, post-rap, post house style he could again call his own, re-leasing *Dangerous*, working hard to reframe his now standard intensity, sweetness, moodiness and volcanic self-consciousness inside a musical hybrid that didn't leave him stuck in the '80s – he'd made the jump from the '70s to the '80s, but that was from the basis of being a medium-sized superstar. His leap into the '90s was from the position of huge superstardom, which made the move harder not easier, and also he was operating in a groove fixated dance pop context that was many genres and sub-genres moved on from where it had been with 1982's *Thriller* and even 1987's *Bad*. Through sheer will, the hiring of Prince-conscious, Quincy respecting, hybrid beat master Teddy Riley as main producer, his enduring competitive fight now transferring into a deeper neurotic fear that he was being left behind as pop star and innovator, he managed to ensure that *Dangerous*, while not as hook heavenly as *Off the Wall*, or *Thriller*, not quite as much an event as *Bad*, was not at all a disaster.

The trouble was, even as Michael proved, again against odds dramatically stacked against him, that he could get on not only without his father, his brothers, or Gordy, or Gamble and Huff, or, most impressively, without Quincy, that he could extend and modernise lessons learnt back at Motown, and then through Philly, and maestro Jones, the pop world's attention was not as such completely interested in a regenerated Michael Jackson. Nirvana, much more of a Glastonbury model of where pop currents swirl around a zeitgeist, more comfortable to a rockist mentality, were of the moment, and Michael was just another star from the as yet not romanticised and recycled pop past fighting to adapt to an increasingly fast-changing, now very much CD-shaped pop world. Such natural results of pop's natural need to replace itself with another version of itself in order to maintain the illusion that it was still alive with future-fancying possibility did not help Michael's frustrations.

There had been many changes in pop because Michael and Quincy worked out how to crash into the opaque MTV building: many more black superstars liberated by Jackson's success and able to create exotic fantasies of glamour and wealth inspired by Jacksonic principles, and many new trends replacing old trends and then in turn being replaced themselves. In many ways, though, not a lot had changed since Jackson's peak imperial phase.

The pirouetting pop of spectacle and gossip that Jackson had set in motion had not led to the kind of music featured at Glastonbury, even in the dance tents, and even when it was acting a little camp and playful and inviting 'surprise' guests like Kylie or the Pet Shop Boys. Jackson pop, linked through thick and thin, across whatever commercial cosmetic surgery and studio revision, to the evangelical fervour and fire-breathing preachers of the rural south, had led – with a little penetrating nudge from his carnal show business fad-following stepsister Madonna and a generous hit of swanky hip hop smarts, both of which were themselves in debt to the luxury sight of the mighty shamanic Michael conquering the world by setting himself inside an illusion of his own mercurial making – to Xtina, Britney, Justin, Kanye, Rihanna, to Whitney, Mariah and Leona. Jackson pop was vulgar, vaudevillian, aristocratically minded, utterly reliant on visual imagery, based on an adoration of traditional Hollywood, and, for all the black-and-blue lusting and thrusting, ultimately committed to a certain sort of domestic, conformist sleekness. It was best heard and seen set inside a television studio, a darkened club or an indoor arena. It was not very open air. It was not at all the elite, progressive pop of Glastonbury. Only death could bring Jackson in any kind of contact with this festival of a completely different section of iTune-era popular music.

A few eager, stunned pop journalists set inside the inappropriate camp preparing for Neil Young and Bruce Springsteen – as far away from Jackson as Kerouac and Pynchon – made a brave, clumsy stab at eulogising Jackson and his achievements. They tried to cleanly separate the groovy, dreamy, gleaming pop music Jackson who bound the rock song with dance beats, the synthesiser with soul, the Jackson that slid swiftly backward while appearing to walk forward, from the sleazy, unearthly and scorned remnant that had been slowly turning to stone for years. Some mentioned Jekyll without Hyde, some mentioned Hyde without Jekyll, some mentioned them both, finding it impossible to talk of the evangelical daylight adventurer without acknowledging the savage night-time demon. If someone concluded the Jackson that represented the very best in American popular music, you couldn't help wonder about the other Jackson, the one that publicly elevated something squalid, peevish and malignant at the heart of America. And then you'd wonder if it was tactful, if it was ultimately a mean disservice to the unblemished pre-grim Michael, at a time like this, in the shimmering, excitable TV minutes following the announcement of his death, to bring up the dark side of the man, and stumble into the seething mysteries of his ego, and the exhaustion, the mock-Biblical grandeur and the exasperating moral zaniness.

Watching others deal with the problem by seeming not to think it was even a problem didn't help me at all to work out whether I had anything to say about Jackson, as opposed to having anything to say about a caricature, a media-assembled monster, a glimpse of a glimpse of someone we only ever really witnessed when he was making some kind of exhibition of himself, gloriously, curiously or repulsively.

It did make me see how the news bulletins were of necessity remembering a very compressed, simplified version, one that could easily be labelled as some kind of tragic legend, that everyone had their own Jackson to remember, and that really the only way to respond to the death in an effusive broadcasting context was to decide which area of his life you might be an expert in, and simply concentrate on that. Find a fragment of Jackson, a shiny, densely actual one or a gruesome, drugged one, something to revere or revile, and stick to examining that.

I agreed to do the radio interview. Perhaps speaking my thoughts aloud on a live show under pressure of particular questioning and the fact that someone else was about to follow me might help me work out what exactly those thoughts were.

It was midnight, about an hour after what during the day had seemed a standard mischievous internet rumour – Michael Jackson had suffered a heart attack, he was dying, he was dead – had turned out to be, once and for all, true. Before I did my phone interview with the radio station looking for a three-minute summary of the passion of Michael Jackson, I heard an expert talk to the BBC about his impressions of Jackson. He remembered watching a suspiciously wrapped up and unexpectedly sturdy Jackson at the O2 launch presentation for his fifty-date residence at the arena. He was struck by how tall Michael was, much taller than the television host Dermot O'Leary, who introduced him. 'Yes, very tall,' he murmured, as though this was enough of a revelation for anyone to take in at this time of day, faced with such surreally disruptive news. 'Very tall.'

Clearly this particular battle-scarred expert had not been as anxious as me in locating what his approach might be to the news. Or perhaps he really did consider that Jackson's height was significant. Or he was just very tired and emotional. This was in stark contrast to idiosyncratic Jackohistorian Uri Geller, slickly zooming into position with a hustler's pace as leader of the rapidly developing posthumous cult. The hideous and all-knowing spoon-bender was so wideawake I could feel my very soul bend to his glossy will. He clearly was on a mission, as if there was a momentous spiritual vacuum opening up now that Jackson had, no word of a lie, vanished off the face of the earth. Geller obviously had his eye on filling that vacuum himself.

Within minutes of the big Fox News flash, and the slightly more modest BBC notice, that Jackson was dead, Geller was revealing that he clearly was some kind of genuine post-Jackson magician by seeming to appear live on three or four news channels simultaneously. He had two pieces of what he told, and indeed sold, as very big news. One, he had once been in a room with Michael – I'm not sure if I lost focus or he did, but each time he told the story, this room seemed to be in a different place, a hotel, his house, Michael's house, cloud cuckoo land – and had asked Michael, as you do, if he was a lonely man. Michael had replied, as you do, 'Uri, yes, I am a very lonely man.' There was a stunned pause from the interviewer, as though this somehow was this incident's equivalent of Jackie O's decision to keep on her blood-splattered clothes while Lyndon B. Johnson was being sworn in as president on the jet carrying JFK's body from deadly Dallas to devastated Washington.

Uri had more to give. He had once, unofficially, hypnotised Michael so that he could ask him a certain question that needed to be answered definitively – had Michael ever interfered sexually with young children? From deep inside one of those deep comas Michael must have had some experience of, Uri, deep inside his own tunnel-vision, got the answer he had presumably been expecting – a simple, sure 'no'.

There was another pause, as though this was this incident's equivalent of the news that Diana was in fact pregnant when she died. The look in Uri's eyes as he dropped this news from the great height of his smugness numbed me enough for me to proceed with the radio interview.

I'd decided to develop some theory I had, or was about to have, about the idea of Michael Jackson and a cartoon world that seemed to be the best way of briefly summing him – and his gleeful love of another boy who was seemed stuck at about the age of ten, with strangely coloured skin and a slightly wonky family. Perhaps in Michael's cartoon world Bart Simpson was his friend: how close, and what they might have got up to, we can only speculate, but it was no wonder that he contacted the *Simpsons* producers, first of all offering to write his pal Bart a number one single (which became 'Do the Bartman', credited to Byron Loren for contractual reasons, which did reach number one in the UK) and secondly to see if he might actually appear on the show. He eventually appeared in a third season 1991 episode entitled 'Stark Raving Dad', well before stars routinely gave their voices to the show as themselves. Jackson, again, ahead of his entertainment time. (The episode was shown again on Fox on 5 July as a tribute to Jackson.)

Michael didn't quite play himself. He was the voice of the large lumbering mental patient, Leon Kompowski, a bricklayer from New Jersey, who suffered from the delusion that he actually was Michael Jackson. Therefore in this cartoon Michael Jackson was 'Michael Jackson' and possibly even further removed from how Jackson looked at the time as the Jackson at the time was from the *Thriller* Jackson.

Jackson apparently was not at all unnerved that he was cast as a crazed twenty-two-stone white man, and his only requests were that in a joke about mentally fragile pop stars Elvis replace Prince, and the inclusion of a scene where he stays up all night writing a song with Bart. He also asked that an apparent sound-alike (John Jay Smith) be credited with supplying the voice, always a big fan of keeping people guessing.

When Homer meets Leon in the New Bedlam mental institution where he has been sent after being mistaken for a free-thinking anarchist, Leon introduces himself by saying, 'Hi, I'm Michael Jackson, from the Jacksons.' Michael is using his soft, sappy, defenceless voice, especially incongruous coming out of the large, shapeless Leon. Homer replies, 'Hi, I'm Homer Simpson, from the Simpsons.'

In the episode, Bart has not brought his sister Lisa a present for her eighth birthday. She's very hurt by this. When Leon and Homer are released from the institution, Bart gets Leon's help to write a special song for Lisa's birthday. Jackson did write the song, the short, very sweet 'Lisa, It's Your Birthday, 'which Lisa says is the best birthday present she has ever had', but he did not sing it, also for contractual reasons. (No doubt paid to speak but certainly not to sing.) The song for Lisa was sung by a plausible and genuine sound-alike, Kipp Lennon.

The forced amusement initially shown by the disc jockey interviewing me on the other end of the line soon drained away when it became clear that all I was going to talk about was Michael Jackson as Leon Kompowski. It disappeared completely when I began to wonder whether 'Lisa, It's Your Birthday' was truly one of Michael's better songs in the '90s, and his guest appearance a little hint of a sign of the awareness Michael had, at least up to the early '90s, of how to play around with people's minds and their perception of his unusual existence.

I wondered on air, rambling a little I admit, how many minutes of Michael Jackson music that will truly stand the test of time, compared to, say, the Beatles, or Dylan or Prince, how long it would take in order to play the very best of his songs – I decide just over an hour, and to include 'Lisa, It's Your Birthday', when I am thanked for my time, and that time is in fact over. I have, perhaps, been seen as being just a little too ironic considering it is still, certainly in America, the day that he has died. I have, it seems, misjudged the mood, even though I am very sincere about that thought concerning how many minutes of classic music Michael Jackson actually released, certainly in relation to the amount of very professionally designed secondary music, more than filler, but less than stupendous, that was arranged on his handful of solo albums, not counting greatest hit collections, he made since 1979's *Off the Wall*. It is some sort of compliment that he transformed himself into such a musical legend based on such a very few undeniably excellent pieces of commercial art.

Perhaps I should have said, 'It's hard to believe he had such a huge hit, his first solo number one, with a song about a rat from a horror movie.'

Or 'The Jacksons' 1978 album, *Destiny*, can be seen to anticipate Michael's first solo album, *Off the Wall*, and it's got its moments, not least 'Blame It on the Boogie', – but that album and it's Jacksons' successor, 1980's *Triumph*, full of the quaint, stringent synths and antiseptically infectious funk of the time, although as glossy, as built on the sweat and anonymous precision of the best session players available, cannot compete with *Off the Wall* and *Thriller*, and the record-breaking solo destinies of Michael, who crowned himself the king of pop but deserved the title nonetheless.'

Or 'He loved to record his vocals with the lights out. Perhaps it was all those years living in the glare of the spotlight that made Michael more comfortable working in the dark.'

Twenty-three

My radio appearance had ended with me not being hailed as someone who in this incident has access to the equivalent of the Zapruda film of the Kennedy assassination but as someone who was spotted lurking a little too close to the Dallas book depository. Before I made any kind of decision about whether I would do anything like that again, and already the requests had come in to appear on early morning TV and radio shows, from those ignorant of the unfortunate *Simpsons* incident, I re-read an article I had written for the *Observer Music Monthly* a few weeks before he died.

It was written after an appearance on the ruthlessly easygoing teatime *Richard & Judy* TV show, which required a certain sort of professional control regarding the overwhelming complexity of pinning the liquid Jackson phenomenon in any kind of fixed place. I wanted to see if it could help me get my bearings, and better appreciate that what was expected from me must not contain a grain of suspicion or sarcasm, and no hint of an old-fashioned easily misunderstood rock critic shrug, of the vagrant thought that wasn't this a tremendous amount of fuss to make about a largely discredited pop singer.

Twenty-four

(*Column written for the* Observer Music Monthly *April 2009*)

I don't know about you, but when I was on *Richard & Judy* to talk about Michael Jackson, which I didn't dream but maybe you did, I said that I would be going to see him at least once, maybe once a week, when he plays all those immense sideshows at the O2 Arena between July and February. I was on the show with a godfather of Jackson's children, the former child actor Mark Lester. He played Oliver in one of Jackson's favourite films, Carol Reed's 1968 musical production, and is now a very level-headed osteopath living in Cheltenham.

I was aware of the strangeness of the moment, a strangeness I quite enjoy, leading as it does to a certain intoxicating lightness of being, and also that, because I was on the *Richard & Judy* show with a friend of Jackson, it was not appropriate to consider the paranormal side of the Michael Jackson phenomenon nor indeed the oozing creepy side. It didn't seem correct either to explain at length my theories on how the pop universe is such an amazing thing it stretches with scintillating elasticity from the polluted wastes, the hell, of where Jackson now lurks to the glittering life enhancing purity, the heaven, of, say, Camera Obscura, and that there should be a kind of abstract rating system that fences off the nefarious nature of such as Jackson and draws attention to the ideal, idealistic pop of Camera Obscura. It didn't seem right to say, you know, if you love pop, whether the Carpenters, Love, Buzzcocks or Girls Aloud, you should listen to the new Camera Obscura single, 'French Navy'. We were there to discuss the disorientating impending resurrection of Jackson without reference to any hell he may or may not be setting up at home, in a castle the size of his ego.

When discussing Michael Jackson in certain controlled and light-hearted showbiz situations it becomes necessary to block out vast troubling areas of the gothic labyrinth of his life, the grimly occult tangles of stress, loneliness, accusation, freakishness, kinkiness, eccentricity, hypocrisy, addictions, abuse, legal disputes, financial shenanigans, dubious deals, weight loss, skin conditions, panic attacks, scandals and sundry deceptions. Even when the sordid sensationalist details of his unnatural personal saga are touched upon, it is still very much as a response to how a celebrity squirms inside a shredded tabloid representation of sleaze, as though the sicker details of Jackson's life, and indeed his literal physical sickness, is somehow not real, merely a kind of unpleasant side effect

of the toxic notoriety that comes with such far fetched international success. The full craziness contained in the thought that this creation, this trembling mortified hybrid of fact and fiction, commerce and neurosis, vacancy and allure actually roams the planet is ignored even when the accusatory tabloid horror at his repulsive otherness is at its most vehement. Jackson's brittle alien presence is taken for granted even as it is being mocked or marvelled at.

As I was talking to Richard and Judy I found the way I was internally censoring my thoughts about Jackson so as to suit the circumstances, wearing my own mask in a way, led to a kind of agitated celebration of this spoiled child star as the ultimate science fiction glam rock star – I stopped short of revealing my suspicions that he's a true spider from Mars, an eerie Warholian manifestation of supernatural self-consciousness, infected charisma, fractured originality, brutalised sensitivity, epic self-pity and performance craftiness, a sneaky, fraudulent version of a human being, a vain, unscrupulous interplanetary wanderer trying to make sense of a planet he just happens to be visiting on his way to other worlds. While here he has disguised himself as an extraordinary entertainer, needing unconditional adulation as a form of nourishment, generated a following of pseudo-religious proportions, and made a few sometimes appalling blunders, almost to the extent of giving away that he is not human. While getting carried away with the self-publicising self-glorifying search for adoration that feeds him he has forgotten the location of his space ship. He cannot make his planned getaway and the whole adventure leads to being found out, panic stricken incarceration and an eventual autopsy revealing that when we thought he was a child prodigy he was in fact over two thousand years old.

And then there is his skin, the skin Bowie as the thin white duke fancied but could never achieve without actually dying and coming back to life. When you think about Jackson's skin too closely it causes a kind of vertigo, an anxiety that its spooky journey from dark to light and lighter and somehow thinner will not stop, leading to a kind of transparency where we will end up seeing his insides, his nerves and brain and heart and blood, and clues perhaps as to how it all turned out this way, how the innocent boy with the sweet voice and the promising moves became an obscene living metaphor for the self-harming violence of fame. I mentioned none of this to Richard and Judy, of course, and listened as Mark explained how normal it is to spend time with Michael, who is – despite the scars, the decaying vigour; the burnt deadness in his eyes which are stretched back further and further from the haunting remnants of his nose; the surgical masks; the *Planet of the Apes* wigs; the smeared lipstick; the baby dangling; the malignant obsessions; the forlorn protestations of innocence; the ultimately defaced essence – quite normal.

Mark takes the position of those inside the Jackson camp – he's a nice person who had a bad childhood, there's persecuting cruelty and racism implied in the media-organised assault on his reputation and status, he's the most brilliant entertainer of his generation, the vitally vivid if tantalisingly vulnerable singing dancing idol that has influenced the image manipulation song selling media hypnotising actions of every single mass appeal hyper-pop singer since the mid '80s. It starts to sound moderately plausible, give or take that unsettling hole in Jackson's chin, the surreally chiselled jaw line, the tip of the nose that is undoubtedly glued on, and which I heard – allegedly, a key word in this story – once fell off when he was rehearsing a dance routine, to be stood on by a member of his dance troupe who thought he had stood on a snail. And then there's the latest abnormal nose, which rumours have it – rumours, another key word in this story – was built out of part of his ear.

Nevertheless, a sensible Mark proposes that the gentle, traumatised, unfairly dishonoured Michael is preparing a magnificent return to what he does best, by which I decide he means transform unique internal anxieties and insecurities, a liquid sadness and compacted anger, his fascination with waifs, strays and mutants, into dazzling showmanship. Mark almost officially represented those many who want to maintain the history that Jackson was the extravagant, irresistible latest in line after Garland, Holliday, Presley, Brown and Wonder, and honour the pop-holy version of the young, dream star that ignores how Jackson himself betrayed this version perhaps by assuming that it led to an immunity from punishment for various aesthetic, commercial and moral sins.

A recent MTV poll to establish the greatest album of the past thirty years seems to follow this route and exile all the horror and disfiguring and blight into a vacuum. Forget about what he has done to himself, and allegedly others, just think about the music. Think about the videos. Think about the production of Quincy Jones. *Thriller* was voted number one. Craig David's debut album *Born to Do It* was at number two, which along with the vastness of the pop universe, which its position confirms, needs some explaining, followed by Appetite for Destruction, OK Computer, Nevermind, Morning Glory, U2, Stone Roses, the Arctics, Amy, Kanye, Strokes, etc., etc.: the vast pop universe from a fairly fixed local temporal perspective. All led by Jackson. And Craig. I don't think *Thriller* would be in my top 100, and I don't listen to Michael Jackson – although Ian Brown singing 'Billie Jean' and 'Thriller' with elegant wistfulness provides a blissful melancholy echo of the idea of Jackson as soulful, mysteriously motivated hero worth celebrating. I find myself strangely drawn to seeing Jackson at O2 because of his fame, and the way it has eaten into him, and it seems his fans.

Perhaps, because it's my job, allegedly, I would see the first show on 8 July, two or three along the way, and then the final show on 24 February next year, just to see what change there is in his appearance, the show, the audience's relationship with him, the old and new media's treatment of him, what we can tell of what we still call his mind, to what extent the final curtain really is the final curtain, and whether indeed it is still a real Michael Jackson performing or some kind of Jacksontron, or Thrillerbot. Some say it wasn't actually him at the press launch for his O2 series, and so maybe he will he be played by a series of performers each one representing a certain period in his life, a little like how in Todd Haynes's Dylan film *I'm Not There* it took six actors to scratch the surface of Dylan.

When Michael was the eleven-year-old superstar, the Jackson 5 darling with something sinister lurking in the background as yet largely undiagnosed, the nose on his face was totally his. (This MJ could be played by Keira Knightly and a young Obama child.) It wasn't touched before he became the beautiful smiling and humble thirteen-year-old singing his first number one to Ben the rat. (Will Oldham and Taylor Swift as angelic Michael not the rat.) The first adjustment to his nose in the late '70s was apparently a botched job in response to a nose broken during a dance rehearsal. In the crotch-grabbing moon walking glove-flashing '80s, as his fame exploded, his nose imploded. (Usain Bolt, David Blaine, Justin Timberlake, Cate Blanchett, Beyonce and C3PO to play the imperial Jackson, leading via Susan Boyle, David Copperfield, Peter Andre and Bonnie Tyler to Peter O'Toole, John Barrowman, Mickey Rourke, Katie Price, Cheryl Cole and David Van Day as the ruined and exiled post-nose Jackson.)

Each new release requires new facial surgery, allegedly. Much about him, including his talking voice and wealth, shrivels up. His eyebrows wither. He adopts the harried mannerisms of victimised bully. Any comebacks must come accompanied with appearances on television specials loosely related to celebrity reality shows that are set up to convince those that question his intentions and sexual preferences but which tend to confirm that he is wrecked, corrupt, bewildered, fragile, absent. At best he's an experiment gone horrifically wrong in just how a child star can mature into artistically satisfying adult superstar and then age in public without losing touch with the reality his music and videos once so generously illuminated.

To admit completely that it has all gone beyond Marlon Brando/Howard Hughes/Gary Glitter/Bernie Madoff/Robert Mugabe wrong for Michael Jackson means that our own memories, our own past and the way he fits directly and indirectly into recent history as pioneering superstar presence, have been stained rotten. Perhaps the lingering faith in Jackson as enduring if unstable pop icon as opposed to broken genius with ruptured reputation, a faith that leads to fifty sold-out shows at the O2, is because to admit he is an untamed immature beast means we identified with and supported and ultimately financed something more disgusting and degenerate than delightful. To help Jackson survive the disaster of his downfall and rebuild him as triumphant entertainer is to help us clean up and reorganise history, and absolve us of our own responsibility in allowing such a miserable disintegration to happen.

As Mark finished describing Michael, it seemed quite natural to admit to Richard and Judy that, yes, I would be going to see the Jackson shows. If only for those astounding first few seconds, the moment he first appears, surrounded by a cast of thousands and a mighty bass line handed down from above and below, tricking the audience into believing in his magical majesty, washing away all the nastiness, all the rumours and doubts, causing the audience to re-anoint him as their pure and precious King . . . or the first few seconds when his body falls to pieces . . . or the first few seconds as he climbs into the space ship he has finally located, and flies back into the stars . . . or when he incredibly begs for forgiveness . . . or when he doesn't turn up.

Twenty-five

Perhaps I needed to make the role of the mature, clear-sighted and musically open-minded Quincy Jones in the pop construction of Michael Jackson the centre of my response, and examine how it was the very particular history of melting, merging, made over, improvised and composed American music that Jones lightly and proudly carried with him that ultimately created a kind of common-sensical but considerably electric focus for the woozy, self-aggrandising visions of Jackson.

Jones once described being a record producer as being 'part babysitter, part shrink. I'll tell you what it is — it's love. It's loving to work with people you respect. It's a serious love affair — that trust between a producer and a performer. Because sometimes what you're doing is like an emotional x ray of a human being.'

He built Jackson, the biggest-selling solo performer in pop history, in the studio, with Jackson and for Jackson, creating the sonic fictions we most think of when we think of Michael Jackson, the riffs and horns and feel and rhythms and sudden bursts of grabby action — songs that obviously come out of the Motown and Philly Michael, where Quincy found obvious clues as to why people liked him and his voice, he couldn't miss the charisma and otherness, but Jones treated the idea of Jackson as if he already appreciated that in years to come Jackson would be as massive an entertainment name as anyone he had worked with in music. And that means he treated Michael as someone who would belong in a list that contained Sinatra — his first job for Frank was to arrange 'Fly Me to the Moon', the first music ever played on the moon, — Basie, Gillespie, Clark Terry, Tommy Dorsey, Cannonball Adderly, Milt Jackson, Sarah Vaughan, Lionel Hampton and Ray Charles.

Charles was a couple of years older than Quincy, but he was a key figure in Quincy's '40s introduction to a variety of urgent new outsider underground music rapidly coalescing from all points on the compass to form rock and roll. Charles showed Jones how the blues were used to chase away the blues. Quincy was once asked if working with a pop crossover act like Jackson was an unusual move for him, because of his background in jazz. 'Not at all. I've always done that. When I was thirteen years old, during World War II, we were doing that in nightclubs of Seattle with Ray Charles. We played everything, blues, jump, country, southern soul, strip music, R&B, pop music. Everything! A lot of jazz people came down on me and were talking about how I was stretching out to do Michael Jackson. I said, that's not a stretch. I've been doing it my whole life. I loved Louis Jordan and Debussy, Dizzy Gillespie and Sinatra. I never did one style.'

Quincy grew up amid the type of poverty that means he was driven to frying up cockroaches in order to eat down Seattle back alleys teetering on the edge of civilisation. Jones's clever music-loving but emotionally disturbed mother was institutionalised and his father was a master carpenter. He was musically precocious as a child, neighbourhood vandalising leading to a love for the pure elevating wonder of sound. He would sneak into Seattle dance clubs when he was a small boy. He babysat for a local music teacher so he could read the teacher's books on arranging by Glenn Miller. He was weaned on Cab Calloway, Woody Herman, Skinnay Ennis, became fascinated as a young trumpeter why saxophone sections sounded the way they did, why bass trombones went so low. By 1956, at twenty-three, he was Gillespie's musical director on his state sponsored tours of the Middle East and America.

For Jones, Jackson might be the next stage on from Gaye, Donny Hathaway or Wonder, but he could see how they themselves owed a debt to the explorations and innovations, the wit, ingenuity, humour, spirituality of Miles, Coltrane, Bill Evans and Adderly, to the hip and aware bop and bebop as 'one of the greatest solutions to the racist shit back then'. For Jones hip hop was just bebop flipped through the edited and editing sensibilities of a few driven assimilating rebelling synthesising generations.

Quincy relished the constantly updated space-age beauties of the recording studio, and if pushed hard to come up with the ultimate reason why the music of Jackson had such appeal and sold so many copies I would say it would be because of the way Jones, like all the truly great record producers, treated the recording studio as the central instrument of a pop record. The recording studio could replicate the adrenaline-driven transformative urgency of someone like Jackson, because the capabilities released by a recording studio were all about the notion of transformation – and of turning feeling and thinking into sound, which to some extent existed in the same place as feeling, outside the body, inside the soul, beyond easy definition.

If we think of the *Off the Wall/Thriller/Bad* Jackson as the equivalent of a kind of sculpture that turned into a fixed but constantly fluid state, a particular vision, in one sense, then Michael Jackson is a gallery looking for a very particular shape and texture. Quincy Jones is commissioned as the artist dreaming up the idea and design based on the specific taste and desire of the gallery, and then in turn using others to help build and execute the finished piece – to make it real. Quincy built this model of Michael Jackson, one that ended up being an intensely accurate symbolic rendition of Jackson's complex relationship with himself and his audience, inside the recording studio. Michael Jackson is a complete studio creation, and perhaps the trouble we have understanding any kind of 'real' Jackson is because the Jackson we think of only existed inside the imaginations of those using the recording studio as an instrument to create a multi-dimensional illusion that would be labelled as 'Michael Jackson' – and which Jackson himself believed in a little too solemnly – but which was not actually a person.

It was a sonic fabrication, a powerfully drawn character, an invented personality created inside the recording studio that took on a life of its own. The Michael Jackson we had to deal with, and indeed he had to deal with, was made up on this incredibly sophisticated instrument, and the fact it ending up walking the earth was the equivalent of a character leaving a novel and having to exist in an outside world. (In that sense, comparing this recording-studio construction of a myth to how the Beatles were conceived inside a recording studio and then entered the real world suggests one area where Michael Jackson did break through his own limits and enter history as a dramatically positive figure.)

Quincy, as the artist being hired by Michael Jackson as the figurehead of a company representing the interests of Michael Jackson to come up with the best possible musical combination of originality and accessibility, is perhaps closer to the Michael Jackson we think we are talking about when we think of the Jackson of this period. Quincy is Jackson because he is making up from scratch the musical Jackson, even if under the instructions, direct or indirectly, of Jackson himself: perhaps, more accurately, the recording studio is Jackson, so perfectly did Jones use it to build a very particular character. Jackson and co. would later obviously commission other musicians, technicians and engineers to fabricate

Paul Morley

a sonic version of himself, but no other recording studio operator and technical illusionist came close to Quincy in inventing such a convincing Michael Jackson.

It needed a considerable team of technicians and players for Quincy to operate this recording studio instrument, and a mysterious combination of scientific knowledge, immense patience and imaginative flexibility, but all pop music, whatever the instrumental line up, whatever the sonic ambition, whatever the apparent organic essence of the sound, is made on and because of this complicated, intimidating instrument. To be able to control it so that you can create sound that has a completely distinctive sonic signature, so that you can make out the artistic owner of a song even if you are only hearing the drums or bass, requires a set of skills that were at the time, because of accelerating technological advancements, brand new, and which within years were already largely obsolete. For Quincy, the studio was a kind of church, and it produced a kind of prayer.

'I love recording studios. That's why I never had a studio in my home – to me a recording studio is a sacred, hallowed place. I used to have a saying, "Let's always leave some space to let God walk through the room." Because you're looking for very, very spiritual and special moments in a studio. It can't just be some place you hang out and take for granted.'

Jones's experience in the recording studio went back to the days when they were the equivalent of a penny farthing and travelled the couple of decades to an era when they were a sort of space shuttle. Both extremes of mobile sophistication were still devoted to the magical idea of capturing sound, which is a series of thoughts about itself, a sequence of pulses and noises that disappear as soon as they appear, and keeping it in a state where it could last forever. The key was to ensure that this risky technological capturing didn't just merely literally copy a sound but somehow factored into that sound an individual atmosphere and a kind of metaphysical soul print that accurately represented the emotional and psychological intention, the psychogeographical and intellectual history, the personal story behind – and in a way in front of – the making up of this sound.

Quincy first worked in a recording studio in 1951 with Lionel Hampton. A member of Hampton's band, he toured with him, at a time when Hampton was bigger than Armstrong and Ellington. He started recording when you recorded in mono straight to 78-rpm disc. The sound had to be mixed absolutely correctly as it was all happening; there was no mixing desk. What you heard was what you got.

Stereo recording changed everything. For Quincy, it was the future, even as the major labels ignored it. Jones became a passionate advocate of stereo, and pushed it hard. He worked on one of the first stereo records, in 1958, *The Genius of Ray Charles*. He produced Lesley Gore's 'It's My Party'. Jones worked in the early days of the vocal over dub. It would take an hour just to get one overdub sorted out. He'd call pal George Martin during Beatles sessions so that they could congratulate each other for managing 'to have gotten one extra voice on tape!'

Jackson first worked with Jones on the soundtrack for the film version that an all-black cast was making of *The Wizard of Oz*. Jackson was the scarecrow. Rumours naturally suggested he liked his costume so much he would wear it home. Jackson took to Jones and his love for music that seemed to share Jackson's own sense of music as a kind of saviour. He wanted him to produce his first solo album, an important part of how he could distance himself from his older brothers, and his stressful role as compliant miracle kid. It took management intervention to persuade a dubious record company that Jones, the writer of movie scores for *In Cold*

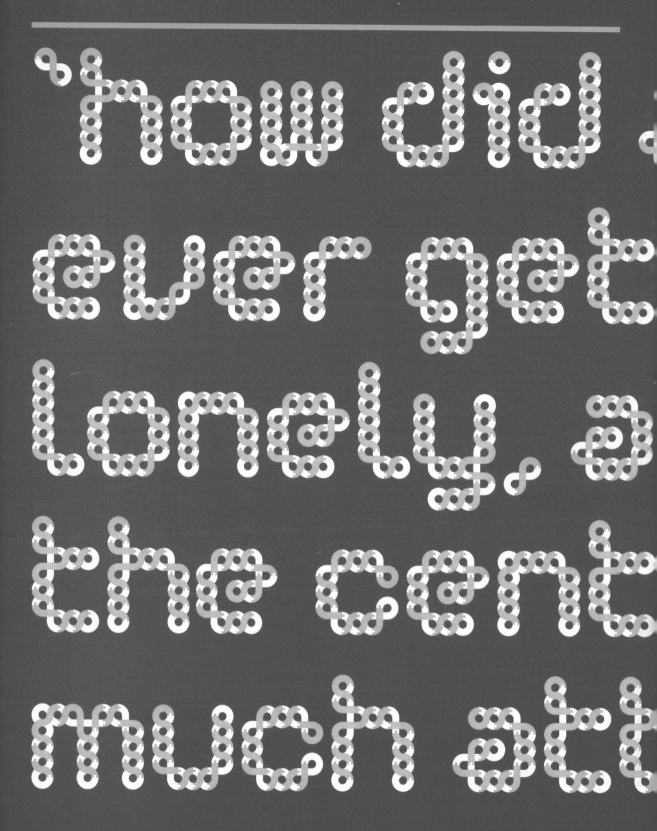

'how did i
ever get
lonely, a
the cent
much att

Paul Morley

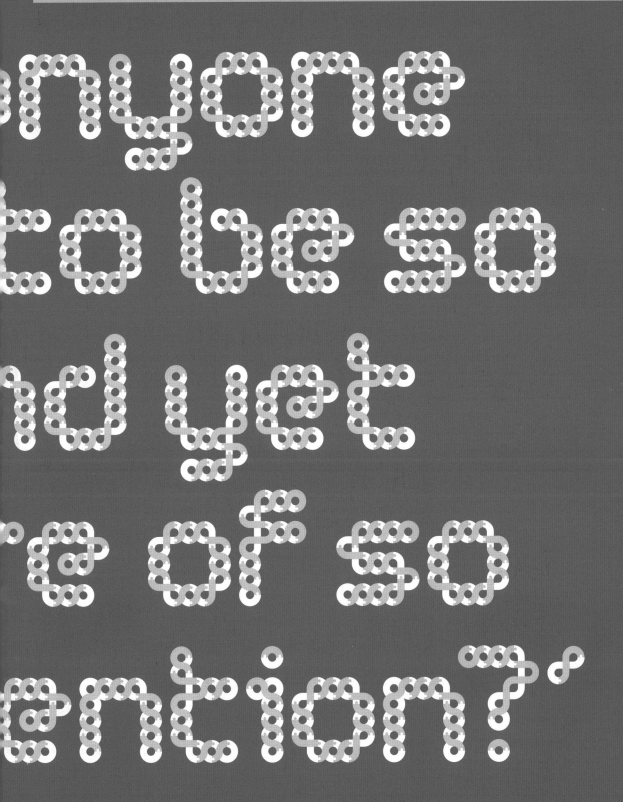

nyone
to be so
nd yet
e of so
ntion?'

Blood, of music for TV shows like *Ironside*, was the man to usher Jackson to a new pop level.

'The record company said Michael couldn't get any bigger,' Jones once said. 'We fixed that.'

Off the Wall's urgently inviting opening track, 'Don't Stop Til You Get Enough', written by Michael, with the demo intro percussion of Michael's sister Janet and brother Randy still intact, immediately thrusts the possibility of a new self-determined self-styled Michael into place, with a composed but explosive, epic but relaxed, busy but spacious sound, perfectly tailored to cleanly set up his urgently demanding vocals. All the disciplined thrills, fills and spills elements of the new Jackson sound were already in place – lush strings from disco, insistent horns from big band jazz, plucked, crystalline guitar from funk, elemental bass from soul and R&B, worked up Latin-singed cymbal simmering percussion from everywhere, voice from gospel, pop, Motown, Philly, Jackson's own history, all of it held in space and fixed in time by Jones in his recording studio with his carefully assembled team of engineers and session musicians.

Jones calmly recalled that his big band experience helped him organise all the sounds, and whatever else the track was, it was an incredible, inspired act of meticulous organisation. Outside the studio, on the radio, in everyday life, it just sounded like a great, uplifting, pop record, almost purely a gesture of defiant spontaneity capturing moments inside moments as they happen, even though its appearance of one-off exuberance had been carefully pieced together by Jones from assembled bits and pieces of technology, history, musicianship, ideas, excitement and, of course, Michael. (Quincy encouraged Jackson to also sing newly low on these songs, as on 'Rock with You', another break with the Motown system, which favoured the purely high Michael. The commitment Quincy gave to perfecting the deluxe Michael Jackson studio sound, without which Jackson was just anybody, paralleled Jackson's own professional dedication to working for hours on his dancing, perfecting every kick, gesture, movement so that they came together precisely. Jones factored into the intricate but accessible Michael Jackson sound a multitude of sonic moments and platforms and deviations that could inspire sudden motion and frozen reaction that best showed off Jackson's body breaking abilities. He turned Jackson's fluid but jagged movement into sound.)

The Quincy Michael never strayed far away from this detailed studio blend of shine and energy, drama and attack, tension and release, electronics and ecstasy, expert musicianship and studio trickery, pop air and jazz grace, whether he was mooching as a melancholy lost little boy through a broken-hearted ballad, or maintaining his monumental relentless self-regarding energy as he shot forward into his truly fantastic future life.

Off the Wall was a solo album – solo Jackson meeting, shadowing, dissolving into solo Jones – but the sound was made by a team of fairly anonymous musicians used to performing isolated studio duties on the instructions of a producer searching to generate and capture unpredictable energy, and by technicians given the task of ensuring all the work put into the song writing and playing was recorded, mixed and balanced in ways that finished off the music with an unparalleled sound that could only belong to those songs and that playing. 'The collective is always more powerful than the individual,' said Jones, who gathered together many of the same musicians and technicians when Quincy and Michael were reunited for the second solo album.

Twenty-six

After Michael Jackson's death, common digital mourning practices emerged on a variety of platforms. Testimonials and goodbyes poured into Michael Jackson's MySpace page. Facebook saw a similar influx of grievers on Jackson's main fan page and in newly created groups. At its peak, the conversation about Michael Jackson's death on Twitter proceeded at a rate of seventy-eight tweets per second. What can be said about this massive body of tweets? What sorts of emotions did people express about Michael Jackson's death?

Appendix B
Typology of Tweets with examples

Objective: Reporting sadness as news, part of updates on tweeter's life
It is a sad day

too caught up in wimbledon . . . but still saddened by MJ's passing.

Feeding the baby and feeling sad about Michael Jackson! He left is too soon!

Shocked by Michael Jackson's death. Such a sad, sad day. Going out for a couple of sales calls, late.

Emotion: Simple expression of sadness
I am sadden by MJ's death . . .
RIP Michael

Emotion: Personal sadness/extreme sadness
I'm devastated about Michael Jackson. What a sad day!!!

it sunk in . . . MJ is gone.. as don lemmon put it, 'Michael Jackson's music is the soundtrack to my childhood' . . . my life. i'm sad . . .

Emotion: Rant, expressing frustration at the media
i'm sick and tired of hearing about MJ's death, yes he died, that's sad. Just leave the man alone already!

i get mj's death was tragic but does it have to be shown everywhere?

Commentary/Editorial: Regret
It's so sad that he died so young

Commentary/Editorial: Chastising others for what appeared like forgiveness of his 'sins'; sad used as 'pitiful'
So Michael Jackson died today . . . like i care.. I am more saddened about Farrah Fawcett's death then a shiesty child molesters death . . .

Am I the only not pretending to be sad about Michael Jackson? He was a child fucker . . . remember?

I hope I'm not offending my friends for not being sad over MJ's passing. I won't be sad when OJ dies, either.

Humour: Making light of something about the event
Is watching the rerun of Michael Jackson night on *American Idol*. Suddenly sad in a completely different way ;-)

From 'Detecting Sadness in 140 Characters: Sentiment Analysis and Mourning Michael Jackson on Twitter'

Twenty-seven

Off the Wall as the sound of Michael Jackson and as a commercial monolith would take some beating. The first day that Quincy and his team started recording *Thriller* at the Westlake Audio's A studio on Beverly Boulevard, he turned to the leading contributors there for the start of recording – including Michael, so the story goes, his favoured and favourite long-time recording engineer Bruce Swedien, the Cleethorpes-born composer Rod Temperton who wrote central Jackson songs such as 'Rock with You' and the title tracks from *Off the Wall* and *Thriller*, drummer Leon Ndugu, percussionist Paulinho Da Costa, Louis Johnson of the Johnson Brothers – and said: 'OK, guys, we're here to save the recording industry.'

'Now that's a pretty big responsibility,' noted Swedien, whom Jones first worked with in 1958, 'but he meant it. That's why those albums and especially *Thriller* sound so incredible. Everybody who was involved gave 150 per cent. Quincy's like a director of a movie and I'm like the director of photography and it's Quincy's job to cast it.'

Jones's methodical choice of cast, mixing superb black funk and soul players with ace local white musicians, meant that the sound for all its consumer-friendly technological gloss would be centred around a masterly superimposed fusion of dandy, wised-up black power and spic-and-span, almost neutered, white decoration. This tendency to use whatever musicians worked, regardless of their colour, background or genre, was something he began back in the late '50s when he was recording his own big band album *The Birth of a Band* and *The Great Wide World of Quincy Jones.*

Thriller is in many ways – for all its showbiz-changing operatic excess, its formulaic machine-tooled approach to swish, swaggering dynamics that were clichés in jazz but deeply refreshing in pop, and now its permanent dazzling reputation as the biggest-selling non-greatest-hits album of all time, the peak-performing vinyl age product of all time, the last of its type in a way – as much an earnest, jaunty example of studio-processed and programmed electropop as it is a classy piece of Prince-minded groove-based African-American showmanship. It's connected to the history of Kraftwerk as much as it is connected to the history of Little Richard, Otis Redding, the Beatles, Stevie Wonder and Jackie Wilson. (Jackson and his people did ask Kraftwerk if they would produce him. They declined.) It is also in some form a Toto album

featuring Michael Jackson, a campy, corny middle-of-the-road grown-up rock–soul album smartly disguised as an awesome Michael Jackson dance pop extravaganza.

Toto were known as the 'session cats revenge band', the house band to the music industry, an uncharismatic team of top-level Los Angeles session musicians formed in 1976 to make a name for themselves. They had played for Jackson Browne, Eric Clapton, David Crosby, Sheena Easton, Earth, Wind and Fire, Rickie Lee Jones, the Jefferson Airplane, Rod Stewart, Loggins and Messina, Spinal Tap, Paul McCartney and on Quincy Jones's own records.

Toto guitarist Steve Lukather, keyboardist David Paich and drummer Jeff Porcaro were the main members of the house band Quincy used for the solo Michael records. Jackson wrote 'Beat It', and he sings it like he means it, like he's found a way to get out from under all the pressure and dance all the way to the moon, and it's notorious for the point-blank guitar solo given as a gift by Eddie Van Halen ('I did it as a favour. My band and management thought I was mad. Maybe Michael will give me dance lessons some day.'), but the backing band is Toto. It was Porcaro who wrote the track that ended up being charged with following 'Billie Jean', which in turn had followed 'Beat It', which actually, on a compact disc, followed 'Thriller'.

It's the rock of Toto more than the rock of Van Halen that Jackson and Jones used to smuggle the still-blackened style of Michael into the timid rock world. Lukather played all the guitars on 'Beat It' apart from Van Halen's one-take solo, instructed to find a way to bind the on-the-fly solo and some haphazard percussion. Van Halen himself referred to Toto as 'collectively, the best musicians on the planet', and it was this level of bland dispassionate expertise that Jones exploited as part of the opulent Jackson template.

Paul Morley

Thriller is perhaps the album that broke all the records because the elegant, ace Quincy, military minded, in the right place at the right time, working with the right commercial phenomenon, managed to fix the sleek clear-cut session-playing with the honed horny disco-funk with the revolutionary new technology with the contemporary atmosphere and make everyone involved believe that the work they did on this album, in their area of expertise, given all the creative freedom they needed, whether mix engineer, drummer, guitarist or Michael Jackson, would be around forever. This is all Quincy's way of saying he's a believer in togetherness. Then again, rumours have it that in order to get Michael to sing 'Billie Jean' the way he wanted him to sing it, hard and clear – without the annoying whoops, coos, squeaks and gulps Michael were convinced made him sound strong and in touch with some sort of street – Quincy laid into a wretched Michael curled up on the studio floor. Michael did it Quincy's way.

Michael wrote 'Billie Jean'. (Even if he mostly just turned up while everyone got on with building the tracks, hummed a lyric, hung around for a bit, and left, he's credited with both 'Billie Jean' and 'Beat It', the two stand-out tracks. Maybe he claimed them totally because they were the stand-out tracks. Maybe they are the stand-out tracks because Quincy was given the most information about what was required, even if they were just anecdotes Michael told about a couple of recent experiences.) Michael had something on his delicate, indignant mind. He's seeing red. Swedien recorded the song as though it was an absolute work of art, full of life and twice as spare, getting as tight and powerful a drum sound as he could come up with, using the glassy clean, spanking, skanky guitar solo David Williams (the BB King of the rhythm guitar) recorded for the demo all the way to the finished product. When David replayed the solo, it was never the same. It was such elements that gave the album, for all the attention to form and detail, little assertive splinters of spontaneity that keep the sound breathing even as it is set in mighty stone.

Bruce was left to mix it. (You were just happy to have him around, working for you.) You can tell to this day listening to the track, which is always more than it seems, all that fanatical control, the craze for neatness, all those sharp flashing things, a special level of exclusion, a cooling, illuminated groove, even after all the time and controversy and surgery there's been to wear it down, standardise it, defeat it, that he fell in love with a sound, a song, and his innocent, music-loving commitment, an integrity beyond corruption, is to achieving a dashing, chic sonic personality so that even if you just hear a few drum beats of the track, you know instantly what the track is, and then when the firm, festive, boss bass starts up, too much seems to be happening, considering so little is going on, and you get this warm, good feeling that everything will turn out all right, and such a feeling can somehow separate you from annihilation.

After a day or two Bruce had mix two of 'Billie Jean' which he thought was 'a killer'. Michael, Quincy and Rod Temperton came into the control room to listen. There was a lot of love for it and happy, relieved dancing. Then Michael motioned for Bruce to follow him out of the control room and whispered to him that it was perfect, but it needed a bit more bass, just one more mix. After that was done, Quincy had a thought. He asked Bruce to 'add a little garlic salt to the snare and the kick. Just a squirt!'

Swedien was soon up to mix twenty. Half-inch tapes stacked to the ceiling. A week later, mix ninety-one. Perfection! He played it to Quincy, who seemed happy, but there seemed to be a 'but' hanging in the air. Quincy asked, just for the fun of it, to listen to one of those earlier

From the Rolling Stones to the Clash, Lucien Freud to Damien Hirst and purple hearts to ecstasy...

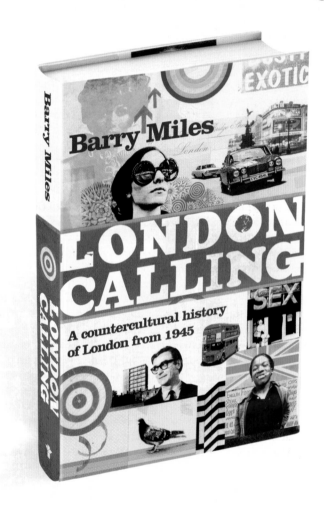

The major new history of the counterculture in the capital from the leading authority on the underground.

OUT NOW IN HARDBACK

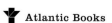 Atlantic Books

mixes. How about mix number two? What the . . . !? Everyone in the control room agreed that this was the one, as though all those other mixes had never even existed, but it would not have been so clear that mix two was the one without those other mixes proving that, even though there were all those possibilities, in the end there was only one true way of getting it done.

'Well, here's the deal,' reported Bruce. 'When *Thriller* was released to the whole world by Epic Records on Tuesday, November 30, 1982, it went to Tower Records with mix two of 'Billie Jean' on it. And then when the single of 'Billie Jean' came out it was mix two!'

The success of *Thriller* as an utterly persuasive musical product and as a piece of commercial entertainment was perhaps down to the fact that Quincy, watching over and watched over by Michael, in control in his own way of all the things he needed to be in control of, made more of the right decisions about sound and content than is usual among all of the thousands of decisions that need to be made when you work on such an enterprise and search for form and meaning.

Somehow, its very inconsistency as a complete album highlighted its amassed power as simply the place where Michael's greatest songs first appeared, one after the other, one ending, because this was actually a two-sided record, the first side, and another starting side two. 'Thriller' and 'Beat It', because of the videos that were now so much a part of the effect, completing the overall illusion, and the histories and myths they've ended up being part of, now seem far too big, rich and cinematic, too much their own worlds, to have ever been simply tracks on a vinyl album, routinely lifted off to be 7-inch singles.

Even the tracks that weren't the newly franchised disco synthrock of 'Wanna Be Startin Something', 'Thriller', 'Beat It' and 'Billie Jean', even including the Paul McCartney

duet and the (naturally, knowingly) sub-Prince 'Baby Be Mine', seemed perfectly positioned without shattering the illusion to showcase, to isolate, to intensify the effect of, the tracks that we can now not think of in any other way, as if they have been around forever, and will be around forever.

Twenty-eight
Posted by Father Maxxitone on 25 August 2009

'As a priest, musical fanatic and follower of Christ I can only pray that Michael's soul has been received by the Lord Jesus Christ. I had broke down into tears and prayer when news of Michael's sudden death had approached. I believe Michael is indeed in heaven, and I cannot believe in anything else until I reach the heavenly gates myself. As a student of music, I myself have been captivated by Michael's angelic vocals, sweeping dance moves and graceful songwriting. Studying him as a man, as a humanitarian, as a father . . . a man of such humility and love . . . I cannot picture him in the ghastly pit of eternal suffering. I pray for his children, family, and friends who have been affected by his passing. I also pray for his fans who seemed to have taken it hard. Our God is a god of mercy, love, care, and fairness, and we must remember he sent all of us here on a mission. He sent Michael here to Entertain, bring joy, and show his kind heart to people.
May he rest in eternal paradise.'

Twenty-nine
The day after Michael Jackson died, I was asked by the BBC 2 arts review programme *Newsnight Review* if I would go on to the show that evening to talk about Michael Jackson. To Clare, the producer making the call in all innocence, because surely this was my job, as rock critic and regular *Newsnight* panellist, I must have sounded infused with such wearisome self-pity I might actually be related to Jackson himself.

The truth was I had decided overnight, not least because of the *Simpsons* debacle, that I was not going to agree to any requests to comment in the media on the life and death of Michael Jackson. It wasn't like anyone would really miss me – losing out on some vital piece of the analysing puzzle without which none of the collected punditry building up by the minute would make sense. And the thought of it was causing me an indistinct sort of grief, although maybe I was transferring the feelings I more naturally if subconsciously felt over the death of Jackson over into my professional life.

I explained to Clare that I didn't think I would be much use on the programme, as my thinking about Jackson had become so knotted, and fractured, and a little fishy, as though somehow my response to the death bore as much relation to a really concise and hopefully insightful *Newsnight Review* contribution as Jackson's latest nose did to a normal nose. I had come to the conclusion that in fact Jackson had died at some point between 1992 and 1994, but that due to some uncanny elemental force, the death had not quite 'taken'– Jackson had not been completely removed from life or the planet, and began a strange twilight period where he still haunted the planet, half dead, barely alive, and the rest of us were forced to postpone the grief that was natural to give back then, when it seemed the right time for him to die. We had all been compelled to live through a fifteen-year period where we could not put the whole thing where it really needed to be – actually, in a grave, his grave, so that we could deal with Jackson as it should have been for all these years, as a dead superstar. The raw, giddy response to his death, I told Clare about fifteen hours after it had happened, was a massive outpouring of relief that finally we could all grieve and mourn. Reality had somehow realigned itself to where it should have been all along. He was dead, but then he'd been dead before.

I said that consequently my thinking was too twisted up around itself for me to be able to do any light dancing through the musical progression. I'd lost track of whether I was responding to something that had any merit and logic in itself, responding to his music and its essential qualities, as if the story really was as it seemed to be, as if it actually was a case of a creative trailing away after *Off the Wall* and *Thriller*, as *Bad* turned to *Dangerous* turned to *Invincible*, as meaty, integral bits of Jackson's soul and body were left behind every time he pulled off the completion of a Jacksonically conclusive, internationally successful, career-boosting or sustaining or rescuing pop track, whether it was 'Black or White', or 'Scream', or 'Smooth Criminal' – and that I was in danger of dwelling for hours at a time on the meaning of those self-mythologising one-word album titles, and losing my track, and deciding in the end that he was just some grotesquely self-important post-modern day P. T. Barnum who had decided a) attention is good, b) controversy is better, and c) outrage is a gift that keeps giving, and all those attractive and/or not-so-attractive pop songs were nothing more than well- or not-so-well-designed pop songs that were part of the greater plan to simply keep drawing attention to himself, that his music was just him pouring his emotions over his body and then passing it on as if everyone else should care, that the drugs first liberated him and then ruined him, that the more knowing he got the more glassy eyed and screwed up he became, that he and he alone had knocked the stuffing out of the idea that rock and pop had any spirituality or sense of mission, or he was in the end merely a spectacular, sophisticated and sometimes quite raucous collective hallucination calculated to survive for about fifty years and then splutter to an end before releasing a series of oozing flashbacks, tattered souvenirs and fleeting impressions of his role in the late twentieth-century entertainment age that would last to the end of time.

And then there was a new theory I'd had about Michael Jackson's lyrics, whether they were written by him or commissioned to fall in with the raging, tender, paranoid, moonstruck, aphrodisiacal, wistful, victimised, passive house style, the defiance and toughness that acted as a protective armour, the way they seemed to auto-biographically feed off his private life, his secret psychology, his deepest feelings, confronting the rumours about his sexuality, the media reports of his dysfunctional habits, the mocking of his taste and whimsies, the way they seemed to tantalisingly confirm that as cruel and con-temptuous as the media could be about Jackson's physical and emotional deformities, they were on to something.

I had concluded that in fact these lyrics were themselves written or selected by him in reaction to his increasingly fixed image as malfunctioning celebrity and sexually anxious paranoiac. They were not about any real Michael, they were Michael making up this tragic, defiant image of Michael as projected on to him by those that were either adoring or condemning the shtick. The words he sang were just another part of his deviant gamesmanship and another method of actually hiding far away who and what he really was: he hid behind the pretence that his songs were faithfully and generously about his feelings, grievances and tribulations. This was what he wanted us to think. There were no clues at all in any of the songs about his secluded behind the scenes true nature except of course that none of them were actually really about him. Only about a fictional portrayal of him. This was how clever and sly a psychedelic huckster he really was. I had no clear follow up theory about why the hell he would bother being so oblique, other than that he was very cold.

So I was going to find it hard to fondly recall the time he moon-walked on that MTV TV and blew the world's mind, as if that was what really happened. I couldn't see Michael Jackson for all the Michael Jacksons that the news of his death had discharged. All I could see was how an over-dressed and over-done, tacky and shapeless Michael Jackson existed because of the way an image had been constructed by various forces and the tension that continually existed between him and the media and the music business – which he both needed and profoundly distrusted.

Perhaps thinking about all of that released Jacksonia vapour that had occurred once he had died had sent me into a near trance-like state, one that put me very close to actually understanding the vast, tiny mind of Jackson himself, all the clutter, and emptiness, elation and dullness, anger and absence, all that Him, and not-Him, all that Tom and Jerry, E. T. and Wendy, Audrey Hepburn and Vincent Price, White Rabbit and Snow White, ghosts and corpses, swans and treasure, jealous fairies and treacherous pirates, sex and waste that resided there, all those memories torn from their moorings, his inability to fix himself to reality, the way he would float clear of the concrete, the multiplication of doubts, the unthinkable thoughts, the horror of the flesh, the suicide he felt only as an idea never an action, he wasn't lucid enough to go there, the time hanging limp in the still air . . . it was as though I could understand how Michael lived without any limits to his mind and imagination, nothing that could ground him in the necessary everyday. Nothing bound his experiences to his memories and emotions in ways that could give him serious clues about how to function and behave as a reasonably sane human being.

Oddly enough, I still got booked for the show. Perhaps Clare thought that after ranting at her for some minutes I had got it all out of my system, and on the night I would crisply slip into a tidy ' phenomenally ebullient child star betters himself like none before, only to dissolve into the apogee of weirdness' conclusion.

The broadcast went relatively smoothly, although I must admit I was a little disconcerted when one of my fellow panellists commented that what was interesting when it came to Michael Jackson was that in fact there were 'two Michael Jacksons'.

Two? Two! What had I missed? For a television moment I almost sank back into the unravelled spiralling mind of Michael Jackson, all that susceptibility and paralysis, all that frantic menace and insecurity. I caught myself just in time, and interjected that even as recently as the *Invincible* album in 2001, he wasn't that far off being up to his old tricks, give or take the fact that there was nothing left of the body of the Jackson 5 boy. Still, we all grow up, and our appearance changes, one way or another. (You put a photo of me now next to a photo of me at ten and you would conclude that in sad, unfathomable ways, I was not what I once was. I too have a very different nose and my hair is in a very different place.)

Meanwhile, even though I had decided I had absolutely nothing to say about Michael Jackson, and I was damned well not going to say it, I had agreed to write a comment piece about the life and death of Michael Jackson for *The Observer*. I arrived back home after the *Newsnight Review* appearance and had ten hours to come up with something, reeling as I was from the 'two Jacksons' comment, an observation that was either true, grounded and revealing in its elementary simplicity, or completely missing the point that Michael Jackson was legion. He was many. And now he was dead he was on his way to becoming many more.

Thirty

(*Comment piece written for* The Observer *dated 28 June 2009*)

As soon as he was gone, he was everywhere, regaining a flashy, bewitching agility he hadn't had since the early 1980s when he really was a kind of king. He was everywhere, and everyone had something to say, even if they didn't really know what to say. As soon as it was clear that he was really dead, and that it was now Michael Jackson 1958–2009, the instantly surreal truth of course being obtained and announced not by a traditional media outlet but by a furtive, deadpan celebrity website, a whole host of Michael Jackson's were released into the air. The loved Jackson, the gloved Jackson, the wealthy Jackson, the bankrupt Jackson, the Motown Jackson, the moon-walking Jackson, the MTV Jackson, the despised Jackson, the genius, the mutant, the addict, the oddball, the victim, the black, the white, the creepy, the glorious, the pathetic, the gentle, the monster.

You could take your pick which Jackson you want to remember, which version of the monster, or the genius, or the dissolving man behind the mask. He was everywhere, but now that death had returned his full powers as a spinning, gliding master of self-publicity, any truth about who he really was and what he'd been up to was shattered into a thousand glittering pieces. Once we stayed up late to watch the premier of the *Thriller* video. Now we stayed up late to watch another form of extraordinary choreography intended to turn one fascinating, paranoid, fiendishly otherworldly entertainer into an immortal.

The crazed rush was on to try and fix just one Jackson in place; the trailblazing star, or the abused innocent, the loneliest man alive, or the greatest entertainer of all time. The uneasy combination of frantic web action and obsessive, hasty, flamboyantly superficial news coverage meant it was possible actually to witness a certain sort of immortality start to take form. The tweeters, the websites, the pundits, the acquaintances, the impersonators, the colleagues, the hangers on, the fan club members, the news readers, the correspondents, the international celebrities all performed their duties so obediently that the whole event seemed to follow a script with the full approval of Jackson. (Imagine how well he'd planned the funeral.)

It was immediately clear that the nature and timing of this end had been coming for such a long time. Even while the whole thing was deeply disconcerting and in the middle of it all someone had actually died, it was also the most obvious thing in the world. Now that it had arrived, this punch line to all the scintillating music and living, seedy chaos, everyone knew their place, as if Jackson's final mortal act as extremely self-obsessed entertainment illusionist was to ensure that the news of his death was itself a kind of glittering if slightly tawdry spectacle.

In those first remarkable moments, death had allowed the myth of Jackson to surge into life, and his career got the focussed injection of publicity he had recently been unable to consistently generate without sacrifice. The twenty-four hour news channels couldn't believe their luck, all this archive, tension, scandal, revelation and gossip. All this Uri Geller. Jackson played a massive, needy part in shaping an entertainment universe which now largely consists of constant gossip about the antics and eccentricities of damaged celebrities, and his death was confirmation that the presentation of round-the-clock news, certainly when it comes to popular culture is little more than formally presented, gravely delivered, hastily assembled tittle-tattle.

Everything had been destined to lead to this untimely, shady death, and once that death arrived, a certain kind of order was established. Jackson was where he'd been heading all along – a sudden tragic end, a twist of mystery, a sad final trip low across the LA sky to the coroner, coverage that seemed in part pre-recorded ready for the big day. The whole thing concluded the only way it could – in a resounding blast of grotesque but compelling publicity for a figure who had become all that he had become, the king and the imprisoned, the adored and the humiliated, the accused and the indulged, because of publicity. Jackson had been publicised to death. As soon as he died, the response came in the form of pure publicity, an almost relieved acceptance that finally the damned thing had at last been resolved.

He was no good to us alive, falling apart physically and mentally, making repeated attempts to repair his image and reputation, reminding us again and again that the neurotic energy, dangerous perfectionism and desperate ambition he'd turned into dazzling, video-age show business had eventually turned back on him and started to eat him up. There was only one real way to rescue Jackson from the enduring pain of decline and reclusiveness. It wasn't going to involve taking on fifty dates at the O2 Arena, and no doubt revealing a poignant lack of wit, speed and power, and escaping to exile after a couple of disastrous shows.

When he was alive, it was never clear quite how to approach the perverse, shape-shifting, scandalous, ruined, faintly repulsive idea of Jackson, how to deal with the transformation from irresistible child star to weird, shattered, self-piteous, fallen idol. Dead, in acceptably mysterious and fairly dubious circumstances, he had joined those he had loved and admired for their life after death adventures, Garland, Dean, Monroe, Presley, Lennon, Diana – and because one of the many Michael Jackson's seems to have had the kind of pointless, chaotic fame that we now think of as being the result of time spent on reality television, there's another chain of celebrity disaster he also belongs to that drops all the way down to Jade Goody. It was the loopy minor celebrity element there definitely is in late period, now final period, Jackson – a celebrity Big Brother appearance, even a pantomime, would have been more beneficial than all that demanding singing and dancing he was facing – that actually helped give his death something Presley's and Diana's couldn't have. An element of the busy, hustling, fragmented hyper self-aware twenty-first century, as reflected by TMZ, Fox, Perez, Hilton and Google.

He'd hung on long after parts of his mind, business and body were falling off, but his sense of timing was in the end immaculate. He sprang to life in the '60s, got himself into position in the '70s, was anointed in the '80s, started to disintegrate, and then hung on for dear life until the media and the web, and the way it covers itself as it covers events beyond its control, was in the right ever-vigilant, tabloid minded, freakishly amoral, multi channelled, search saturated, tweetist state to properly cover his death with the correct combination of pomp and prurience.

The media had become as bizarre in its obsessions and anxieties and worries about its image as Jackson himself. The cultural stars were in alignment. Even as he lost ultimate control he somehow took absolute control of the coverage of his life and death, disappearing behind hundreds of versions of himself, now always in our lives whether we liked the idea or not. He had been disgraced as a living legend, but death had given him back, one way or another, the kind of grace he craved. The grace that comes when your fame, and your name, cannot be taken away.

Thirty-one

Quincy Jones contributed a lovely piece to the *Los Angeles Times* Calendar Section days after Michael had died. The truth was Quincy and Michael had not worked together for two decades, and even though Quincy was diplomatically quiet about what he thought had happened to him in the years since they had been together, you could guess that he was not at all impressed. He'd fallen for his focus and innocence, Michael's strategic attention to detail, when they had first met. Such things had fallen off the bus a long time ago.

Quincy understood how that time in the '80s when they all worked and dreamed together, planning their fantasies inside a studio and seeing them gush all over MTV, was the perfect convergence of forces. 'We owned the '80s,' he boasted, 'and our souls would be connected forever. There will be a lot written about what came next in Michael's life, but for me all of that is just noise. I promise you in fifty, seventy-five, a hundred years, what will be remembered is the music. It's no accident that almost three decades later, no matter where I go in the world, in every club and karaoke bar, like clockwork, you hear "Billie Jean", "Beat It", "Wanna Be Starting Something", "Rock With You" and "Thriller".

He knew that it was his Michael that was the ultimate reason why when Michael died it was more than just the surprise death of a celebrity. Michael Jackson could not have been considered in any form the greatest if it hadn't been for Quincy: Quincy grabbed from Michael the finer parts of his amorphous magnetism and poured it into the songs. Michael was never the same again, as though Quincy, to get that music, had needed to suck something out of Michael that severely affected his already teetering temperament. Michael needed Quincy, but Quincy needed Michael to make sense of a personal musical story that without his albums with Michael would have been missing something that made sense of everything he'd learnt. He was a Michael Jackson away from missing his moment. But Michael was a Quincy away from reaching his prime.

If Quincy, as the most sensitive and understanding of Michael's bosses, teachers, fathers, brothers, band members, aides, friends, was a sort of teacher, it is interesting to go back and find those that taught Quincy – to see that Michael Jackson didn't just come out of *The*

Wizard of Oz and Smokey Robinson, out of the religious fervent rural America south and the electronically groomed screaming far out. If Quincy is central to the story of Michael Jackson, or at least to a story that isn't reduced to the slimy rubble of hearsay and insinuation, a mainstream music story, then his teachers, the ones that encouraged his quest for excellence, and his own particular ruthless search for acceptance, are also important.

There was Ray Charles, and boots stomping the floo juke joints. Quincy would claim underground '40s trumpeter Clark Terry as an important mentor, and Count Basie as a kind of father – in the Los Angeles piece he mentions meeting Basie just before he died, and being so proud that Basie was so proud of him, that he'd been a jazzer that had ended up coordinating the biggest-selling album of all time.

But Quincy's more conventional teacher was a brilliant French woman, Nadia Boulanger, born into a musical family on 16 September 1887 who died in 1979 renowned as one of the most important composition teachers of the twentieth century. Among those this master musician taught were: John Adams, Burt Bacharach, Aaron Copeland, Philip Glass, Leonard Bernstein, Elliot Carter, and Quincy, so her influence on American music is considerable. Other students she taught included Igor Stravinsky and Maurice Ravel. Her pupils would be exhausted and depressed by the demanding rigour of her lessons, both fearing and admiring her.

She apparently told Glass he would never be a composer, which actually encouraged him to prove her wrong. She told Quincy to forget about writing symphonies and concentrate on jazz, although it's not clear whether this advice extended to pop and producing 'We Are the World'.

Jones studied counterpoint, orchestration and composition under the inspirational Madame Boulanger while he was in Paris in 1957, a year before Jackson was born – meeting Picasso, James Baldwin, Josephine Baker along the way – and such studies means that the producer of the biggest-selling pop album of all time has an intellectual approach to form and content, style and fashion, sound and meaning, energy and emotion, and can refer to Stravinsky as much as be linked to every conceivable American musical form, to Louis, Bird, Duke, Frank, Jay Z. He understands the pure dynamics of musical decades stretching way back before the '50s and this far into the twenty-first century.

Quincy once said, 'Stravinsky said that the big responsibility of an artist is to be a great observer and really pay attention. Pay attention ! The things that have guided my life are to pay attention, be true to yourself, and figure it out. That's really what it's about. My life was messed up when I was young, but so what? Get over it. Figure it out. Just inhale every second of life.'

Nadia taught him to think like this. She famously could not tolerate lack of attention. 'It is a vital part of self-awareness. It's a force of concentration and it means you do not repeat the same actions day to day. I'd go as far as saying that life is denied by lack of attention, whether it be to clean windows or write a masterpiece. I have the impression that the more I try to think about the essentials of music, the more they seem to depend on general human values. It's all very well to be a musician, it's all very well to be a genius, but the intrinsic value which constitutes your mind, your heart, your sensibility, depends on what you are. You may have to lead a life in which no one understands who you are. Nevertheless I believe that everything depends on attention. I only see you if I pay attention. I only exist in my own eyes if I pay attention to myself.'

These are some of the thoughts that Quincy would have been opened up to as taught by

Madame Boulanger, a lover of Monteverdi, Bach and Debussy, who herself was renowned as a master of sonic precision, training her students to develop the muscles of the ear and the focus of the mind so keenly that notes, harmony, rhythms, melodies be pressed deeply into the conscious and the subconscious mind. You can imagine some of these ideas and theories being pinned up in the holy recording studio as Quincy swept up the various forces and energies that went into the making of *Off the Wall*, *Thriller* and *Bad* – some sense of something burning and moving way beyond the obvious and cynical that perhaps supplies one of the best answers to the question of why people loved this music so much, not just because of its synthetic attractiveness, electronic richness, concentrated hooks and pulsating rhythmic attack.

'To think that a man with everything against him can overcome all obstacles by courage, with will, energy, vital powers! I find that more impressive than the result itself, it's a joy to see all that effort bear fruit. And then, you must take time to savour. To eat is to taste. Stravinsky used to taste. He didn't eat fast. He savoured. I almost never taste. I eat a peach while giving a lesson and I don't notice what I eat. And then there's something extraordinary, a peach. Two years ago I had a cherry that was a masterpiece of a cherry. From time to time I think of it. I've never eaten its equal.'

'Do you know what Valery wrote? "We are told that the sea is flat, we do not see that it is standing up in front of us. It's probably the same thing with sound. It produces phenomena of the same order."'

'But the essential condition of everything you do, and not only in music, the touchstone, must be choice, love, passion. You do it because you consider the marvellous adventure of being alive depends entirely on the atmosphere you yourself create, by your enthusiasm, your conviction, your understanding.'

Thirty-two

Throughout the summer, the calls kept coming, from TV, radio and newspaper, from those hoping to hire me for a few minutes, to talk about some incident generated by the after-effects of Jackson's death. Can you talk about Jackson in relation to the memorial, the fight over the children, his burial, the fact that Mark Lester is claiming he is in fact the surrogate father of two of the children, did the British kill him because he couldn't cope with the thought of performing all those London shows, what about the fact that Daddy Joe wants to create a new Jackson singing group with Michael's kids, what about his doctor having all that propofol delivered to his girlfriend's apartment, what about the *Ben Hur* show and Robbie Williams taking over some of his dates at the O2 Arena, what do you think of those who want their O2 tickets as a souvenir, prepared to pay £75 for a ticket that now won't mean show number thirty-four of the Michael Jackson season, what about the Jackson benefit show, the tribute show that Jermaine is arranging, the way that the Jackson family seemed to be setting their sights cheap and cabaret low in terms of the way they carried the torch forward, Madonna calling him the greatest artist that ever lived, delivering an emotional speech at the MTV Video Music Awards, feeling he was abandoned, we all abandoned him, and put him in a box, and labelled him a strange person, what did I think of that, apparently she can't stop thinking about him, we should have helped him, how could we have helped him, does that mean he's set some weird kind of precedent, is she sincere, is she guilty about something? (A talk radio jockey responds to the idea that we should have helped Jackson with a curt 'Speak for yourself'.)

I get the feeling that the requests will come forever, that there will always be some reverberation that requires instant pundit commentary – just how great was Jackson – the greatest? – an

Paul Morley

Ali, an Otis, a Diana, a Ledger, just how important is he as a man, an entertainer, what do you think of the rehearsal footage of him, as he prepared himself for the O2 shows, did he seem ready, did you hear that in fact according to the post-mortem he was all things considered relatively healthy for a man of his age suffering his levels of stress and considering the drugs he was addicted to?

I reply to some of the requests, explaining at some length that I have nothing to say or I don't know what to think about Michael Jackson and his casket, or Michael Jackson and the troubled tribute shows, or Michael Jackson and his wills. I take some time to run through all my thinking about Jackson, how I'm sloppy with chronology, I'm not the right person to summarise his contribution, I don't really like his music – this thought was often greeted at the other end of the phone as though I had in fact said Shakespeare was not as good a writer as J. K. Rowling – I can't keep a straight face, Quincy was the key, the Jacksons that are left are a disaster, Latoya makes me especially nervous. The truth is, I end up saying, I have nothing at all to say about Michael Jackson.

I get a little paranoid and feel that these producers and researchers calling me to book me on to some show to fuel or diffuse or scoff at some new piece of Jackson-associated peculiarity get a little annoyed at me playing games with them, as if they've worked out that I'm still stuck playing tedious old-fashioned games of self-reflexivity – nervous of letting go and being exposed as someone who for all his reputation as a pop writer has nothing original, surprising or relevant to say about this pop event of the year. I'm pretending I've got nothing to say even as in fact I can't shut up pushing forward various responses and theories. God, I think they think, my paranoia no doubt inflated by flying close to the palpitating Jackson paranoia, I probably still believe in that fashionable post-

Nietzscheian French nonsense – there are no facts, only interpretation. All this deferral, but yet really not deferral, the deferring of deferring, all this spinning around, all this self-consciousness about committing myself to an actual conclusion about whether I do or do not like/admire/miss/resist/hate/understand Jackson, all this clotting up of decision and then indecision, this elaborate avoidance, this ironic evasion – it's like Camille Paglia said years ago, about all the men that get up to this game-playing nonsense, it signifies an alienation from emotion. Could there be anything worse than a fifty-odd-year-old male white rock critic fascinated by Foucault and Derrida, those blasted Eros-killers? Like she said, as an attitude toward life it betrays a perpetual adolescence.

Actually, that must make me ideally qualified to talk about Michael Jackson, even though I'm trapped inside all this anxiety about whether/if/when/how I commit to an argument, an opinion, a simple anecdotal statement, an artless, outspoken opinion. I worry that I'm giving too much away, or not giving enough away, that I don't know where to begin, and actually have no idea what it all means and where it will all end.

I reject all the requests to talk about Michael Jackson. I stop even replying to the messages. I have nothing to say about Michael Jackson. There is no actual Michael Jackson to actually say anything about, not in the ways we like to think.

....

Then I agree to write this essay.

Thirty-three

I sometimes wondered whether Michael Jackson ever considered what kind of fuss would be made when he died, and then after. Did he spend time calculating whether he could have any kind of influence over the reaction to his death, as if it was something that could end with a virtual burst of rapturous applause, mixed with such shock that he could pull off such a move, so profoundly threaten his internal balance, produce such a climactic acknow-ledgement of the limits of his consciousness?

I wondered whether in his haywire and exotic later years, with the assured if battered instincts and perceptions of someone whose entire existence was based around thinking and behaving as a watched and available entertainer, he considered that it was more likely that his best chance for a glorious, life-affirming come-back, a flamboyant reconfirmation of his powers, was to die in circumstances that were sad, seedy and suitably sensational. To die would be to live.

How carefully did he consider the idea that a certain sort of death, one achieved in a kind of privacy that was also completely public, would lead to the greatest encore of all, one that could last for ever? A peaceful relatively ordinary death, at a time of life some would consider acceptable, might not be the best way of sealing his myth. He needed to die fairly young, sadly before his time – or biblically old, decades after his time, way beyond a hundred years, encased in hi-tech sonar-fuelled technological life support and surgically transformed into a nerve-less, sexless, odourless sheet of transparent skin – to complete the tragic meta-theatrical arc of a life grievously distorted by the weirdest of appetites and impulses.

This did not mean he would take his own life, not directly, not with desperate, shattered purpose, not as an explicit premeditated act of escape intended to release him from merciless pain and misery. Nothing that cynical, if suicide can be called cynical. It would mean that he was aware that the death of someone like Michael Jackson – his own death, allowing for the fact that he maintained a connection to himself, to the fact that he was Michael Jackson, even as he had peeled away from the idea that he actually was Jackson, living inside that skin, inside that

reputation – would be a crucial conclusion to his life-as-performance, and that the way he exits the stage, leaving an audience with a last tantalising sight of his presence, would have an enormous impact on how he is remembered.

For someone as famous as Jackson, for someone who has managed to make the whole world a stage, someone so terribly self-conscious about making people aware of him, to the point that he seemed content to allow people to become aware of him because he was weird and distressed, death is a major part of the whole strategy. Death is everything, because it will ensure that everything he fought for, to be so alive millions of people would know all about how alive he was, would not lead to nothing. Death would be a key element in ensuring no one ever forgot how hard he worked as an entertainer to let people know he was alive.

Did he think a lot about what form his death would take, and what unpleasant kind of death would be the most useful in how it contributed to maintaining enough interest in him, as extreme pop star, celebrity monster and object of fascination, so that he would not, if you think about it, die? He would simply make one more alteration in his appearance, one more conceptual adjustment in how he presented himself to the world. His death would be the extravagant equivalent of an outrageously manipulative costume change, a stunning example of spine-tingling performance magic that would ensure no one would ever forget the name Michael Jackson.

Did he spend much time dwelling on how and when, and why, he died would have a huge impact on his posthumous reputation, and so therefore the design of his death, whether accidental or intentional, was as important a part of what it was he did as any piece of music, as any video, television interview or award ceremony? Was there some kind of personal preference for how he died, a sense that the more mysterious and suspicious his death, the better it would be for the life he would lead once he was dead – a strange, murky Los Angeles death announced first by a celebrity website and then distributed around the news world in sensational pomp-filled seconds, a fitting death for someone whose life ultimately seemed like one long preparation for a squalid, endlessly analysed and ultimately expressive departure?

Did he anticipate how he would be remembered, and hope that the coverage of his death would mean that he was honoured for his glossy, tremendous music and eruptive movement, and not the kinkiness and decadence, his attempts to be normal and live a normal life which ended up merely intensifying his abnormality, his inability to function? Did he ever dream of just what would happen to his body, who and what would be the first outlet or organisation to make the announcement, would he be on his own when he died, surrounded by family, or in the middle of a sudden panicky flight to exile?

Perhaps the moment would come when he was on his own in a penthouse suite in Las Vegas after a 2034 comeback that seemed chilling and yet heroic in its recreation of late twentieth-century show business perfection. A common, anti-climactic heart attack. Perhaps a successful assassination by someone or some organisation he had defiled or let down – a late payment on some mammoth loan he entered into to maintain his Neverland home.

The worst thing of all, from the point of view of his reputation, would be to die of natural causes. By being Michael Jackson he naturally required supernatural causes.

Perhaps he knew, even to the extent of indirectly setting up the circumstances, that his death would have to be appallingly grim, an unstoppable descent of darkness, and unbearable lightness, due to a chaotic combination of sedatives, anaesthetics and pain-killers, a few days before his big, improbable comeback was due to take off, leaving open the necessary myth generating possibilities that it could have been murder, suicide, fake, accident, full of alleged this and alleged that, and even just the result of a certain lack of concentration, an amount of neglect from those paid to look after him on an ordinary afternoon that suddenly became extraordinary.

Thirty-four

I saw Michael Jackson die. That's not quite the exact truth, but then as Michael Jackson sort of sang, nothing ever really is. While he was alive, there was nothing exactly true about Michael Jackson, nothing that could ever make you think, that's who Michael Jackson is, he is that one thing, and only that. He is simply what his name, and his successful compelling popular music, makes you think he is. He is no more and no less than what he wants us to think he is.

And then, because he died, and I saw it happen, in my own home, spread over time, a turbulent mind-boggling decline reaching a sudden unavoidable climax, you could now *not* work out the truth of what he *had* been, who he was, exactly how he would be remembered. There was no exact truth, perhaps, because there were too many near truths, all of them overlapping and competing with each other, all of them with the same weight, the same value, the same level of integrity, the same lack of integrity, the same gigantic transparency.

Or there was no exact truth because there was nothing true, and truly settled, about Michael Jackson and his relationship to the rest of us, a relationship which ended with his death, which I witnessed. Michael Jackson lived, and died, sang, and danced, at the edge of reason, and so far out was his life and death that everything about him was a construct built out of lies, rumours, publicity, hints, avoidance, revelation and perversity. Everything about him was a lie, an evasion, an escape, a revenge, an outrage, and here perhaps was an ultimate example of how distinctive entertainers essentially find a way to tell risky even dangerous lies about themselves and their lives in order to seduce those less prepared to so comprehensively make up their identity. The great entertainers invent themselves so thoroughly that there is little about them that is in any ordinary sense solid and stable.

The great entertainer vibrates with predatory slyness and subterfuge, even as they find ways to present this surreptitious energy as a sincere kind of generosity and humility. They appear to give everything they are in order to entertain and amuse the masses. Really, they are always taking, feeding their neediness with the love and attention of their audience. Their whole act is always a lie, and is always about finding ways to camouflage this lie, this dazzling forgery, as something reliable. Entertainment is a way of disguising necessary deception and a consistent fabrication as something honourable and honest, and Jackson symbolised how trying to keep that arrangement going at the level he was at can often lead to the entertainment, and the entertainer, buckling under the pressure.

I think as soon as I saw Jackson die, on my television, in my imagination, or at least as soon as it was announced that he had died, a death that had been building up since he was a boy, or even a baby, or even before, I started to wonder just what the truth was. About the death, which was obviously an interesting kind of death because I had seen it happen, and it was an infected grandiose drama, and it was built in the image of famous assassinations, dubious accidents, cryptic deaths, possible suicides, bizarre comas, blatantly the kind of death with implied causes, suggestive anomalies and a whiff of the criminal that would never be solved, and I don't think I was alone in seeing it unfold, but also about the life. I couldn't help it.

I started to have thoughts about whether it would ever be possible to understand the truth about someone who was so embedded in the idea of show business as a sort of seductive fraudulence. Now that he was dead, would some sort of truth take shape, because, after all, the death seemed true enough? Or would the death take us further and further away from truth, because, after all, his death may now have been a fact, but it was soon apparent that this was the kind of death that is not about truth, but about the kind of distortion, disinformation, small talk and mercenary exaggeration that is at the heart of commercial entertainment? This death was still part of the process of building an image, of continuing the work of shepherding his manufactured presence and the soundtrack and accompanying images that are at the heart of the fabrication into whatever shops will be like in the future.

Within seconds of his death, which was televised, live, more or less, people around the world started to talk about Michael Jackson, about his nebulous, disordered life, and then about the death which had the appearance of something oddly methodical, as if it had been previously measured so that it would achieve maximum promotional impact. There was certainly something to talk about, and those that were talking, the newsreaders and then the pundits, guests and those that claimed to be friends quickly called upon to offer thoughts and reflections, seemed ready to summarise the reputation, music and demented family life of Michael Jackson, as if it was relatively straightforward. They talked as if there was a way of seeing truth, or at least working toward the truth, about this character, and the way his whole life meant that in the end he would die, live, on TV, hidden from view, but as exposed as anything. And, clearly, there was now someone to cherish, to praise, to honour, a good, decent man, someone who cared about the less fortunate and deserving, who was selfless and giving, not the soft-voiced, evasive, self-indulgent mega has-been dedicated on building an entertainment empire as if there was something of the Walt Disney about him.

Thirty-five
Michael Jackson is buried with full make-up on, wearing his precious white glove and sunglasses, draped in beads and pearls with a huge gold belt around his waist.

Thirty-six
As soon as Michael Jackson died, he came to life. As soon as he stopped, he started. The whole thing, this awful conclusion to a life spent spiralling into chaos – this freaky circus event, this historic item of news, this pure emblazoning blast of transmitted energy based on a momentarily unbelievable piece of inform-ation – was timed to perfection, suggesting that the essence of life, of existence, of maintaining balance, of locating and projecting charisma, is all about timing. At his very best, Jackson was a master of timing, of moving his body through space in a series of considered spontaneous sequences that indicated he was in so much control of his existence he could do whatever he wanted. Look how he moved, a vision of self-control, a genius at turning emotion into move-ment. At his devastating, distressing worst, he was confounded by time, and couldn't keep up with it. It broke him up. He could barely move. It surrounded him and took away his freedom. At the moment he died, time had taken all the power away from him, but he hadn't given up entirely. As soon as he died, there he was, facing up to time, and moving in a whole new way. He'd planned it that way, that the moment of death was not the end. It was where the story of Michael Jackson really began. Everything before the death was part of the getting ready.

He died. It was a kind of performance, as much a part of his career as a brash, exuberant early '70s Motown single, a flash, sophisticated massive selling Quincy Jones album, a frail but feisty post-'90s comeback, a startling near-sickening surgical adjustment, a self-consciously semi-crazed TV interview. We couldn't see his death, it was the most hidden thing of all, beyond even the reach of the scandal-hunters and celebrity-chasers, but we could imagine the moment, fantasise about how he made the move from one original state to altogether another, marvel at the final sounds he heard, and his final thoughts.

Perhaps his final thoughts were something Quincy had once told him Madame Nadia Boulanger said: 'Nothing is better than music. When it takes us out of time, it has done more for us than we have the right to hope for. It has broadened the limits of our sorrowful lives: it has lit up the sweetness of our hours of happi-ness by effacing the pettinesses that diminish us. It brings us back to the pure and new.'

Or maybe something of his own: 'If you enter this world knowing you are loved and you leave this world knowing the same, then everything that happens in between can be dealt with.'

Or something Paris Hilton once said: 'Of course it will work. I am a marketing genius.'

Thirty-seven
There are thoughts I had about Michael Jackson before he died, and there are thoughts I am having now that he is dead. Some of these thoughts are the same, and some are very different – there are those thoughts you could only have when he was alive, when there are still all sorts of absurd, amazing possibilities about how such a life can proceed, and those thoughts you can only have when he has died, and one set of possibilities are replaced by another. There are the thoughts you can have about how the body of Michael Jackson changed while he was alive, and how the body changed once he was

dead. There are the thoughts you can have about an enslaved Michael Jackson slogging through 2009 and into 2010 performing night after night, month after month, at the O2 arena, a constant cycle of pretence, strain and razzle-dazzle that the poor bamboozled media couldn't keep up with, as if Jackson was using the shows to overwhelm them with his presence until they were unbelievably forced to actually ignore him. Or he was using the show to pay off debts, to pay off the crooks, banks, courts and blackmailers, so that each show was his way of printing enough cash to fulfil his financial obligations and stay alive and perhaps have enough left over at the end to withdraw to Neverland and never, ever, ever, ever leave. One final amount of enforced work, the kind of grinding fleet-footed blank-eyed routine and sweat that was the desperate middle-aged version of the chained child star efforts, and then some freedom, the rest of his life, where he could design the perfect sort of exotic superstar exile and let the myths and rumours about the length of his fingernails, the state of his skin, the job requirements of his nurses and maids, the number of caged wild animals, the songs he'd been working on for thirty-four years and the peculiar architecture of the underground cells grow, until they completely buried him.

There are the thoughts you can have about how the This Is It shows he was apparently preparing for, in all good, fit and healthy faith, were a complete distraction from his real plans. This Is It was Jackson's last and greatest act of misdirection – everyone was looking that way, where he seemed to be setting up the show, the flashest trick of all, the biggest of his showbiz dares, where he was hiring the dancers, musicians, sorting out the set list, developing the arrangements of the songs, rehearsing his moves, selling the tickets, attending the launch, confounding those that thought he was not up to it, seemingly laughing in the face of all the

doubt and suspicion and the accusations, working on the comeback show of all comeback shows that would prove once and for all that he was the mighty eternal king, ruler and creator of all pop culture he surveyed, and not now simply the pitiful, repulsive curio outmanoeuvred by the likes of Miley Cyrus, the Jonas Brothers and the Pussycat Dolls.

While we are all looking that way, beginning against our better judgement to believe that he might actually be serious about undertaking this impossible, unprecedented marathon, he was somewhere else altogether in a very different frame of mind. He was planning a very different sort of This Is It, a very different way of spending the rest of 2009, and indeed the rest of his life. Perhaps for a while he really did engage with the idea of announcing just how physically and mentally limber he was by lightly knocking off these fifty shows, completing something that even in these jaded times would be considered to be awesome. Perhaps he really did conceive of the technological methods that stand-ins, models and holographic versions of various Jacksons could be used, so that his fans weren't disappointed. He could invent the kind of show involving electronically faithful reproductions and genetically modified Jacksons that once more confirmed how ahead of his showbiz time he was, anticipating how to produce a convincing meta-Vegas show that could run forever as an official Michael Jackson Production even if he was not actually physically a part of it.

Deep down, he was fully aware that there was no chance he could put himself through so much pain and pressure, no matter how physically strong he might actually be, regardless of how ingenious the multi-dimensional representation of his music and dancing was. He could not coast through these shows, miming, sending along body doubles, hiding behind a tidal surge of special effects. He was

Paul Morley

risking losing everything, and becoming a laughing stock, reducing his show business currency to the value of Milli Vanilli and Vanilla Ice.

He willingly let the financial and practical reality of the shows, the expectation and anticipation, gather so much momentum that the whole plan engulfed him. He allowed himself to be cornered by the commitment that was expected from him. In the end, he let This Is It become something that was both a cryptic suicide note, and the abstract cause of death.

Once Michael Jackson had died, it wasn't as though he actually disappeared. He might have added a certain depth to his invisibility, but there would be no stopping the traces of visibility he'd always sent out into the world from wherever he was hiding. If there is one thing that it very sure about Michael Jackson it's that his death does not mean he has gone missing. Death has not plunged him into anonymity. Death has put an absolute stop to the idea that Michael Jackson can ever be inconspicuous.

It wasn't as though his death meant we stopped thinking about him. It just meant that we thought about him in a different way, and in fact one of the first thoughts I had when I found out that he had died, as my thoughts about a living Jackson started to mingle with the new thoughts about a dead Jackson, was that it made more sense to be thinking about him as a dead star than as a living legend rotting by the day. As a dead star, he was pristine, he was complete, he was in his element. It was everything he was meant to be. Death had made him more real than ever. He was now the most real he had ever been.

I thought about how there were so many different versions of Michael, held by so many different people, that perhaps this was the secret of the immortality he craved for himself, and then arranged by dying at what, so the story goes, was just the right Jackohyperbolic moment. At the point of death, there were so many Jacksons that even as some were removed, as reputations and myths were debunked, as various versions started to fade away, as memories of his greatness faded, or memories of his horrible demise were erased, as some people just started forgetting, because they had other things, and other celebrities, on their minds, there were always memories and versions and highlights and a lingering love of Jackson that still existed. He could not be completely wiped away because as an idea he was multiple, and too scattered and luminous as a presence to truly disappear.

Thirty-eight

An obscure moment of silence, a final sigh, a last twitch, a catastrophic drop in temperature, an ugly scrapping of motion, and a gnarled, breathtaking pause that no one could ever know anything about. Michael Jackson, the winning singer, the celebrated mover, the worshipped hero, the accused tycoon, the soiled living legend, the warped icon, the faded legend, the troubled, scarred recluse, now all by himself, backstage, off to the side of space and time, as if everything was finished, the show was over, the curtain down, the applause given and gone, the colleagues, nurses and assistants let go, the lights out, the night stretching on forever. Now that it was all over, this grand dramatic commitment to performance, this intense self-sacrifice, after giving so much of himself, taking all the energy he could muster in the act of pleasing himself by pleasing others, it seemed like the end of the world. It seemed like he had nothing more to give. There was nothing left.

He removed his dazzling costume. Picked out the fake hair and pulled off bits of his body artificially added to ensure he resembled a human shape even as he'd left behind the conventional proportions and colouring of a man his age, race and size. Shed with a sinister shudder the sad glitter of mortality. Lay naked and exposed inside his own incandescent isolation.

He found the kind of relieved calm he searched for all his life, and sank into himself so profoundly, the steadiness and peace he achieved rinsed away decades of pain, suffering, anxiety and chaos. He was on his own, so lonely he would never be able to explain to anyone just what it felt like to be so lonely, and so at the end of his tether. He looked in a mirror. There was no one there. He'd disappeared.

And then a sudden red-hot transformation, an electric emergence of an authorised immortality, a powerful confirmation that Jackson without the skin and bones the head and heart the tortured body and soul that had ruined him was to be somehow more than he had ever been. The curtains opening. The lights flashing on. A radiant show business commotion of pumping liquid ecstatic sound and a constant clatter of gossip.

He had arrived. He was where he belonged. Right in front of us, demanding our attention. He had stormed into our minds, where he felt instantly at home, where he could move around and manipulate our emotions and memories with ultimate freedom and flexibility.

At this moment, as a desperately arranged deep sleep dissolved into an abyss, a moment so real it was something you could only describe by making up the details, something he had been preparing himself for his whole life, as if he could actually permanently postpone its occurrence, the Michael Jackson we now think of, the one that's dead and gone, was born.

This is what we had been waiting for, what he had been waiting for – one kind of death, a severe removal of necessary signs, the kind of action leading to ultimate inaction that will never be understood, a great mystery leading to perpetual rumours and endless questions, and then, immediately, this new state of being, this life after death, this new form of immaculate stardom. Some kind of survival replacing the moment he knew, deep in himself, deep in a coma of someone's making, that everything he was, this man who so easily changed his shape and skin, had made the most dramatic change of all. Michael Jackson had entered, through the darkness of some messy, miserable final moments, a different life, one that seemed instantly to hint at making sense of his role in our lives, of his tenacious, reverberating position in our imagination.

He had, after all that, found his way home. He shut the door. He thought of nothing and no one. He was in control. He didn't move a muscle.

I looked at him for a while and then I left him where he was.

Paul Morley

CONTRIBUTORS

OWEN HATHERLEY writes on political aesthetics for Building Design, *The Guardian*, the *New Statesman* and elsewhere, and blogs at Sit Down Man, You're a Bloody Tragedy. He is the author of *Militant Modernism* (Zero, 2009).

Beatgirl scribbler MIRIAM LINNA operates Norton Records with Kicks co-founder Billy Miller. Both make noise with the A-Bones. Their Kicks Books line has just published *SWEETS* by R&B legend Andre Williams.

MATT THORNE is a novelist and critic. He is presently working on a book about Prince.

ELISA AMBROGIO grew up in Marlborough and Hartford, Connecticut, and currently lives in Seattle, Washington

ANDY MILLER is the author of three books. His writing has appeared in *The Times*, *The Telegraph*, *The Guardian*, *Esquire*, *Mojo* and the *Second Pass*, among others. He plays guitar and sings with the Gene Clark Five.

FRANCES MORGAN is a critic, musician, DJ and formerly of *Plan B* magazine. She contributes to *frieze*, *New Statesman* and *Electric Sheep*, and has recently helped to launch *Vertigo of the Modern*, a new fiction magazine

DAN FRANKLIN is an editor at Canongate Books. He is currently working on a project investigating the heavy rock underground.

LAVINIA GREENLAW is an award-winning poet and novelist.

MARK FISHER writes regularly for *The Wire*, *frieze*, *New Statesman* and *Sight & Sound*. He is the author of *Capitalist Realism* (Zero, 2009). His weblog is at k-punk.abstractdynamics.org.

TIM LAWRENCE is the author of *Hold on to Your Dreams: Arthur Russell and the Downtown Music Scene, 1973-92* and *Love Saves the Day: A History of American Dance Music Culture, 1970-79*. He also leads the Music Culture: Theory and Production programme at UEL.

RUBBISH RAVER is rubbish and would prefer to remain anonymous (for now).

NICK KENT is the author of *The Dark Stuff*. His memoir, *Apathy for the Devil*, will be published in 2010.

SIMON REYNOLDS is the author of *Totally Wired*, *Rip it Up and Start Again*, *Bring the Noise* and *Energy Flash*. He can be found at blissout.blogspot.com

KEV KHARAS lives and works in London. He writes for *NME*, *The Quietus* and *The Stool Pigeon*, among others, and runs the No Pain In Pop website.

ROB CHAPMAN's definitive biography of Syd Barrett will be published by Faber in 2010.

LINIERS lives in Argentina. His graphic fiction is published by Random House Mondadori.

PAUL MORLEY is the author of *Nothing*. He wrote for the *NME* from 1977–83 and founded ZTT Records with Trevor Horn.

HUW GWILLIAM is a freelance graphic designer with a love of music. He doesn't get many opportunities to mix music and design in his day job. http://tr.im/coverversions

KEVIN CUMMINS is author of *Manchester: Looking for the Light through the Pouring Rain*.

JEB LOY NICHOLS is a musician, novelist and artist. He lives in Wales.

LOOPSJOURNAL.COM

Website
Visit loopsjournal.com for specially commissioned articles, exclusive video content, event news and to sign up for the *Loops* newsletter.

Twitter & Facebook
Follow *Loops* at twitter.com/loopsjournal and find us at facebook.com/loopsjournal.

Music Sampler
We have an exclusive Domino Records digital music sampler available for free with issue 02. For more information and to download the tracks, visit dominorecordco.com/loopsmp3s. This sampler is available until 31 July 2010.

Cover Illustration
Kam Tang

Editors
Lee Brackstone
Richard King

Design & Art Direction
Wallzo

Rights
Lisa Baker

Publicity
Anna Pallai
Colleen Maloney
Jodie Banazkiewicz

Erratum
The editors would like to apologise to Tom Fleming of Wild Beasts. In issue 01 of *Loops* the piece 'Wild Beasts and the New Vorticists' was incorrectly credited to Tom Fleming and Hayden Thorpe. The piece was the work of Hayden Thorpe alone. We are looking forward to a contribution in a future issue from Tom Fleming.

Thanks
Simon Armitage
Hans Juergen Balmes
Louise Behre
Laurence Bell
Angus Cargill
John Dyer
Becky Fincham
Fiona Ghobrial
Hanif Kureishi
Jonathan Lethem
Aris Maragkopolous
Jack Murphy
Silvia Novak
Stephen Page
Simon Reynolds
Jon Savage
Paula Turner
Julian Vinuales
Darren Wall
Dave Watkins

Publishing
Loops is published twice yearly by Faber and Faber Ltd (Bloomsbury House, 74–77 Great Russell Street, London WC1B 3DA) and Domino Records (PO Box 47029, SW18 1WD). Typeset by Palindrome. Printed and bound in the UK by Butler Tanner & Dennis, Frome.

ISBN
978-0-571-25479-8